Adorno

Adorno

A Political Biography

Lorenz Jäger

Translated by Stewart Spencer

Yale University Press
New Haven and London

For information about this and other Yale University Press publications, please contact:
U.S. Office: sales.press@yale.edu   yalebooks.com
Europe Office: sales@yaleup.co.uk   www.yalebooks.co.uk

Set in Minion by Northern Phototypesetting Co. Ltd, Bolton, Lancs
Printed in Great Britain by St Edmundsbury Press, Bury St Edmunds

Library of Congress Control Number: 2004107530

A catalogue record for this book is available from the British Library.

10   9   8   7   6   5   4   3   2   1

Photograph credits

© Theodor W. Adorno Archive, Frankfurt am Main for the photographs on pages ix, 7, 89 (photo: Almayer), 108, 165 (photo: Ilse Mayer Gehrken), and 178 (photo: Ilse Mayer Gehrken)
© Elisabeth Reinhuber, Oberursel for the photograph on page 35
© Barbara Klemm, Frankfurt am Main for the photographs on pages 202 and 205
© Ullstein Bild for the photograph on page 211

Contents

'We do not know what grants us insight; the tightly closed seed needs the damp, electrically warm earth to grow, to think, to express itself. Music is the electric earth in which the spirit lives, thinks, invents. Philosophy is a precipitate of music's electric spirit; its need to base everything on a fundamental principle is increased by it, although the spirit has no power over what it creates through it but is none the less happy to create it, thus the true product of art is independently more powerful than the artist himself, returning to the divine through its own manifestation and being linked to the individual only by virtue of the fact that it provides evidence of the mediation of the divine in him.'

Beethoven to Bettina von Arnim

'The word "beautiful", this declaration of love to the whole of nature . . . '

Otto Weininger

Acknowledgements

I should like to thank Sigrid Weigel of the Berlin Centre for Literary Research for the welcome that she gave me at her institute in October 2001. I am also grateful to my colleagues Gerhard R. Koch, Henning Ritter and Wolfgang Sandner, as well as to Tilmann Allert of the Johann Wolfgang Goethe University and, last but not least, Reinhard Pabst, who provided me with a great deal of information concerning Adorno's youth.

Prologue

Teddie

In a thumbnail sketch of Richard Strauss dating from 1929, Adorno evoked his childhood memories of the composer's works. They were surrounded, he recalled, by an aura of modernity, by a secret that the boy could not decode but that he could only suspect. The adults around him did not make his understanding any easier. He had been told that in *Salome* the head was that of a calf, while *Othello*, he was reassured, was all about a handkerchief. Where the information was lacking, his imagination had to take over: 'But more than all this,' wrote Adorno, 'my imagination was kindled by the word Elektra. This word was explosive and full of artificial, seductively evil smells, like a large chemical works close to the town where we lived, whose name sounded very similar. The word glittered cold and white, like electricity, after which it appeared to have been named; a piece of gleaming electrical machinery that poured out chlorine and which only adults could enter, something luminous, mechanical and unhealthy.'[1] This passage captures something of the general situation of the time, notably the growth of modern industry in Frankfurt in particular. And it also says something about Adorno's own family. His mother was a singer and, as such, responsible for the musical side of things. Bernhard Wiesengrund, his uncle on his father's side, was a scientist who in 1894 had published a book under the title *Electricity: Its Generation, Practical Use and Measurement. A Brief Outline for the General Reader.* For the young Adorno, *Elektra* was the epitome of modernism, immediate and yet remote, a title in which art, society and productive forces all came together without any distinction between them.

Hugo von Hofmannsthal's *Elektra* had received its first performance in Berlin in 1903, the year in which Adorno was born. This was also the year in which Mahler began work on his Sixth Symphony and met Arnold Schoenberg, who had recently completed his *Pelleas und Melisande*, a work that

'Philosophy is really there to redeem what lies in an animal's gaze', Adorno wrote to Max Horkheimer on 24 March 1956

explores the frontiers of music and teeters on the brink of atonality. The following year witnessed the publication of Frank Wedekind's *Pandora's Box*, a sequel to his drama about the figure of Lulu, *Earth Spirit*, that had first appeared in 1895. Also in 1904, the twenty-year-old Anton von Webern completed his Eight Early Songs (as yet without opus numbers), and Alban Berg became a composition pupil of Schoenberg. It was Berg who, with the constant support of his own pupil Adorno, later wrote an opera based on Wedekind's two Lulu plays. And it was not only composition that began to change, so too did the reception of music when in 1906 a 'complete' *Trovatore* was issued for the first time on eighteen shellac records. These were the years in which modernism, not only in music but in the other arts, too, broke away from Impressionism and began to formulate its own, more astringent, rules. Of Picasso, who was then working on his *Woman Ironing* and *Old Guitarist*, Adorno was later to write: 'I should not like to differentiate between, on the one hand, the magic and the shock that these wildly painted and strictly ordered constructions exercised on me when I first stumbled upon reproductions of them and, on the other, the insight into the necessity of this oeuvre, which obeys the compulsive law of the immanent development of painting as much as it obeys that of the historical disaster.'[2] Meanwhile, at the opposite end of art, there began a development that Adorno was later to describe as the culture industry, when the art of advertising became one of the subjects taught at German colleges of arts and crafts. In 1903, sociology acquired a distinctive profile as an independent science and as a subject for essayistic journalism with its finger of the pulse of the times. Georg Simmel wrote his essay on 'Cities and the Life of the Spirit', Émile Durkheim lectured on society and morality at the Sorbonne, and Max Weber examined the methodological problems associated with the social sciences and especially the question whether sociology was capable of 'neutral' research. In Germany a precursor of the country's Automobile Association was formed and, in the United States, Henry Ford founded the company that was to give its name to a whole era of rationalized, organized capitalism. At their party conference, the German Social Democrats condemned the 'revisionism' of Eduard Bernstein, who wanted to replace the socialist revolution by evolution and by reforms to the existing system, and reiterated their determination to abide by the principle of the class struggle. Also in 1903, Rosa Luxemburg marked the twentieth anniversary of the death of Karl Marx, beginning her article with one of the most famous tenets of Marxism, the eleventh of his *Theses on Feuerbach*: 'The philosophers have merely interpreted the world in various ways; the point, however, is to change it.' The 1903 Nobel Prize for physics went to Pierre Curie for his work on radioactive matter: nature itself was acquiring more sinister aspects. The brothers Orville and Wilbur Wright became the first to fly in a heavier-than-air machine: mobility and danger were increasing in equal proportion. Thomas Mann published his short story *Tonio Kröger*, in which he drew a contrast between the artist and the bourgeois. The Russian Social Democrats split into two separate parties, the revolutionary Bolsheviks under Lenin and the Mensheviks who sought to change the world through reform. And the teddy bear was exhibited by Margarete Steiff at the Leipzig Fair – it derived its name from the American president Theodore Roosevelt, who was said to have spared a bear's life on one of his hunting expeditions. 'Teddie' was to be Theodor Adorno's nickname and pet name, both within his own family and among his wider circle of friends.

The opening of Adorno's late philosophical study, *Negative Dialectics*, sounds like a belated echo of the sentence by Marx cited by Rosa Luxemburg: 'Perhaps it was an inadequate interpretation which promised that it would be put into practice.'[3] What are Adorno's writings if not a philosopher's attempt to square up to the events of 1903, to examine all their possibilities, to justify them from a normative point of view and ultimately to note that this particular constellation of events had finally had its day? And at the same time do they not also provide evidence of his conviction that none of us can escape from the circumstances of our birth?

1   Heartbeat of Expectation

Oscar Wiesengrund (1870–1946) was a well-to-do businessman who worked in the wine trade. Although of Jewish descent, he had converted to Christianity and also had his son baptized, albeit at the insistence of his Catholic wife, Maria née Calvelli-Adorno (1864–1952), the daughter of a Corsican fencing master who had settled in Germany. Her sister, the pianist Agathe Calvelli-Adorno (1868–1935), lived with the family. Adorno was fond of tracing back his family's roots to the Genoese doges, the Adornos della Piana, claiming that through them he was related to the royal house of the Colonnas – and ultimately, through Heracles, to Jupiter. Thus, at least, his friend and pupil, Peter von Haselberg, reports.[1] Rather, we should speak here of a romanticized family tradition. But what is beyond doubt is that the family contained within it a great potential for talent. One untypical aspect of the marriage was the difference in age between Adorno's parents. For a man who was to devote himself to aesthetic theory, the Italian legacy, however fictitious it may have been, was an early and crucial influence – it was Kant, after all, who described the Italians as 'preeminent in their artistic taste'.[2] In much the same way, Viktor Hehn speaks of Italy as 'the home of beautiful voices, the sign of a noble organization'.[3] Italy's artistic tradition extends from classical antiquity to the Renaissance and right up to the present day, providing a model for the whole of the rest of Europe. It was in the synthesis of Italian melodiousness and German rationality that Adorno later saw the precondition for the historically unique Viennese tradition, a tradition that he regarded as extending seamlessly from Mozart to his teacher, Alban Berg.

During his youth, Oscar Wiesengrund had spent some time in England. According to Haselberg, he was 'a small, slim and tough individual whom you could well imagine would be possessed all his life by a lively Anglomania, but it must be said that this love of England was widespread in Frankfurt before the First World War and was also fashionable as the expression of a slight reserve towards the Prussians'.[4] Following his conversion to Christianity, his Jewishness remained no more than a memory, albeit the memory of the history of a stricter concept of God, inimical to myth, a history that brought with it a feeling of being 'chosen', a history, in short, of persecution, exile, messianic hope, a desire for justice typical of the Old Testament prophets and a sense of ethical calling that the Jewish nation ascribed to itself. No less important was the memory of the position of the outsider that had allowed the Jew to play the role of an interpreter of dreams and symbols at the Egyptian and Babylonian courts, the memory of reading and learning from the scriptures and from the written word in general, and of the search for the traces of God in history. This view of history, which invests sufferings and hope with a sense of drama unique in the history of the world, is responsible for the element of pain and longing in individual thinking. And the additional sense of being a foreigner – even when that sense is mediated, as it was in the case of Adorno's parents by his mother's Mediterranean provenance and his father's Jewishness – invariably means that a child is necessarily more self-aware. The cultural background of neither parent could be assimilated and accepted with naïve insouciance but always required reflection. We see something similar in the case of another precociously talented writer, Hugo von Hofmannsthal, whose family could likewise point to Italian and Jewish forebears.

No less important was the family's cosmopolitanism, a life-enhancing experience that finds expression in 'Heliotrope' from the collection of prose and aphorisms, *Minima moralia*, that Adorno wrote during his years of exile in America. 'Heliotrope' tells of Else Herzberger, a friend of the family, to whom the then fifteen-year-old Adorno dedicated his first two settings of poems by Theodor Storm:

> When a guest comes to stay with his parents, a child's heart beats with more fervent expectation than it ever did before Christmas. It is not presents that are the cause, but transformed existence. The perfume that the lady visitor puts down on the chest of drawers while he is allowed to watch her unpacking, has a scent that resembles memory even though he breathes it for the first time. The cases with the labels from the Suvretta Hotel and Madonna di Campiglio, are chests in which the jewels of Aladdin and Ali Baba, wrapped in precious tissues – the guest's kimonos – are borne hither from the caravanserais of Switzerland and the South Tyrol in sleeping-car sedan chairs for his glutted contemplation.[5]

Even if it extended only as far as neighbouring countries, the vast breadth of the world had already opened up to the young Adorno.

Music formed the family's cultural centre. The film director Alexander Kluge, who was one of Adorno's pupils, once recalled how Adorno's mother, whom the philosopher always described as 'the former singer from the Imperial Court Opera',[6] toured the whole of Europe singing the part of the Forest Bird in Wagner's *Siegfried*. Some of the anecdotes concerning Adorno's own knowledge of music go beyond mere admiration and border on the incredible, with Thomas Mann, for example, reporting on his collaboration with Adorno on his novel *Doctor Faustus*: 'But his knowledge of tradition, his mastery of the whole historical body of music, is enormous. An American singer who works with him said to me: "It is incredible. He knows every note in the world."'[7] Adorno's knowledge was acquired at an early age and acquired, moreover, without effort or conflict: 'The music that we are in the habit of calling classical,' he wrote, 'I got to know as a child by playing duets. There was little in the symphonic and chamber music repertory that did not find its way into our domestic lives with the help of large oblong volumes bound by the bookbinder in a uniform green. They seemed to be made to have their pages turned, and I was allowed to turn the pages long before I knew the notes, simply by following my memory and hearing.'[8] Adorno had begun in fact with the violin and viola, followed by his earliest attempts at composition. His knowledge of harmony was self-taught.

Traces of music can also be found in Adorno's childhood memories of Amorbach. It was here, in one of the most beautiful towns in the immediate vicinity of Frankfurt, situated in the eastern part of the Odenwald, that the family spent its holidays. The sympathetic portrait of the town that Adorno later painted is at the same time a fairytale-like transfiguration of a Teutonic myth that appears here in a child's contented vision. 'Wolkmann [literally, 'Cloud Man']: a mountain that is the image of its name, a giant generously left over.' With these words in praise of a mountain, Adorno – who much later, in the course of a conversation with Monika Plessner, described himself as a 'man of the mountains' – began a brief essay that includes the earliest scene from his childhood. Never again was he to speak with such warmth about pre-1914 Germany, a country that was then calm, provincial and old-fashioned in a positive sense of the word. Even the local smithy formed a Wagnerian universe in miniature: 'It was in Amorbach that the prehistoric world of Siegfried, who according to one version of the legend was murdered beside the Zittenfeld spring deep in the wooded valley, entered childhood's world of images. The Heune Pillars below Mainbullau date back to the age of the migration of the peoples, or so I was told at the time, and were named after the Huns. This would be more beautiful than if they came from an earlier, nameless period.'[9] The ferry – that 'archaic form of transport' – recalled the villain of the *Nibelungenlied*: 'There was no simpler or more sober means of reaching the opposite bank than the vessel from which Hagen threw the chaplain into the Danube so that he was the only one of the Nibelungs to be saved. The beauty of the expedient has a retroactive force. The sounds of the ferry on the water that one listens to in silence are so eloquent because they were no different thousands of years ago.' The man, who in his mid-thirties wrote his critical *Essay on Wagner* while looking back on the countryside that he had left, had undergone an early process of socialization that was so effortless and so successful that it might have been child's play. In Amorbach he got to know the painter Max Rossmann, whose favourite lines from Wagner were from Hans Sachs's *Flieder* Monologue in *Die Meistersinger*: 'Dem Vogel, der heut' sang, dem war der Schnabel hold gewachsen' – literally, 'The bird that sang today had a well-formed beak', but conveying the idea of natural artistic inspiration. (Adorno, in fact, misquotes the line as 'Dem Vogel, der da sang'.) It was because of this, Adorno went on, that he felt that these lines summed up Amorbach for him. 'The little town is only eighty kilometres from Frankfurt, but in Franconia. – A picture by Rossmann, *The Mill at Konfurt*, unfinished and significantly dilapidated, appealed to me. My mother gave it to me before I left Germany. It accompanied me to America and back. I met Rossmann's son when I returned to Amorbach.'[10]

During his years of exile in America, it was the Franconian countryside along the River Main that returned in Adorno's dreams as a symbol of longing. Not only Wagner, but modern poets, too, seem to have encountered a sympathetic response in his parents' home, a home, moreover, that was without doubt more cultured than is normally associated with the vaguely contemptuous term 'middle-class culture'. Soma Morgenstern – an amusing, if not always entirely reliable witness – claims to have heard Adorno remark that his Aunt Agathe was 'very knowledgeable about Baudelaire, to whom she introduced me during my childhood years'.[11] Whenever Adorno wrote about questions of culture and education in years to come, he never failed to recall the preconditions that lay beyond traditional educational establishments: an opera, he believed, was something people could understand only if they had fallen in love with a soprano in their youth. And, according to *Minima moralia*, anyone wanting to find *Die Fledermaus* a thing of beauty 'must know that it is the *Fledermaus*: his mother must have told him that it is not about the winged animal but a fancy-dress costume; he must remember having been told: tomorrow you can go and see the *Fledermaus*'.[12]

Adorno's mother and aunt were both Catholic, and it was as a Catholic that he too was brought up. As Reinhard Pabst has shown, he was allowed to choose the family's Christmas trees in the Taunus mountains. He also took part in

Corpus Christi processions and scattered roses for the 'dear Christ child'. The reader should resist the temptation to smile at this: the range of culture to which he was exposed is clear even here. More than that: we can speak of 'culture' only when its ideas are related to a truth whose nucleus is expressed in religion. It was the dimension of a more sophisticated sphere of right living, as imparted to him by his Catholic education, that turned Adorno into the man we now remember him to have been.

Adorno's middle-class adolescence was shattered by the first great disaster of the twentieth century: war. He wrote very little about the period between August 1914 and November 1918, and what little he did have to say on the subject must be read, rather, between the lines. One such passage occurs in the middle of a discussion about the aesthetic problems surrounding the term '*pianissimo*' in an essay on Webern: this *pianissimo*, he wrote, 'should not be taken as it sounds, should not be taken just as a reflex of the gentlest stirrings of the soul, although it is this, too. Often, especially in Webern's orchestral pieces, but also in individual phrases in the following pieces, namely, the Violin Sonata op. 7 and the Cello Sonata op. 11, this *pianississimo* – the slightest of all sounds – is the threatening shadow of an infinitely remote and infinitely powerful noise: thus there sounded, in 1916, on a forest path near Frankfurt, the rumble of guns from Verdun, which carried as far as there.'[13]

Adorno's relations with his teacher Reinhold Zickel were also overshadowed by the war. The boy was ten when he started lessons with Zickel and soon developed a personal liking for him even though, as he was to write retrospectively, 'many National Socialist ideas were not entirely alien' to him.[14] It was above all around 1920 that Zickel, whose Protestantism was of a gloomy, somewhat sinister kind and who valued his pupil as someone with whom he could discuss the burning issues of the day, left his most lasting mark on Adorno by introducing him to poetry: 'With an integrity for which the word "heroic" is not too much but whose colour also indicates something questionable, he placed his whole life in the service of the idea of being a poet.'[15]

During the war Zickel was severely wounded on more than one occasion. 'I still clearly recall a visit to the hospital; the transparent face, the expression of selfless goodness in contact with death.'[16] Zickel was one of those who returned from the war in the certain knowledge that the old bourgeois order was played out. As such, he was the first person to confront Adorno not only with the fact that the world had changed but with the sharp-edged, unromantic features of the new reality: 'He overturned the self-evident nature of the preconditions of our liberal culture under which I had grown up. In particular, I shall never forget a conversation in which I spoke of tolerance and he made me aware for the first time of the idea of an objective truth beyond the laissez-faire of popular opinion. I had been babbling on with my usual fluency, but this left me literally dumbstruck.'[17] In 1921 or thereabouts Adorno dedicated his String Trio to his teacher, to whom he owed his earliest insights into linguistic criticism. These insights he later found confirmed by Karl Kraus. 'In an essay on the subject of what we expect from poetry I had used the word "restlessness", and with unerring love he placed his finger on the cliché-ridden, formal and at the same time badly versified nature of it.' And Zickel was the first to encourage Adorno's own attempts to write poetry: 'One poem that I submitted to him spoke of the moon, "Sleepy song plays round the corners of her mouth / Over the houses with tittering staircases." A literary expert objected to the tittering staircases, claiming that they reminded him of servant girls. Zickel said: "Then let him think that." What struck me about his defence, then and for all time, was that the beauty of a work of art has nothing to do with the desideratum that the objects depicted should be aesthetic.'[18] The moon, the twitch of a smile, the tittering – these are the topoi of the Expressionist poetry of a writer like Alfred Lichtenstein. They plunge the city into a nocturnally alienating light that allows new forms of movement to assert their unsettling sway.

By November 1918 Germany's defeat in the Great War was a foregone conclusion. In Kiel sailors mutinied against the naval command that ordered them to set to sea again. The movement of workers' and soldiers' councils quickly spread to the rest of Germany, culminating in the declaration of a republic by Philipp Scheidemann and the abdication of Wilhelm II, who went into exile in the Netherlands. The Social Democrats under Friedrich Ebert proposed a parliamentary democracy, but it did not remain uncontested, for the example of the Bolshevik Revolution in Russia had repercussions in Germany, too. The extreme left-wing Spartacists, who later formed the core of the German Communist Party, wanted not a bourgeois democracy but social revolution. In January 1919 they attempted a putsch under the leadership of Rosa Luxemburg and Karl Liebknecht, but it was bloodily suppressed. Thanks to his decisive policies, the Social Democratic minister for defence affairs, Gustav Noske, was able to prevent the country from becoming a Communist dictatorship, but it was not long before the forces on which he had to rely – above all, the Volunteer Corps – had become uncontrollable. The young democracy groaned beneath the burden of the Treaty of Versailles, which had declared Germany solely responsible for the war and which resulted not only in territorial losses but also in considerable financial penalties. There followed a period of

Adorno, his mother and his aunt outside the summer house in the grounds of the Hotel Post in Amorbach in around 1918

attempted putsches from both the left and the right. These lasted until 1923, when the Communists sought to seize power in Hamburg and Hitler attempted to do the same in Munich. The occupation of the Ruhr by the French gave a new impetus to German nationalism.

Historical changes are felt with particular force when they coincide with key periods in a person's life. Adorno was fifteen and on the brink of independence when the prospect of Communism hung over Germany. He retained a lifelong memory of this period, even if he was later to describe that memory in increasingly circumspect terms. For Adorno, the defeat of the Spartacist movement remained a political trauma of the first order. In his late lectures 'On the Doctrine of History and of Freedom', for example, he speaks of the 'possibility of freedom' developing within a lack of freedom. What he had in mind here was an ideal Communist movement projected back into history, embracing not only the slaves' uprising under Spartacus in ancient Rome but also the Peasants War in Germany and the attempted rebellion by the communist radical François-Noël Babeuf at the time of the French Revolution. 'And it is very difficult to say whether within the infinitely complex structure of history things could ever really have turned out differently and humanity could really have extricated itself from the mire. I myself believe that in my youth I experienced a moment at which this was very close to coming true.'[19] We can imagine two philosophical routes, running in opposite directions, one of which stresses the rational context, ordering and weighing up the data, while the other privileges the unsettling irruption of hitherto unknown thoughts. The first of these alternatives takes as its theme the cosmos and order, while the second is concerned with the individual event and with history. The first will tend towards ontology, whereas the second will observe the unique event and interpret its symptoms accordingly. A convenient shorthand way of referring to these two approaches is 'Athens' and 'Jerusalem'. Of course, these are abstract types, and every true philosophy will take over motifs from both. Be that as it may, the political developments that had taken place in his youth had alerted Adorno to the breakdown of various kinds of order that he had once thought stable and left him feeling sceptical about all theories of an existence that was unhistorical or outside history.

Adorno's family and his contacts with his teacher provided him with a safe haven for art and intellectual discussion, while conflicts raged all the more violently elsewhere. 'In a sense,' he wrote in 'The Bad Comrade' in *Minima moralia*,

I ought to be able to deduce Fascism from the memories of my childhood. As a conqueror dispatches envoys to the remotest provinces, Fascism had sent its advance guard there long before it marched in: my schoolfellows. If the bourgeois class has from time immemorial nurtured the dream of a brutal national community, of oppression of all by all; children already equipped with Christian-names like Horst and Jürgen and surnames like Bergenroth, Bojunga and Eckhardt enacted the dream before the adults were historically ripe for its realization. I felt with such excessive clarity the force of the horror towards which they were straining, that all subsequent happiness seemed revocable, borrowed.[20]

Adorno later believed that Eckhardt in particular was 'a typically anti-Semitic name'.[21]

In the meantime, Adorno had been confirmed in Frankfurt's Protestant Saint Catherine's Church and attended classes in religious instruction in order to avoid feeling isolated, but he was still regarded as 'the Jew' by several members of the class and subjected to anti-Semitic abuse.[22] He later recalled that this group had set itself up in opposition to the official 'top-of-the-class liberals' and represented an 'unspoken, conspiratorial hierarchy', a set of leaders who 'expressed their views on elections to the liaison committee and on similar occasions'.[23] The experiences gleaned during his childhood and adolescence meant that later, too, Adorno could envisage conflicts only from the standpoint of something that was abhorrent not only in political terms but also in terms of character: 'The five patriots who set upon a single schoolfellow, thrashed him and, when he complained to the teacher, defamed him as a traitor to the class – are they not the same as those who tortured prisoners to refute claims by foreigners that prisoners were tortured?'[24] Another distinguishing feature of Adorno's later sociological writings is their tendency to interpret social conflicts as expressions of a malicious hostility in which there is no longer any trace of mutual respect. Even in his first study, which he wrote when he was sixteen and published in a school newspaper under the title 'On the Psychology of the Relationship between Teacher and Pupil', the reader senses that the revolutionary background of this period left its author emotionally shaken and gave his thoughts their particular colour. From the very outset he writes about socialism, international understanding and materialism and of the 'basic religious ideas' to which these political doctrines must be related. It was not only a question of a practical struggle. Rather, the greatness of the present age was revealed by the fact that 'we have again learnt to fight for an idea'.[25]

The early works of a writer or artist are particularly revealing if they coincide with the beginning of an intellectual engagement that gains in succinctness with the passage of time. The title of Adorno's essay 'On the Psychology of the

Relationship between Teacher and Pupil' contains remarkable pointers to the events that were to unfold towards the end of his life, in 1968 and above all in 1969, when relations between teacher and pupils at the Institute for Social Research broke down with disastrous effect. The reader will also be reminded of the titles of some of Adorno's other books and articles, including *The Loyal Répétiteur: Didactic Writings on Musical Practice*, 'Kierkegaard's Doctrine of Love', 'Philosophy and Teacher' and 'Taboos on the Teaching Profession'. Teaching and schooling are concepts around which Adorno's thinking revolves in the main. They define the dramatic element in his life. In the first of these essays he describes a social conflict which, as he says, already owes its structure, in part, to 'prejudice' – and prejudice was not to forsake him for the whole of the rest of his life. But we also hear a pre-echo of another motif here, namely, that of maturity and childhood. And the comments that Adorno makes here, not only on the psychology of the child and adult but also on the conflict between 'age, maturity and knowledge' on the one hand and the child and adolescent school-child on the other, were later to be deconstructed. Adorno was often particularly productive when he was able to call on his memories of childhood and use them in a theoretical context. His ability to play with the dialectics of childhood and maturity gave him the means by which to react and intervene in an anti-cyclical way, for, if need be, he could fall back on older experiences, on episodes from his childhood and on events that predated the tribunal of theory and at the same time insist on the strictest theoretical orthodoxy. His writings often acquire their underlying point from the clash between these opposites and from their ability to criticize one element by reference to the other.

In the case of his essay on pupils and teachers, it is significant that he does not simply repeat the turn-of-the-century criticisms that were familiar to him from contemporary literature, be it Hermann Hesse or Emil Strauß. Quite the contrary, for the rebellious attitude on the part of adolescents was particularly suspect in his eyes. In *Minima moralia* he describes how the rebels of today reveal themselves as the conformists of tomorrow: 'Those, however, who were always truculently at loggerheads with the teachers, interrupting the lessons, nevertheless sat down, from the day, indeed the very hour of their matriculation, with the same teachers, at the same table and the same beer, in male confederacy'.[26] Through its 'sobriety, rationality and coldness', school had a 'most violently inflammatory effect on the young soul that needs warmth'.[27] But here, Adorno argued, there lay an objective and inevitable conflict, for 'as long as a mature individual is forced to achieve something in life, he must acquire knowledge during the preparatory period, i.e., a knowledge and understanding of facts and laws'.[28] In the conflict between teacher and pupils, Adorno saw a form of confrontation in which both sides drew on the irrational forces of hatred, envy and the desire for revenge. The pupils who in their uncouth camaraderie 'fight' the teacher and 'destroy him emotionally' encourage the latter to make the sort of 'emotional gesture that a person makes when physically fending off a swarm of troublesome little gnats'.[29] The subject of Adorno's first independent thoughts was the tension-laden scene in the classroom, with its contest between reason and irrationality.

2   In Search of Vocational Training

Anyone who stares for any length of time at the mullion and transom of a cross-window and then closes his eyes will see a negative: the bright openings appear black, while the wood is now white. There is a newspaper article by Siegfried Kracauer entitled 'Sentimental Suite on the Bergstraße' that operates on this principle. It was written in the early 1920s, at a time when Germany was still isolated. The country's financial meltdown meant that there were only limited opportunities for travel. And Europe remained a dream. Within this defeated country – Walter Benjamin spoke of 'poor Germany' – Kracauer offered his readers a fleeting portrait of the South. The countryside around the Bergstraße enjoyed a more favourable climate than any other part of Germany, allowing Kracauer to see in it an imaginary Italy. The narrator's young companion is called Gianino.[1] It is a portrait of the nineteen- or twenty-year-old Adorno, who plunges the day into an Italian light, 'for here,' writes his enthusiastic older friend, 'was the South, the South incarnate, we penetrated it ever more deeply, like figures in a painting in which we swaggered strangely. . . . In the little Jugenheim café we dreamt away the late morning and early afternoon. There was a piano in the room and Gianino could not resist the temptation to play it, picking out our favourite tunes, and, to the thin counterpoint of rattling cups, joviality oozed viscously from the black keys into an extinct world.'[2] Later that evening a Romantic poet recites a Gothic ballad from the feudal past but he fails to get on with the friends, who are already living in a different cultural world: 'High-spiritedly Gianino hummed a ragtime number in quarter-tones, and up there the gawping poet danced to it and was still dancing indefatigably when the rest of us, freezing in our coats, waved goodbye to him and set off home with quickening step.'[3] What Kracauer was describing was an intellectual idyll, the idealized picture of a Southern, Western, modern Germany, an imaginary space in stark contrast to the social reality of the country, which was shaken by disturbances and attempted putsches and that groaned beneath the yoke of the Treaty of Versailles and the occupation of the Ruhr. Readers who know Adorno only from his writings, above all his sharply critical essays on jazz, will have difficulty imagining this scene, for the piano rag from the turn of the century was one of the elements from which jazz emerged in the 1920s. But one of Adorno's pupils during the 1960s, Elisabeth Lenk, similarly reports on the way in which the great thinker, 'whose aversion to light music was notorious', conquered her heart 'by sitting down at the piano and improvising jazz in a masterly fashion'.[4]

'The war was barely over when Georg got to know Fred as the result of a newspaper ad. According to the ad he was looking for someone to provide extra coaching for a young boy.'[5] Thus begins the second chapter of Kracauer's posthumously published novel *Georg*. The main character is a man in his early thirties who lives in Frankfurt and who thinks seriously about philosophy and theology. From the very first moment he is enchanted by the younger man: 'For an instant, Fred hesitated in the doorway to appraise the stranger. A slim, fair-haired young man in a kind of sports outfit, who stood there as nonchalantly as if borne in on the breeze.'[6] But it is not only Fred's boyish attractiveness that Georg notices. There is more to Fred than his cheekily modern name suggests. A thinker like Georg is bound to see in him a desire to learn about philosophy. 'Leaning against his mother's chair, he answered the questions put to him in a dull tone that contradicted his large sad eyes, which peered out from beneath long eyelashes. Their expression implied a secret that was buried inside the youth, much as he himself was buried inside the coarse materials that he was wearing.'[7] This secret demanded elucidation, and what follows could be described as a philosophical socialization that recalls the poetic and philosophical socialization practised at this time by Stefan George. Their lessons in algebra and history are soon accompanied by tender embraces as their bodies nestle together. Although the childlike demon in Fred still occasionally breaks free, he is immediately able to turn on the charm again. Each seduces the other, leading to the admission: '"I'd like to spend my whole life with you, Georg."' Again and again they kiss each other. So comical with shaved cheeks.'[8] Who is Fred, who on one occasion is also called Freddie? A code name for Teddie?

Kracauer was interested principally in the transition from philosophy to a diagnosis of society and in a sociological and theological definition of the boundaries of scientific rationalism. He had studied architecture and, after 1914, designed war memorials, before emerging as a writer on philosophy with his essays on the meaning of war. 'I was nearing the end of my time at secondary school,' Adorno recalled, 'when I got to know him towards the end of the First World War. A friend of my parents, Rosie Stern, brought us together. She was a teacher at the Philanthropin, where the staff also included Kracauer's uncle, the historiographer of the Frankfurt Jews. As was no doubt our hostess's intention, lively contact was established between us.[9] Every Saturday afternoon, the two of them would read Kant's *Critique of Pure Reason* together.

> I am not exaggerating in the slightest when I say that I owe more to this reading than to my academic teachers. Pedagogically speaking, he was exceptionally gifted and brought Kant alive for me. Under his guidance, I learnt from the outset to see the work not as pure epistemology or as an analysis of the conditions underpinning scientifically valid judgements, but as a kind of coded essay that revealed a historical state of mind, with the vague expectation that something of the truth itself might be found in the process.[10]

The truth, which lies somewhere between this account and the revelations contained in Kracauer's novel *Georg*, may be found in the correspondence between Kracauer and Leo Löwenthal, later the Institute for Social Research's literary expert. In the early 1920s Löwenthal was still entirely in thrall to the Jewish reform movement under Franz Rosenzweig that was centred on the Free House of Jewish Learning in Frankfurt. Kracauer played an essential role in its shift of emphasis from a purely theological concern to a socio-theoretical one. Löwenthal, too, found a mentor in Kracauer, and Kracauer in turn could confide in him – and him alone – when he needed to unburden himself on the subject of the pangs of unrequited love that he felt for Adorno.

Kracauer's engagement with Rosenzweig's *Star of Redemption* forms one of the cruxes in this correspondence. The book, he wrote, was 'systematic rot, of course, that kills idealism only to reestablish it again afterwards. But individual points appeal to me greatly'.[11] Adorno added a few lines to this letter, striking a note of decadent coquetry reminiscent of the young Hofmannsthal:

> I'm so tired, but in a relaxed way at last, that I don't even feel like taking out *Elective Affinities*, although this is an important enough work for me. Anything more demanding than detective stories and old issues of *Die Woche* is beyond me at present, and there's little in between. We could undoubtedly recover our strength good and proper in this beautiful and special region, if it weren't for the fact that the economic situation makes every minute uncertain and we weren't afraid that the brutal dollar might put a premature end to our idyll. Friedel [i.e., Siegfried], who has retained more wit than I have, is reading Rosenzweig and reporting on linguistic philosophemes from it that I wouldn't understand even if I understood them. Even so, I mean to read the book as it deals with matters of the utmost importance.[12]

Kracauer's letters to Löwenthal contain the most impressive and lively accounts of the gifts and dangers posed by the young intellectual that the eighteen-year-old Adorno now was. Where else would we learn about the dance lessons that Adorno received in November 1921? According to Kracauer, he was 'learning Jimmy',[13] by which he meant the shimmy, a ragtime dance of the period. And where else can we read that Teddie 'longs very much to love a woman'?[14] When Kracauer and Adorno wrote a joint letter to Löwenthal in December 1923, congratulating him on his marriage, Adorno added a few whimsical lines about the 'ideology' and 'psychological insights' of marriage, prompting Kracauer to append a note of his own:

> Teddie thinks that such precious guff about philosophy is naïve and prefers it in light conversation, in other words, in letters, seminars, conversations with young ladies and so on; as you know, his (actual) writings are couched in a language that makes the drolleries derived from the convolutions of Benjamin's brain seem like the stammerings of a slobbering infant in comparison. If ever he makes a real declaration of his love and abandons the state of perfect bachelor sinfulness in order to enter a state of equally perfect marital sham, there's no doubt that he'll phrase it in such difficult terms that the young lady that he means and that is meant for him will have to have read the whole of Kierkegaard – especially *The Sickness unto Death* and the *Fragments* – in order to understand him – or in order to misunderstand and reject him – there's bound to be something in it about the 'leap' and the 'power of faith of the absurd', so that she'll inevitably think that Teddie, the philosopher, is declaring *her* absurd, something that will give rise to the worst possible disappointments.[15]

The wilfully witty tone of this note conceals the deepest pain that his love was starting to cause him. 'I was and am very sad because of Teddie,' Kracauer wrote to Löwenthal on 12 April 1924. 'Do you know, I think I feel an unnatural passion for this man, which I can explain only in terms of the fact that on a non-physical level I'm homosexual, after all. Otherwise, could I think of him in these terms and suffer because of him like a lover pining for his beloved?'[16] His unhappiness was made up of trivia, but behind it lay their incipient estrangement. Kracauer's novel had the young Fred embark on a business career that could hardly have been more trivial or superficial. A more embittered and unjust parting of the ways is hard to imagine.

Even so, Kracauer saw a very real danger. Adorno's Achilles' heel was his almost unlimited trust in ready-made theories such as Marxism, psychoanalysis and the teachings of the Second Viennese School. Even while suffering the pangs of extreme jealousy, Kracauer was aware of this: 'Only on Thursday, he granted me an hour (an hour!) of his time, which he spent reading me a critique of Musorgsky – a critique in which my entire terminology was repeated back at me, but in an artificial, ready-made way, skilfully adapted to suit the particular case. Appalling – I'd no choice but to tell him so. He was supposed to ring me on Friday – he didn't.'[17]

Kracauer dedicated his essay on 'The Detective Novel' to Adorno, while Adorno for his part inscribed his postdoctoral thesis on Kierkegaard to his friend. Both are works that inhabit the narrow dividing line between theology and social theory and, to use an expression from dialectics, deal with the 'sudden transformation' of the one into the other. This was one of the ideals of the age in both literature and philosophy. Kracauer had discovered social reality by interpreting it as the loss of meaning. The detective, he believed, represented pure rationality divorced from any theological dimension. This was an idiosyncratic approach to the phenomena of the bourgeois world that culminated with glorious absurdity in his reflections on the hotel foyer as the typical setting for detective stories. Kracauer was attempting nothing less than to prove that the hotel foyer, in each of its aspects, was the antithetical counterpart to the house of God and that the wholly rational world of the crime novel was a distorted image of a religious community:

> In both cases one arrives as a guest. But whereas the house of God is all about the service of Him to whom one betakes oneself in it, the hotel foyer serves all who betake themselves to no one in it. It is the setting of those who neither seek nor find the man who is constantly sought. . . . Here the impersonal nothing that is represented by the manager replaces the unknown in whose name the church congregation assembles.[18]

This is the world of the New Objectivity and, at the same time, a critique of that world. But Kracauer also rejected the purely theological way and was sharply critical of the translation of the Bible undertaken by Rosenzweig and Martin Buber, both of whom worked at the Free House of Jewish Learning in Frankfurt. He countered their attempts at religious reform by proposing his behavioural ideal of 'people who wait', a theologically open and uncommitted intelligentsia. His own route led him to sociology, but his writings continued to strike a lofty note reminiscent of religion.

Kracauer has been described somewhat simplistically as the 'media man' of critical theory, even though he never really gained access to the inner circle of the Institute for Social Research. But if one looks at his *Theory of Film* and at the countless film reviews that he published in the *Frankfurter Zeitung*, the label

makes sense. Yet media theory also meant a lifelong involvement with the business of propaganda, a business that affected people's lives from the time of the
First World War and throughout the whole of the Cold War. 'The crowd very
excited,' Kracauer had noted in 1912 at the time of the elections to the Reichstag:
'The stupidest people become animated, not for any profoundly practical reasons but through mutual suggestion. But at least they're all stirred! To that
extent politics is a good educational aid because thanks to something outside
them it makes people excitable who are otherwise lethargic and indifferent.'[19]
To that extent, 'even war' was 'a blessing,'[20] because it had an educational impact.
As he observed the announcement of the results of the Reichstag elections, the
twenty-three-year-old Kracauer was looking for meaningful groupings that
would ensure that social organizations retained their cohesive strength. 'The
Group as a Vehicle for Ideas' is the title of one of his most characteristic writings. It is the interplay between ideological mobilization, the media and sociology that provides the key to understanding his works. His study 'Sociology as a
Science' appeared in 1922, at a time when his discussions with Adorno were at
their most intense. Its aim was to provide a completely new basis to the material findings set out in the writings of Max Weber, Georg Simmel, Robert
Michels and Ernst Troeltsch. Sociology, ran the argument, devoted itself to
researching the 'rules' that governed the lives of 'socialized men and women'.[21]
As a result, it could not be equated with the science of history, which investigated the individual case, or with psychology or the philosophy of history.
Even if we grant Kracauer this provisional definition, there remains the question as to the specific research that can be conducted on this basis. One could
think of family structures as well as questions of leadership succession or other
aspects of social reality.

But Kracauer preferred above all to study those groups that are formed by
ideas and which as a result can define and determine the consciousness of their
members. The first example that he gives of a sociological investigation is an
outline history of the Jesuits: 'Sociological research into the Order of Jesuits . . .
will enquire into the influence that the spiritual exercises prescribed by Ignatius
necessarily have on the general behaviour of the people subject to them, [and]
will throw light on the circumstances that in general can affect the growth and
decline of a society structured along lines similar to those of the Order of
Jesuits.'[22] Even here we find that a decision has already been taken in favour
of an unequivocal research strategy, with Kracauer advocating a type of sociology that enquires into ideologies and mentalities and into their implementation
by specific techniques of shaping our consciousness. In this, he was in accord
with his contemporaries in the early 1920s, when German reality was exposed

to the conflicting demands of rival ideologies. This was a programme of socio-logical research on the part of a man who was soon to set about moulding public opinion in the pages of the *Frankfurter Zeitung* and who later, during his years of exile in America, investigated the impact of the propaganda broadcasts of *Voice of America* that were transmitted to Eastern Europe. 'It matters little', we read in 'Sociology as a Science', 'where and when people live: if they belong to professions, positions and classes of the same sociological make-up, their essen-tial nature will reveal common features. The education to which they are sub-jected influences their thinking, feeling and the direction of their will. Indeed, it even creates a particular Weltanschauung.'[23] *Weltanschauung* – a particular philosophy or world view – was one of the key words of the 1920s. Another of Kracauer's categories is also worth mentioning in this context. His study of the detective story begins with a picture of a meaningful life, a life of spiritual depth. The person who leads such a life is said by Kracauer to be '*ausgerichtet*' ['orientated' or 'focused'].[24] It is not just a descriptive term but is, above all, nor-mative: to be 'focused' is the highest virtue that the theologically inspired soci-ologist and contemporary commentator can envisage. Taken together with his reflections on the way in which the group is conditioned by ideas, this argument results in an atmospheric portrait of the Weimar Republic in which public debate was determined by 'focused' individuals and by groups conditioned by a particular *Weltanschauung*. Kracauer's sociology was a response to a situation that it simultaneously idealized. He would presumably never have become the great media specialist that he was or the author of an ideologically critical his-tory of the German cinema, *From Caligari to Hitler*, if his contemporaries had not been prepared to believe in him.

But if we stop to ask ourselves why these brilliant analyses, including his leg-endary study *The White-Collar Ethos* (1929), ultimately remained politically ineffectual in the Weimar Republic, we shall have to examine the texts them-selves. One particularly incriminating piece of evidence is a diary entry by the then twenty-two-year-old Kracauer in which he contemptuously denies his contemporaries the 'will to experience': they led passive lives, he believed; their experience was of an inferior kind.[25] As he wrote at the time, these people included no stars that shone with their own light. Such arrogance may be typi-cal of students, but the prejudice returns in *The White-Collar Ethos*. Here Kracauer argues that this social stratum 'now lives without any doctrine to look up to, without a goal that they can enquire after'.[26] This, however, is a life 'that can be called a life in only a limited sense'.[27] It is not the material limitations of the lives of white-collar workers that cause life to become impoverished. Rather, their refusal to espouse the virtues demanded of them by the philosopher prompted him to voice a criticism that was bound to be humiliating to the parties concerned and that meant that he encountered resistance.

Adorno's relations with Kracauer were never entirely free of tension, and during their years of exile the incipient estrangement between them came to a head. Quite apart from their personal differences, there was also a practical reason for their increasing coldness in that Kracauer was by nature a visual person and mistrusted pure theory. And, unlike Ernst Bloch, for example, he could relate to reality. He had written an elaborately illustrated doctoral thesis on eighteenth-century wrought-iron work, and as a film critic he found a further point of contact with the visual world. For his study of white-collar workers, he did not rely on Marxist deductions but visited firms, interviewed bosses and trade union representatives and went to Berlin nightclubs. While working on his biography of the operetta composer Jacques Offenbach during his years of exile in France, he also began to plan a whole town. Even as late as his study *Theory of Film*, he was still interested in visual elements, in faces and buildings.

Like the whole of the generation that began to study after the First World War, Adorno found himself confronted by a highly politicized situation. Within the prevailing intellectual and spiritual chaos, contemporaries sought not only science as a pillar of support. The old points of reference had disappeared with the old Reich. Indeed, bourgeois society seemed to have reached the end of the road not only in Russia but elsewhere, too. During its early years, the Weimar Republic could hardly have been less stable. Inflation turned into hyperinflation. Many observers thought that through the breaches in the natural order of things they could see into unsuspected depths. From all sides came messages of the new, and the old ruling classes and their modern alternatives now fought over the right to mould society. An esoteric history of the Germans, full of future promise in spite of the country's defeat, could be found in the writings associated with Stefan George and his circle. Among the exponents of revolutionary Naturalism were the brothers Ernst and Friedrich Georg Jünger and the playwright Arnolt Bronnen. The aftershocks caused by the philosophy of Friedrich Nietzsche, with its appeal to an aristocracy of the mind, found a counterpart in the reappraisal of Judaism by Franz Rosenzweig and Martin Buber. With its victory in the Russian civil war, Communism had acquired a position of power that made it possible for its promise of justice and fairness to exert a material influence on radicals in Western and Central Europe. Oswald Spengler's *The Decline of the West* exercised minds with its diagnostic claim that the final struggle of the era would be fought with the rule of money. The proponents of esoteric doctrines, including not only such occult variants as that advanced by Rudolf Steiner but also writers more or less closely associated with academic philosophy, sought supporters for their new doctrines of salvation. And was music not the stormy petrel of all these revolutions? The Austrian Futurist Robert Müller had claimed that the First World War was in the same relationship to earlier wars as the music of Arnold Schoenberg was to tradition. In the view of another observer, the poet and composer Jürgen von der Wense, the names of Moscow, Lenin and Skryabin merged for a moment to create the new world's revolutionary harmony of the spheres.

One trend, above all, had been invalidated: that of the liberal bourgeoisie of the pre-war period. For a young man born in 1903, to pursue an interest in philosophy meant seriously enquiring after doctrines and investigating possible kinds of order and their foundations, or examining the legitimacy of the great upheaval that was then taking place. While Bolshevism promised to remove the existing order, there were also attempts to re-establish a new sense of order and maintain its objectivity. Adorno's philosophy was shaped by his critical engagement with these challenges. During the 1960s, when he was able to look back on his own development, he planned to write three essays on the thinkers who had influenced him: Kracauer, Ernst Bloch and, under the title 'Knock Lukács', a study of the Hungarian philosopher Georg Lukács. All three writers came from the German philosophical tradition and had embraced Marxism in the early 1920s, resulting in the latter's change of aspect: whereas the old social democracy had preached a scientifically coloured but, from a philosophical point of view, not especially sophisticated materialism of 'power and matter', forming a kind of alliance only with Neo-Kantianism in which social change was defined as an 'infinite challenge' to the moral individual, Lukács and Bloch introduced the idea of revolution, which was thereby brought into electrifying contact with the Hegelian renaissance in German philosophy. No one can deny that more exciting prospects were opened up here. Evidently it was possible to be both a serious philosopher and at the same time a radical Marxist.

Adorno's principal model in the philosophy of art was Georg Lukács, the author of *Soul and Form* and *The Theory of the Novel*. Kracauer, too, was influenced by Lukács, as, indeed, were many intellectuals of his day. Lukács's first work following his conversion to Marxism was *History and Class Consciousness*, which appeared in 1924 and which was an attempt to write a philosophy for the Bolshevik Revolution and the Leninist party, a philosophy in which Marx was to meet the German humanities. Lukács hailed from the circles around Georg Simmel and Max Weber and was married to a Russian terrorist, who was a member of the Social Revolutionary party. He took over the office of commissar for culture during the Soviet Revolution in Hungary in 1919 and commanded a division of the Hungarian Red Army, in which capacity he condemned a number of deserters to death. There were quite a few Jews among the Hungarian Communists, whereas on the side of the counter-revolutionaries, anti-Communism and anti-Semitism were often barely distinguishable. As Péter Esterházy writes in an epic family memoir, many Hungarians regarded the short-lived Hungarian commune as no more than a 'Jewish business'.[28]

Lukács began as a literary theorist. Indeed, revolution features in his writings as the logical consequence of the written word. In Hegel's philosophy of history, the direction taken by the world spirit was unambiguous: like the sun, it ran from East to West, from China to post-revolutionary Europe, thereby following progress in the consciousness of freedom. In Lukács's theory of the novel, which was written a century later and which Adorno read as a seventeen-year-old in his final year at school, the direction was equally unambiguously reversed: the new world of the bourgeois novel that had begun in Spain with *Don Quixote* passes via France and Germany to pre-revolutionary Russia, where the promise of great things to come is already adumbrated, in Lukács's view, in the works of Dostoevsky. Certainly, the road taken by Lukács led for many a long year to Moscow. It was here that he became a dogmatic proponent of Socialist Realism and the enemy of European modernism. And not just here. There is a tendency to draw a distinction between the early Lukács as a sensitive aesthete and, less positively, the late dogmatic advocate of realism. All the more surprising, then, is it to encounter such dogmatism in the early collection *Soul and Form* of 1910. Here Lukács begins an imaginary conversation on 'Richness, Chaos and Form' in Laurence Sterne by describing 'a simply furnished, middle-class girl's room where new and very old objects are mixed together in a curiously inorganic fashion'.[29] Here we find a stylistic mix of the most promiscuous kind, with Japanese woodcuts hanging beside Giotto, Whistler and Vermeer. It becomes clear from the conversation between two students, Vincenz and Joachim, that this art no longer involves any sense of obligation. The young woman is strikingly beautiful but she has nothing to say, and so the title is 'A Dialogue'. In her lap lies a book – Goethe's aphorisms. Vincenz, the first of the two students to find himself alone with her, reads to her from Sterne's *Sentimental Journey*.

When Joachim enters, he sets the others straight. Sterne is an unsuitable writer: 'It isn't that Sterne is not for me, although it's true that I don't care for him. It's this one here (he points at the volume of Goethe, which is still lying in the girl's lap) that Sterne doesn't go with.'[30] As a narrator, Sterne works with constant interruptions – *Tristram Shandy* owes its birth to a coitus interruptus – and gratefully welcomes every contingency that offers him the opportunity for more and more digressions. As such, he becomes the epitome of the sort of literary modernism that the early Lukács was keen to combat. In putting down the English novelist, Joachim articulates the battle slogans that his creator was later to use against Kafka and the literary avant-garde: confusedly heterogeneous elements, a lack of structure and 'complete anarchy'.[31] What is found here is not an abundance of life, as Vincenz hesitantly objects, but cowardice in the face of limitations: 'Anarchy is death. That is why I hate it and fight against it. In the name of life.'[32] For Lukács, the opposite of anarchy was the hoped-for, expected art of 'a culture in which the whole nature of a man was compressed into an epigram'.[33] The final essay of the 1910 collection sees this art form in the tragedies of Paul Ernst, works that allow a glimpse of the outlines of a new greatness. In contradistinction to the idea of mystic unity with the absolute, the theme of tragedy is the self tested to its ultimate extreme: 'The self stresses its selfhood with an all-exclusive, all-destroying force, but this extreme affirmation imparts a steely harshness and autonomous life to everything it encounters.'[34] The tragic life is, of all possible lives, the one 'most exclusively of this world'.[35] Lukács speaks of the 'mystery of greatness' and of the tragic as the 'privilege of greatness'.[36] This was the blueprint of a life which, without being religious, had a meaning comparable only to that of religion.

Fourteen years later, Adorno found a figure to fill the space left vacant in 1910. His essay on Lenin speaks of the 'greatness of a proletarian thinker' and describes the Russian leader as the 'greatest thinker to be produced by the revolutionary workers' movement'.[37] A defining element of the greatness that Lukács had in mind was the category of necessity. In his study on Bolshevism, Ernst Nolte has spoken of the 'feeling of absolute right and of identity with the laws of history' that characterized the Russian form of Communism that Lenin helped to shape.[38] 'Historical necessity', we read in Lukács's metaphysics of tragedy, 'is, after all, the nearest to life of all necessities.'[39] It was a Central and Eastern European double portrait from which the ideal picture of the Communist official emerged, with the professional Russian revolutionary joining the radical German student. In *The Magic Mountain*, Thomas Mann raised a literary monument to this character in the figure of Leo Naphta, the Eastern antagonist of the Freemason Lodovico Settembrini who in an endless series of speeches praises the blessings of Western lay civilization. Naphta's home address even contains an allusion to Lukács inasmuch as he lives in a building that also houses a couturier by the name of Lukaçek.

He was small and thin, clean-shaven, and of such piercing, one might almost say corrosive ugliness as fairly to astonish the cousins. Everything about him was sharp: the hooked nose dominating his face, the narrow, pursed mouth, the thick bevelled lenses of his glasses in their light frame, behind which were a pair of pale-grey eyes – even the silence he preserved, which suggested that when he broke it, his speech would be incisive and logical.[40]

Naphta emerges as the sworn enemy of individualism and a typical 'bourgeois', a man who prefers the meaningful world of the Middle Ages to the 'capitalistic world-republic'.[41] What he dreams of is the return of a theologically based order, and Mann allows him to have his say in the chapter 'Of the City of God, and Deliverance by Evil'. Naphta's eschatology turns out to be a celebration of cruelty. A wooden sculpture in his room depicts Christ as a grotesque Man of Sorrows, 'the hanging head bristling with thorns, face and limbs blood-besprinkled, great blobs of blood welling from the wound in the side and from the nail-prints in hands and feet'.[42] Naphta is a man of absolute faith, and this faith is justified above all by its destructive energy. More than the coming state of righteousness, he celebrates the punishments of the Inquisition.

By the date of the novel's publication, Lukács had had to contend in real life with the Communist Inquisition, when *History and Class Consciousness* was condemned as 'idealistic'. In fact, this temporary conflict was beneficial, rather than detrimental, to Lukács's growing reputation in Europe. Following the failed Communist putsch of 1919, he had been living in Austria – an appeal by mainly German writers had saved him from being sentenced to death – and he was now regularly invited to take part in discussions on the philosophy of history. The novelist Hermann Broch sought him out, and Adorno, too, refused to pass up the opportunity for a private meeting.

> My first impression was great and deep: a small, delicate and ungainly East European Jew with a Talmudic nose and wonderful inscrutable eyes, looking very donnish in a linen sports outfit but with a wholly unconventional, deathly clear and mild atmosphere about him, an atmosphere through which the only aspect of his person to penetrate even a little was bashfulness. . . . On one occasion he left me shaken, when he explained that in his conflict with the Third International his opponents had been in the right, concretely, and that only dialectically was his absolute approach to dialectics demanded. In this madness lies his human greatness and the tragedy of the reversal that he suffered. About Tolstoy he said something sadly malicious, perhaps thinking of himself.[43]

As a literary portrait of an exemplary Communist intellectual and his other-worldly, abstract fanaticism that achieved its full impact only when accompanied by an aura of goodness, this is at least the equal of Mann's description of the figure of Leo Naphta in *The Magic Mountain*. And it shows that Adorno was not always receptive to purely Muscovite concerns. He never really found a point of contact with Russian music – in a critique of Musorgsky's *Boris Godunov*, first published in 1924, he noted that the 'category of the individual' was crucial to 'the art of the West' but had no place in the Russian composer's work, with the result that it always sounded like music 'from another planet'[44] – and the great works of Russian literature likewise never seem to have tempted him into interpreting them. Although it was here that 'Western Marxism' began, the expression remained self-contradictory, as Lukács himself was fully aware: although he had repeatedly run extreme existential risks, he used the republication of *The Theory of the Novel* in the 1960s to add a preface in which he mocked the critical theory of the Frankfurt School, claiming that its proponents had 'taken up residence at the "Grand Hotel Abyss"'.

Kracauer and Lukács were the first important influences on Adorno. They were soon joined by Ernst Bloch, whom Kracauer initially regarded as an Expressionist fantast. Adorno later recalled: 'I had not written a date in my copy of the first edition of *The Spirit of Utopia*, but I must have read it in 1921. During the spring of that year, while I was in my final year at school, I got to know Lukács's *Theory of the Novel* and discovered that Bloch was close to its author. I pounced on the book.'[45] Yet, Adorno's initial approach was one of scepticism, a feeling he shared with Kracauer: 'Teddie has bought *The Spirit of Utopia* and finds Lukács greater, something that pleases me,' Kracauer told Löwenthal in October 1921.[46] Bloch was a gifted narrator, and an account that he gives of his beginnings as a writer may perhaps provide the best access to his philosophy. 'Carmilhan' is the mysterious word whispered in the ear of a half-asleep fisherman by spirit voices in Wilhelm Hauff's short story, *The Cave at Steenföll*. The fisherman thinks he is destined for great good fortune, and when the word again wells up from the deep, this time from within the cave, the gaunt man becomes a fanatic who abandons his career and from then on obeys only the promises of the magic word. He is possessed by a hope that proves his undoing. His search for the golden treasure of the sunken ship, the *Carmilhan*, that once foundered off the Scottish coast on its journey from Batavia robs him of his reason and ultimately his life. Bloch once recalled in a television interview that in 1900, when he was fifteen, he wanted to write an opera based on Hauff's short story. As such, the work would have provided a coded account of the century as a whole on its very threshold. Is there a more fitting way of describing ideologies than as half-understood magic phrases at whose bidding people start marching?

Bloch, who grew up on the Rhine, recalled having spent his youth 'on ships', Dutch ships that had come to Europe from Sumatra. The political island is the epitome of all Utopias – an island was also the setting of *Utopia* by the Renaissance thinker Thomas More, whose imaginary island is the prototype of all ideal states. Bloch was more aware of the heretical tradition of the world's religions than either Lukács or Kracauer. 'Prayer is conjuration', we read in one of his key sentences, and, indeed, it is with this sentence that *The Spirit of Utopia* ends. It is difficult to imagine a clearer definition of the magic word. Bloch did not write his *Carmilhan* opera. The pessimism that informs Hauff's short story was uncongenial to a thinker who pinned his colours to the mast of hope. But the exotic magic of sounds that imbues Hauff's fairytale became the law underpinning his philosophy. *The Spirit of Utopia* is a book about such words and sounds. Whole sections are devoted to music, a medium that Bloch felt culminated, via Wagner and Bruckner, in the symphonies of Gustav Mahler. For this reason, if for no other, Bloch's thinking was bound to exercise Adorno, who later praised – and at the same time gently mocked – his friend's style as 'great Bloch music'. 'Dully as a seventeen-year-old perceives such phenomena, I had the feeling that philosophy had here escaped the curse of all things official.'[47] He valued Bloch's way with words in expressions such as '"departure inwards" (*Abfahrt nach innen*), on the narrow dividing line between magic formula and concept'.[48] Even the book's outward presentation led its young reader away from school philosophy: 'The dark brown volume, printed on thick paper and running to more than four hundred pages, held out something of the promise that readers hope to find in medieval books and that I felt as a child at home when I read a pigskin copy of *The Treasury of Heroic Tales*, a latterday book of magic from the eighteenth century, full of abstruse instructions, some of which I can still remember today. *The Spirit of Utopia* looked as though it had been written in Nostradamus's own hand.'[49] Not until 1928 was Adorno introduced in person to the author of *The Spirit of Utopia*.

But Adorno's portrait omits many of the politically more problematical aspects of Bloch's career and personality. During the First World War, Bloch had lived in Switzerland, from where he had published a whole series of articles and pamphlets, not only expressing his misgivings at the policies of the German Reich but advocating the war aims of the Allies, especially those of the French. Initially he even rejected the Bolshevik October Revolution on the grounds that Lenin's seizure of power, which had become possible only because he had promised a prompt ceasefire, delayed Germany's ultimate defeat. In short, Adorno's first teachers were unorthodox, philosophizing Marxists. But that is not all, for all of them had adopted unequivocal positions at the start of the First World War, with Lukács opting for the Eastern solution of a violent revolution, while Kracauer had grappled with the problems of propaganda and people's 'orientation' in his attempt to answer the question about the 'meaning of war' and Bloch had distinguished himself with his active support of the Allies, which then turned into his ardent advocacy of Soviet Russia. Adorno could not have found better mentors for a philosophy suited to the catastrophic days that lay ahead of him.

'For the present he consists for the most part of Lukács and me,' Kracauer wrote to Leo Löwenthal in the winter of 1921. 'Is he perhaps missing something? – The philosophical Eros that you possess. With him, far too much stems from the intellect and from the will instead of the depths of nature. But there is one point on which he is incomparably ahead of us: a splendid outward existence and a wonderful naturalness of character. He is already a fine specimen of a human being; and although I'm not without a certain scepticism about his future, his present life is a source of great joy to me.'[50] This may have seemed different to those who looked in from the outside and who were not initiated into the philosophical language that was to come. When he got to know Adorno in the mid-'twenties, Soma Morgenstern, for example, heard only a 'philosophical Volapük', an absurdly artificial language: 'Quite why he always says "personality" when he means "person", I couldn't work out on that first evening.'[51]

3 Philosophy and Music

Adorno enrolled at the University of Frankfurt in 1921 to study philosophy, sociology, psychology and the theory of music. The university was only seven years old, having been established in October 1914, largely thanks to funding from a middle-class foundation. And it was regarded as progressive, not least because it was the first institute of higher education in Germany to include a faculty of economics and social sciences. Its predecessor had been an Academy of Social Sciences and Trade, dating back to 1901, with the result that an institutional framework already existed to provide the preconditions for a sociological orientation to the humanities.

Adorno graduated in 1924 with a doctoral thesis on 'The Transcendence of the Material and Noematic in Husserl's Phenomenology'. His teacher was the philosopher Hans Cornelius, whose background was in the natural sciences and who was at pains to provide epistemology with a strict scientific basis which in his case boiled down to psychology. He believed that it is possible to make unequivocal statements only about processes within human consciousness: these are structured according to rules and laws and form a coherent framework. All ideas are contained within the 'unity of our consciousness'. The 'framework of consciousness' is the basic term in Cornelius's philosophy. Only within this framework can cognition be legitimized. Cornelius placed psychology at the head of philosophy, from which he expected an analysis and description of the facts of human consciousness. His goal was a free science stripped of all dogmatic preconditions and dealing with the 'directly given facts of consciousness' and the processes that took place within it. His aim, in short, was a psychology free of metaphysics. The whole point of this doctrine is the rejection of every dogmatic claim, every presupposition of the existence of external data. And it was this that was Adorno's premise in his assault on Husserl's phenomenology. There was, he claimed, an unresolved contradiction in Husserl's thinking. On the one hand, consciousness was assumed to be a 'legitimate source of insight', while on the other, it postulated 'from the outset a transcendental world that can be legitimized epistemologically only in relation to consciousness but whose existence is not constituted by the framework of consciousness'.[1] The 'inadmissible appeal to material being in Husserl' was dogmatic,[2] Adorno argued, insisting instead – entirely in the spirit of Cornelius – on the 'legitimate framework of phenomena'.[3] If Adorno later criticized every attempt at ontological philosophy that was geared towards objective ontological structures, his dissertation already included an embryonic form of this motif in its rejection of the 'given' and the enhanced role that it gave to empirical consciousness and its framework. Adorno had attempted to solve a limited technical problem that was to prove basic to his later work. The oral part of his examination was held at the Philosophical Faculty in Frankfurt on 28 July 1924.

We can imagine a type of philosophy that investigates meaning, which it posits as given, be it the love of God, fate or an order of being. Events themselves then reveal elements of meaning. This was an option that many people followed, especially in the neo-religious movements that sprang up after the First World War. Adorno, by contrast, decided in favour of a fundamental rationalism, thereby opting in advance for secular modernism. This had repercussions, for it meant turning his back on metaphysics, abandoning positive religious philosophizing, privileging rational constructs, keeping jealous watch over the autonomy of the individual and, in a political context, adopting a clear position concerning the tradition that was regarded as 'irrational'. Instead, his options were liberalism, socialism and Communism.

'My relations with Teddie, about which you enquire,' Siegfried Kracauer wrote to Leo Löwenthal on 6 June 1924,

are slowly disintegrating; he doesn't know it, but precisely for that reason, they are, . . . for if he noticed, there'd be grounds for hope. He's written his doctoral thesis incredibly quickly over the last few weeks: Husserl, examined and criticized using Cornelius's terminology – clever and sound, but, as he himself realizes, highly inconsequential from an objective point of view. He's spent the last few days dictating – I've hardly seen him, and when I have done, it's been to read to me or to use me in a philosophical regard. Next week he's having a music festival here, and then perhaps there'll be another doctoral dissertation: that's typical of him, he'll always have such a piece to write. The oral examination is in mid-July. He's kept saying that he means to write to you. Has he? I don't suppose so. He'll always forget what's important in human terms because of something of importance that's not important at all.[4]

As for Adorno's work, Kracauer's opinion was only partially justified. True, even here we see Adorno's dependence on ready-made teachings and terminologies, but this does not mean that his work was of no importance. Above all, the doctrine of a 'framework of consciousness' provided not only an epistemological reading, but a musical one, too. For composition, as defined by Arnold Schoenberg, was also about context. As is often the case with Adorno, a philosophical text can be read directly as a treatise on the theory of music.

If it is true, then, that Adorno took his cue from Lukács and Bloch in terms of the claims and social significance of philosophy, this is also tantamount to saying that the role of these two thinkers – the role of politico-aesthetic, Expressionist or neoclassical prophets – was already filled and no longer available for Adorno to play. He took up their ideas, but he rationalized them in the same way that he later attempted to translate Walter Benjamin's complex intuitions into a more rational dialectic. The terms that Adorno used in his early writings on music still bear the hallmarks of Expressionism – 'personality' and soul, inwardness and experience – but they bear within them the potential for being translated into the rational terminology of Cornelius's 'framework of consciousness' and later into that of psychoanalysis inasmuch as both of these conceptual worlds agree in giving a greater role to subjectivity. And the same resistance to assumed objectivity that had been inculcated in him by Cornelius also left its mark on Adorno's early writings on music. 'One cannot build cathedrals if no congregation desires them,' he wrote in 1922 in a review of a piece by Philipp Jarnach, 'even if one believes in God oneself. One cannot achieve objectivity by forcing one's subjectivity into alien forms that are bound up with other metaphysical, aesthetic and sociological preconditions. Otherwise that subjectivity tears the form apart and celebrates its own self-deification. Only on the basis of the self and its continuing decision is it possible to outgrow the self, no objective housing holds us, we have to build our house ourselves.'[5] 'Only on the basis of the self' – this is something that Cornelius, too, could have written, while Adorno's scepticism towards neo-religious aspirations was a feature that linked him to Kracauer. Adorno praised the masterly form of Hindemith's song cycle *Das Marienleben*, for example: 'Yet in spite of this, it seems to me that this encounter with Rilke's poetry, with a devotion that is longed for but not believed in and with aesthetic surrogates for religion that are assembled from every field of culture, has brought an alien sound to Hindemith's world.'[6] And he complains angrily that in Busoni's *Fantasia contrappuntistica*, 'the aesthetically self-sufficient artist feigns a quasi-religious objectivity'.[7] Internal consistency is the decisive criterion for the quality of a piece, while borrowed objectivity is exposed as one of the fundamental untruths of the age, not only in 'secondary religion' but also in the use of folk elements in art music, as well as its opposite, the equally superficial attempt to write 'European' music. An enmity is posited between the hope for objective order and subjective understanding or cognition.

Looking back on his early career, Adorno wrote to the composer Ernst Krenek in the mid-1930s: 'Unless I am much mistaken, you've recently assimilated markedly Catholic ideas. These are very, very familiar to me; I too once thought that through the Catholic *ordo* it was possible to reconstitute a world that is out of joint and on that occasion, ten years ago, I was on the point of converting to Catholicism, a conversion that seemed obvious enough to the son of a Catholic mother. I wasn't able to go through with it – the integration of *philosophia perennis* seems to me hopelessly romantic and in contradiction to every aspect of our existence; and I cannot find any trace of it in Schoenberg.'[8] If there was really any question of a return to Catholicism in the mid-twenties, then the question had already been answered at that time. It was a question, moreover, that had already been answered not least by Thomas Mann's *The Magic Mountain*, in which the position of the Catholic-cum-Bolshevik advocate of the new theocracy was already taken by the figure of Lukács–Naphta. Conversely, the role of the infernal music critic that Adorno was to play in *Doctor Faustus* was still vacant.

Adorno was introduced to his future wife, Margarete Karplus, in Berlin in 1923, an introduction that he owed to a friend of the Wiesengrund family, Else Herzberger, whom he greatly admired. She was a good twelve months older than Adorno, an age difference that recalls the one between his parents. Gretel, as Adorno called her, thereby involuntarily reminding all who heard the name of the fairytale title of several pieces in *Minima moralia*, had been born in Berlin, and it was here, too, that she grew up. She came from an Austrian family of physicians of Jewish descent and had studied the natural sciences, numbering Max Born among her teachers. For her doctorate, she specialized in chemistry and conducted research into the effect of calcium hydride on ketone. She was, in short, a highly gifted woman in whom Adorno found a congenial partner. From 1928 she was also very friendly with Walter Benjamin, who gave her the pet name of Felicitas. And in later years she became friendly with Max Horkheimer. Until 1937 she ran a leather-processing factory in Berlin. Although Adorno had something of a roving eye where women were concerned, he remained loyal to Gretel in a higher sense. Even his hope of immortality, which he hints at in *Negative Dialectics*, was associated with her: 'On the eve of my departure,' he recalled in the 1960s, 'I dreamt that the fact that I cannot abandon all metaphysical hope is certainly not because I am too attached to life but because I'd like to wake up with Gretel.'[9] Gretel Adorno was more closely involved with the development of critical theory than has generally been assumed. During their years of exile in America, she kept a record of her husband's discussions with Max Horkheimer, discussions that were to lead to their *Dialectic of Enlightenment*. And she later worked with both men at the Institute for Social Research, notably on the 'Group Experiment' study. Adorno regularly dictated his writings to her: here her contribution was by no means simply that of the passive agent of his will but, as the first person to hear these works and as a representative reader, she also formulated objections and made a number of critical comments.

'All his life,' Thomas Mann later wrote about Adorno, 'this man of remarkable intellect has refused to choose between the professions of philosophy and music. He felt that he was actually pursuing the same thing in these divergent realms. His dialectic turn of mind and bent toward social history is interlinked with a passion for music; the phenomenon is no longer unique nowadays and is doubtless connected with the whole complex of problems of our time.'[10] Adorno's first composition teacher was Bernhard Sekles, who taught at the Hoch Conservatory in Frankfurt and whose other pupils included Paul Hindemith. Sekles was the dedicatee of the string quartet that Adorno wrote in 1921. In November of that year Kracauer wrote to Löwenthal to report proudly on his friend's talent, which had now found public recognition following the work's first performance by the Rosé Quartet in the spring of that year. Adorno was '18 years old – the scamp'.[11] During the summer of 1922 Adorno wrote a tribute to his teacher on the occasion of the latter's fiftieth birthday, noting that 'all the young musicians of Frankfurt' were 'attached' to Sekles 'as to their leader and friend'.[12] It was Sekles who showed Adorno the way to modernism. 'Even today,' he wrote during the winter of 1921/2, 'he is still falsely accounted a Neo-Romantic because the Jew in him could honourably remain only within the Eastern stylistic tradition, albeit observed very much from the West.'[13] Sekles had begun his compositional career as a Brahmsian characterized by a 'beautiful remoteness from all bombast and overemotionalism'. Behind his playful irony lay 'a hesitant, nostalgic and chaste interiority'. The listener may be reminded of a figure straddling a border: on the one hand, there is urbane irony and a reduction in large-scale gestures and, on the other, nostalgia for the homeland. Many of Sekles's works, Adorno went on, had been 'regarded as "exotic" on account of their droll and colourful impact. . . . For him, the grotesque is not an end in itself but merely the bridge that his soul constructs between its lyrical detachment and the world lest it sink into the abyss; his strangeness is not located merely in his style but reflects the strangeness of his nature in the face of the outside world.'[14]

Sekles's works were an early expression of musical modernism and, as such, one that Adorno, who heard Stravinsky, Schoenberg and Bartók at concerts in Frankfurt, found ultimately unsatisfying. Thirty years later, in *Minima moralia*, he cast a critical glance at his teacher and was unstinting in his contempt for Sekles's exotic orientalisms, which he now judged from a different standpoint and which he dismissed as 'the manoeuvres of a conservatory director with a bad conscience'.[15]

> When my first composition teacher, trying to knock the atonal nonsense out of me, found his tales of erotic scandals about the new composers proving ineffective, he switched his attack to what he suspected as my weak spot, by showing himself up-to-date. The ultra-modern, his argument ran, was no longer modern, the stimulations I sought were already numb, the expressive figures that excited me belonged to an outmoded sentimentality, and the new youth had, as he liked to put it, more red blood-corpuscles.[16]

Adorno soon broke free from Sekles and went off to study with Alban Berg in Vienna.

If Frankfurt, with its new university, represented the intellectual life of the country, including Cornelius's scientific philosophy and the birth of a new generation of Jewish thinkers in Franz Rosenzweig's House of Jewish Learning, and if Berlin was the political centre of the country, where power struggles were decided, then Vienna was the home of German music, with an unbroken tradition stretching from Mozart, Haydn and Beethoven to Brahms, Bruckner, Mahler and Schoenberg, including the latter's pupils. It was a tradition that asserted itself even through revolutionary change. Nor was this tradition mere ballast, something simply dragged along as a dead weight. Rather, it signified a musical norm, music in general, at least to the extent that it sought to fulfil its potential. Adorno was as convinced of the universal importance of this tradition as he was of the line from German idealism to Marx being the ultimate expression of philosophy. Within the German spirit, mediated, perhaps, by the idea of the medieval 'Empire', there had long been a universalist component, a proud certainty that what had been created here was of direct importance for world history. It was a certainty that sustained even Adorno's critical undertaking. He always harboured reservations about Russian music, believing that it appealed, rather, to an emotional type of listener, and he thought that English music had lost its way under the pressure of an economic attitude sprung from a kind of mental asceticism. He revealed a contemptuous lack of understanding of Elgar, for example, sneering in his *Introduction to the Sociology of Music* that 'the English evidently genuinely enjoy listening to him'.[17] Only the French, especially Debussy and above all Ravel, were accorded the role of a counter-weight to Wagner. Among Eastern European composers, only Bartók and Janáček had Adorno's full approval.

It was no accident, then, that Adorno chose Vienna as the city where he opted to study composition. In his *Introduction to the Sociology of Music*, he described the Viennese tradition as a 'synthesis of the German and the Italian'.[18] It was a synthesis that began with Mozart: 'The sensuously Southern element is refracted by a spirituality that distances it while seizing hold of it and thus allows it to speak for the first time. Southern affability that centuries earlier smoothed away the provincial and boorish elements from the German form of musical reaction now receives its own back from the German or Austrian as a spiritualized picture of substantial, undivided life.'[19] The element of the rational and structured in music was joined by the 'naïve element of direct singing from the highly effective art of the Italians'.[20] In this way, Mozart's characteristic humanity was 'shaped by this national duality'.[21] And it was this tension that defined the true spirit of Vienna as a city and determined the universal validity of its music. At the same time, that tension allowed Adorno to rediscover something of his own family history. But Vienna was also the city of psychoanalysis, the city of communicative refinement in general, including the psychological novels and short stories of Arthur Schnitzler and the great school of polemical criticism embodied by Karl Kraus.

It was a performance of the Three Fragments from Alban Berg's *Wozzeck* that provided the impetus behind Adorno's move to Vienna. Georg Büchner's play about the unstable municipal soldier who becomes a murderer had acquired a new and depressing topicality in a world that saw disturbed soldiers returning home from the front. Writers such as Hugo von Hofmannsthal in his comedy *The Difficult Man* and Bertolt Brecht in his play *Drums in the Night* had espoused the cause of these traumatized men who were thrown back on their elemental, natural instincts. Berg's opera used all the resources of modern music to underscore its socio-critical message. When the Captain sings that Wozzeck is 'a good man', the whole of the musical emphasis lies on the mockingly lengthened word 'good'. Adorno left the following account of his first meeting with Berg:

I met him at the Frankfurt festival of the Allgemeiner Deutscher Musikverein in 1924, in the spring or early summer, on the evening of the première of the Three Fragments from *Wozzeck*. Swept away by the work, I asked Scherchen, whom I knew, to introduce me to Berg. Within minutes it was arranged that

I would go to Vienna to study with him; I had to wait until after my gradua-
tion in July. My move to Vienna was delayed until the beginning of January
1925. In Frankfurt my first impression of Berg had been one of extreme
kindness, also of shyness, which helped me overcome the trepidation this
object of my highest admiration would otherwise have instilled in me. If I try
to recall the impulse that drew me spontaneously to him I am sure it was
exceedingly naive, but it was related to something very essential about Berg:
the *Wozzeck* pieces, above all the introduction to the March, and then the
March itself, struck me as a combination of Schoenberg and Mahler, and at
the time that was my ideal of genuine new music.[22]

Alban Berg was a great teacher, fully deserving to be spoken of in the same
breath as Lukács and Bloch. At the same time, he possessed one quality lacking
in Webern and Schoenberg: direct human warmth. And Adorno knew that he
was now being initiated into the mysteries of new music: his letters to Berg are
all addressed to 'Revered Sir and Master'. As he was well aware, Berg showed
him 'unequivocally the character of teaching, the authority of "our school"'.
Behind that authority lay Schoenberg, whose desire for dictatorial power
exceeded even that of Stefan George. Adorno remained in Vienna until 25
August 1925.

Tradition was passed on by Schoenberg, the conservative revolutionary. He
was born in 1874 and had started his career as a composer by writing works that
took Neo-Romanticism to its furthest extreme, but by 1909 he had struck out
in the direction of free atonality. By the time that Adorno arrived in Vienna, he
had devised a new way of ordering the relationship between the notes: twelve-
note composition. A new and strict set of rules was imposed on anarchy, eman-
cipating the dissonance and proposing a new canon of prohibitions. From the
twelve notes at his disposal, the composer chooses a set or row that may appear
in retrograde, inversion and retrograde-inversion. But Adorno's sympathies
were generally with middle-period Schoenberg. In February 1922, the barely
eighteen-year-old student wrote appreciatively of a performance of *Pierrot
lunaire*: 'We know that Schoenberg's ability is unique.'[23] Strict form was 'entirely
imbued with a sense of soul'. But it was not this that was the decisive factor.
What mattered, rather, was the rationality of the work: 'Born into a desperate
age, he finds in his own consciousness those layers from which the work welled
up dully and necessarily in the case of Beethoven. What had once been the
formal precondition of creativity has become its material content for him, and
so in the person of the pierrot he sings of the homelessness of our soul.'[24] From
now on Schoenberg's music constituted the yardstick by which he judged other

A keen ear for modern music: Adorno in around 1925

composers' works: 'But it seems necessary to acknowledge that in terms of its breadth, depth and rigour, this is a work that no contemporary can match.'[25]

Soma Morgenstern has left a not entirely charitable account of Adorno's arrival in Vienna. At a performance of Mahler's First Symphony, Helene Berg had turned to the memoirist: 'Soma, you must help us. A Jewish youth from Frankfurt am Main has arrived. He wants to have composition lessons with Alban.... We couldn't get rid of him. He stayed for a bite to eat and didn't leave even then but kept talking away at Alban so that he's now completely worn out. Alban simply didn't understand what he was saying.'[26] Morgenstern looked round and noticed 'a very small figure' standing beside Berg and 'going on and on at him'.[27] A native of Galicia, Morgenstern revealed a very different sort of

Jewishness from Adorno's, as is clear from his account: 'As he stood there talking to Alban, I was reminded by his whole bearing of delicately built yet clumsy orthodox Jewish boys from a yeshiva in the East.'[28] The young Adorno, Morgenstern went on, was 'of delicate build. Although the weather was very mild, he was wearing a greatcoat of an indeterminate colour. He had a gaunt, bony face, a well-formed head with very short hair, which in spite of his almost boyish appearance was already thinning. His eyes were large, brown, slightly protruding. His hands spoke best for his overall person: narrow, with long fingers, very delicate, of pleasing sensitivity. I saw such hands not infrequently on young Talmudic scholars in the East.'[29] Curious details are recounted, but unfortunately the reader cannot be certain if they are true. When Morgenstern asked him whether he had grown up in a 'God-fearing house', Adorno apparently answered 'with a deep breath': 'Yes, my father is a Socialist.'[30] There is no doubt that Morgenstern was overestimating the significance of his role when he claimed that it was largely on his recommendation that Berg accepted Adorno as his pupil, and in general he is not reserved in stressing his own importance, claiming, for example, that it was he who first drew Adorno's attention to the writings of Franz Kafka. It was their rivalry for their teacher's affections that distorted his views. Certainly, Adorno's letters to Berg are by no means lacking in ironical sideswipes at Morgenstern, so that we may well speak of a well-cultivated mutual dislike. 'Wiesengrund's things', Morgenstern told Berg in the context of Adorno's early compositions, were 'pretty pretentious'.[31] When Adorno's Two Pieces for String Quartet op. 2 of 1925/6 were performed for the first time in Vienna on 11 December 1927, Morgenstern enquired of his teacher: 'How's Wiesengrund's quartet? My girlfriend (who understands these things!) wrote to tell me that it left a very lacklustre impression. Please don't tell him that I said this.'[32] But Berg declined to become involved in the controversy and wrote back to say that the quartet was 'a really splendid piece, it was a great success here & he can be certain that he'll be taken up by Universal Edition in the very near future. He himself has become significantly more manly, but is otherwise the same as before.'[33]

Most of Adorno's works as a composer were written between 1925 and 1930. It may be that for a time he envisaged a career as a composer. This, at least, is believed to be the case by Dieter Schnebel, who reports that the Orchestral Pieces op. 4 were dedicated to Heinz-Klaus Metzger: 'If not, dear Heinz, but something could have become of a Theodor W. Adorno who is heartily obliged to you.' And, according to Schnebel, during the 'fifties and 'sixties Adorno told a number of his friends about compositional projects that he planned for his retirement. Within a private circle, he sometimes played his own music and accompanied his own songs – Schnebel remembered his interpretations as 'almost touching and very impressive'.[34] He even gave public performances of them with the soprano Carla Henius. But Schnebel was in no doubt about the limitations of Adorno's compositions: they were, he believed, already old-fashioned at the time that they were written, being too much in thrall to tradition and 'scarcely going beyond what Schoenberg, Berg and Webern had already written twenty years earlier'.[35] Exemplary in their way, they were entirely products of the school of Schoenberg. According to Schnebel, there were 'orchestral pieces, songs to words by George and Trakl, a string quartet – this in turn a sequence of two pieces. But these works were written at a time when the great composers had already abandoned these forms.'[36] Adorno's compositions expressed his nostalgia for the emergence of modern music, which coincided with his own childhood. Only in one respect, Schnebel believed, was Adorno actually original as a composer, inasmuch as he did more than anyone else to take as his subject the affinity between language and music. In discussing a possible new opera by Berg, Adorno and Morgenstern once again found themselves at loggerheads. Schoenberg had suggested Arnolt Bronnen's *Rhineland Rebels* as the subject for a libretto, a bold and politically risky choice as the Rhineland was occupied by the French. Adorno suggested Hofmannsthal's *The Tower*, a subject related to that of *Wozzeck*: an incarcerated prince, not unlike Kaspar Hauser and, as such, initially barely capable of speech, rebels against his father, the old king. The first version of the play dates from 1925 and was evidently the one that Adorno had in mind: it ends with the Utopia of a Child King. The revised version of 1927 offers a more sombre vision, with both father and son perishing in the chaos of revolution. Morgenstern, finally, recommended Hauptmann's *And Pippa Dances!*, a play about a young woman who finds herself in a community of glass-blowers in the Silesian forests. Certainly, its main female character is closer to that of the pieces that Berg finally settled on with *Lulu*: Frank Wedekind's related plays *Earth Spirit* and *Pandora's Box*. The mutual dislike felt by Adorno and Morgenstern proved long-lasting, with the latter reporting, uncharitably, on their renewed encounter after the war: 'Meanwhile I became aware that standing in front of me was a fat, overweight, prematurely bald and sedate inhabitant of Frankfurt, whose only point in common with my friend Teddie was his narrow, delicate, sensitive hands.'[37] Again: 'Our friendship was destroyed by his ruthlessly rampant ambition, which had persuaded him, inter alia, to remove good old Wiesengrund from his father's name – the kind father to whom he owed his socialism, among other things. People speak of consuming ambition. In his case, ambition had made him fat.'[38]

But it was not only the Second Viennese School that Adorno got to know in Vienna. As for so many other intellectuals of his generation, Karl Kraus became an admired figure, so much so, indeed, that Adorno later dedicated an essay to him. Kraus had made his reputation as a political commentator capable of painting a picture of a whole world of inhumanity and corruption on the strength of the most trivial local concerns. And the Viennese press offered him countless opportunities to recognize the evils of the bourgeois world in its degenerate language. As Adorno was later to write, 'Anyone who was present when Karl Kraus, by words alone, hounded Imre Bekessy from Vienna in 1925 will have discovered something of the concrete power of what appeared to Kierkegaard to be so abstract and so monomaniacal: the power of impotence.'[39] Like the rest of Schoenberg's circle, Berg revered Kraus, and it was he who not only introduced Adorno to the shorter prose works of one of Kraus's friends, Peter Altenberg, but who also helped him to reappraise decadence as an expression of humanity.

Moreover, Adorno's piano teacher in Vienna was Edwuard Steuermann, who accompanied Kraus at his lectures and who was *the* pianist of the Schoenberg circle, all of whose members from Schoenberg to Hanns Eisler entrusted their pieces to him. In his obituary of the pianist, Adorno wrote that it was through Berg that he 'made Steuermann's acquaintance in 1925 and had lessons in piano playing with him; our friendship has lasted with great continuity up to the present day. Words cannot express what I owe him. When he drew my attention to a motivic link in Brahms's B minor Capriccio that I had overlooked and that I had therefore neglected while playing, it became entirely clear to me how far an understanding of the music that one is playing and that is articulated by means of analysis is a precondition for its correct interpretation.'[40] Steuermann brought out the tendencies of new music by roughening up the works, notably by accenting dissonances and auxiliary notes, rather than by downplaying them: 'With Talmudic force he persuades the musical signs to speak, as though through an interlinear version of the text.'[41] As for Steuermann's own compositions, Adorno described them as 'secularized and hence darkened theology'.[42] Steuermann, wrote Adorno, uniquely led a true life among false lives.

Whereas Steuermann and Berg belonged to a much older generation, Ernst Krenek was virtually the same age as Adorno. The latter championed Krenek's works from an early date, admiring in particular their elemental force. They had got to know each other in Frankfurt in 1924 at the first performance of Krenek's opera *Der Sprung über den Schatten*. None the less, Krenek's later reminiscence of their first meeting is unreliable and, given the friendship between the two men, extremely disconcerting. A 'young Jew' came over to speak to him:

> He said a few nice things about my work but quite openly expressed his displeasure at the performance, which was very embarrassing as Rottenberg [Ludwig Rottenberg, the music director of the Frankfurt Opera] was bound to overhear everything he said. It also seemed that this importunate fellow had made a nuisance of himself by distributing pamphlets of a political character at the entrances to the opera house. He had a curiously penetrating look and an over-emphatic, aggressive way of speaking, and I didn't like him at all. He was called Theodor Wiesengrund Adorno, a name I considered risible in the extreme. In later years this man was to become one of my best friends and, moreover, to exert a very great influence on me.[43]

It is difficult to imagine Adorno handing out leaflets outside the opera house, and one can only suppose that Krenek's embittered reaction to the student riots of the 1960s played a trick on his memory. Their views coincided not only in music journalism but also in their shared interest in the French Surrealists.

But Krenek remained sceptical about his friend's political tendencies. As he notes in his memoirs, he saw Adorno as 'someone whom we would now describe as a sympathizer, for everything that he wrote pointed to the advantages of a non-capitalist system, a system which – although he was never as crude as to say so – would clearly be Communist'.[44]

In 1919, Universal Edition launched the *Musikblätter des Anbruch*, the first music journal designed specifically to promote new music. It included portraits of composers and analyzed not only their works but also performing practice and the music industry in general. Adorno took over as editor in 1928, remaining in the post until 1932, but there was an inevitable conflict of interests between the publishing house on the one hand and contributors on the other, as the journal was expected to promote Universal Edition's publications, with the result that its critical freedom was limited – a tiresome and recurrent theme in Krenek's correspondence with Adorno. His co-editor was the musicologist Hans Ferdinand Redlich who, like Adorno himself, was later to write a book on Berg. Once again it is surprising to find how uncharitable are Krenek's recollections of the apparently frequent rows between Adorno and Redlich: 'It is strange that people who on all basic questions are essentially of the same opinion can often not agree on details, which they interpret as points of principle. I have found this to be the case especially with Jewish intellectuals, who often tend towards stubbornness, prejudice and intransigence. This also has its good side, of course, because it signifies uncompromising integrity.'[45]

Adorno's critical writings on music during the 1920s are voluminous in the extreme and include not only concert reviews and assessments of contemporary compositions but also analyses of popular hits that, by treating individual cases, anticipate what was later to become the 'culture industry'. And there are also attempts to adopt an integrated approach to the range of motifs at his disposal, notably by combining philosophical ideas with a critique of contemporary society and, finally, with his thoughts on music. Not infrequently the reader has the impression that individual concepts are being tested for their sustainability. It is in his study of Schubert – arguably his most important essay of this period – that we find one of these new terms being used for the first time: it is the concept of the chthonic. The word comes from the Greek and means anything belonging to the earth. The chthonic gods, unlike their Olympian counterparts, exercise their sway from within the earth. The countryside is chthonic, as are the people who inhabit it and who work the land. So, too, is the language they speak with a regional accent – Adorno did not speak standard German but a cultivated German with a slight dialect. The mountains, the rivers and lakes, the coasts and the plants and animals that belong to this earth are chthonic. But so is the earth as the place where our forebears are buried, so that a certain sadness surrounds the term. The concept of the chthonic was introduced to cultural philosophy by Johann Jacob Bachofen and above all by Ludwig Klages, for whom it was a critical authority to offset against the modern industrial world and the patriarchy that takes its cue from solar myth or from the uranic and the celestial. Fertility, life and vegetation are as much a part of the realm of the chthonic powers as the underworld and the kingdom of the dead. In short, it is an ancient, primordial element to which Adorno felt peculiarly related. Even the essay he wrote for his final school-leaving examination was devoted to man's attitude to nature, while his countless excursions with Siegfried Kracauer were field trips to explore the countryside. If the 'domination of nature' was later to epitomize the false whole in Adorno's thinking, this thesis had a long prehistory. Nature should not be repressed. 'The ensuing conversation,' Thomas Mann recalled a discussion with Adorno on the subject of Beethoven in October 1943, 'passed from humanity as the purified chthonian element to parallels between Beethoven and Goethe.'[46]

The countryside became an exemplar in Adorno's account of Schubert's music, offering, as it did, an alternative to the model of the personality. Landscape, writes Adorno, is 'further removed from the point of reference within the human being', further removed from the 'deceptive totality of man such as he would like to exist as a self-determined spirit'.[47] Schubert's music appears not as a unity but as a scene of diversity or, to be more precise, as the 'landscape of death'.[48] Its textures are crystalline rather than organic and are made up from the outset of the 'volatile, fragile life of stones'.[49] The language of Schubert's landscape, Adorno writes, is 'a dialect without earth'.[50] The composer has 'the concretion of the homeland, but there is no homeland here, only a remembered one. Nowhere is Schubert further from the earth than when he quotes it'.[51]

Anyone who observed Adorno in the mid-1920s was bound to note that he had perfect pitch where modern music was concerned. He had assimilated the teachings of the cultural counter-élite in the form of philosophical Marxism, psychoanalysis and the Second Viennese School. But anyone who looked more closely would see that his attitude was not entirely independent: existing terminologies were taken over and recycled for some considerable length of time, while his work as a composer was nostalgically orientated towards the period of his youth. Adorno thought and wrote within the limitations of existing teachings – one could almost say that modernity became the housing for his thinking. With the passage of time, this housing became more transparent, lighter, more homely and better fitting – but it was never entirely abandoned.

4 A Strict Demand for Justice: The Institute for Social Research

A 'nation of pariahs' was how Max Weber described early Judaism in his socio-logical study on the economic ethics of the world's religions. Unlike the Indian 'untouchables' – the pariahs of the caste system in southern India, who could hope to be reborn in a higher social class if they performed their duties with-out complaining – the Jews used the term to give their destiny an activist thrust. For them, wrote Weber,

> the Promised Land was the exact opposite: the social order of the world was transformed into the obverse of what had been promised for the future and was to be overturned in the future, so that the Jews would again assume their position as the master race of the earth. The world was neither eternal nor unchangeable but was man-made, and its present arrangements were a product of men's actions, above all the product of the Jews' actions and of their God's reaction to them: in short, it was a historical product, destined to make way for a state that was truly willed by God. The early Jews' whole attitude towards life was determined by this idea of a future political and social revolution led by God.[1]

Students of the revolutionary movements that followed the end of the First World War may see a pointer to that period in Weber's diagnosis of the ancient world. During the first half of the twentieth century, an astonishingly large number of the leaders of the socialist, Communist and anarchist movements were Jewish.[2] Trotsky and Zinoviev in Russia, Rosa Luxemburg, Paul Levi, Kurt Eisner and Gustav Landauer in Germany, Béla Kun and Georg Lukács in Hungary had all played a prominent role in the local soviet revolutions. This is not to say that the majority of Central European Jews were Communists. According to an anecdote relating to the October Revolution of 1917, the Chief Rabbi in Moscow had turned for help to the Red Army's new commander: 'The Trotskys are organizing the revolution, and the Bronsteins are having to pay for it.' The counter-revolutionaries spoke in the most general terms of 'Jewish Bolshevism', a catchphrase that had disastrous repercussions under National Socialism, when it served to justify genocide. Yet, in spite of its terrible demagogic exaggeration, it contains a grain of truth.

In 1924 the philosopher Theodor Lessing, who was later murdered by the National Socialists, wrote:

> It is generally believed that the Jew, as history's Ahasuerus Errans, is the born embodiment of revolutionary and radical ideas. In a certain sense this is true. As a small community of late, highly bred people, the Jews shouldered the burden of a strict demand for justice. The Bible and the Talmud inveigh incessantly against the satisfied; and it goes without saying that a displaced nation, attuned to suffering, is bound to take up the cause of all who suffer injustice, at least as long as it remains a suffering community and a community of sufferers: that cause is to represent all impotence against all power. This is the hallmark of strong natures. They take responsibility for weaker ones. That is why the history of European radicalism and of the great revolutions – those of European Communism and anarchy – strikes us as the noblest and finest product of Jewishness.[3]

Since the second half of the nineteenth century, the Jewish communities of Central Europe had represented a pool of potential talent that at least in the West enjoyed equal rights on a purely formal level but which was none the less barred from pursuing certain careers. What were the political means of altering this state of affairs? Zionism proposed that the Jews turn their backs on Europe and establish a state of Israel in Palestine. Political liberalism could make traditional societies more open. The Socialist and Communist way, finally, promised a fundamentally different social order. Within the family of Gershom Scholem, a student of the cabbala and a friend of both Walter Benjamin and, later, Adorno, the journey through life adopted by the two brothers provided an exemplary expression of these political options: while Werner Scholem became a Communist, Gershom quickly espoused the cause of Zionism.[4]

As a discipline, sociology, too, numbered among its great exponents many writers of Jewish extraction: suffice it to recall Émile Durkheim in France and Georg Simmel in Germany. And it was Simmel who in his study on sociology placed his own interpretation on this phenomenon. A group of foreigners, he argued, would almost inevitably adopt a critical or at least a more objective attitude to autochthonous culture:

> Objectivity can also be described as freedom. The objective individual is not bound by any predetermined facts that could prejudice his acceptance,

understanding or consideration of the data. Needless to say, this freedom, which allows the stranger to take a bird's-eye view even of things that are close to him, also brings with it all manner of potential dangers. It has always been the case with uprisings of every kind that the attacked party is said to have been provoked from outside by foreign emissaries and rabble-rousers. To the extent that this is true at all, it is an exaggeration of the specific role of the foreigner: he is the freer of the two, both practically and theoretically. He has a less prejudiced overview of the situation, which he can judge by more universal and more objective ideals, and he is not tied down in his actions by habit, reverence or antecedents.[5]

This description is clearly idealized: not even the outsider can be a purely objective observer but is bound to pursue certain goals and ideas that influence his view of the situation. It would be highly unusual if all autochthonous individuals were marked by particular mental images and that only the outsider was free of such images and able to judge things objectively. The outsider, too, struggles to find recognition. He, too, will not be able to ignore his own social goals when formulating his theoretical ideas.

The Institute for Social Research stood at the crossroads of the revolutionary and scientific traditions. It owed its existence to a foundation established by a Jew, and the majority of scholars who were associated with it were Jews. Moreover, they were not just Jewish by extraction: a number of them were also practising Jews. Foremost among this latter group were the psychoanalyst Erich Fromm and the literary scholar Leo Löwenthal. Others, including Max Horkheimer, who was the Institute's director for many years, saw themselves initially as secularized Jews before returning to the religion of their forefathers towards the end of their lives. At various times, Jewishness and critical theory were interchangeable terms, albeit not always as they were with the later Horkheimer, who asked the question: 'In what does Jewish culture consist? To what extent is it superior to European and American civilization, which is now in the process of disintegration? Modern Jews have given up something higher in order to accept something lower. That is in the nature of assimilation. The Jews were a nation that was held together without any force of its own, held together by the thought of fidelity to themselves alone.'[6] Above all, the Old Testament idea of the ban on graven images was interpreted as a key concept of critical theory: the Utopia of a just society should not be depicted in images.

Much later, during his exile in America, Bertolt Brecht painted a satirical portrait of the Institute's foundation. It was penned followed a meal with Max Horkheimer: 'A wealthy old man – the wheat speculator Weil – dies, unsettled by the world's poverty. In his will he endows a large sum to establish an institute that is to investigate the causes of poverty. He himself is the cause, of course.'[7] Brecht saw the situation with a jaundiced eye, but he was not, in fact, so wide of the mark. The capital used to endow the Institute came from the cereal merchant Hermann Weil and was intended to further the plans of his son Felix, who was a friend of both Horkheimer and Friedrich Pollock and an advocate of radical socialism. Weil had made his fortune from the international grain trade. During the First World War he was one of the government's top economic advisers. In her account of the early history of the Institute, Ulrike Migdal writes that on 17 May 1917 Weil 'crowned his career as an adviser to the Kaiser Wilhelm II, whom he continued to serve until 21 October 1918'.[8] Migdal sees in Weil one of the leading propagandists of the ideology associated with victory and endurance, a man who in his reports and expert submissions repeatedly predicted that the Allies would suffer from food shortages and that this in turn would ensure the success of the German forces. In May 1917 he published an article headed 'Onward to Victory',[9] in which he named England as the 'principal warmonger'. He saw the causes of the catastrophe besetting Europe in nutritional economics. It was not political factors that had caused the war, he believed, but a report submitted to the American Department of Agriculture on 4 August 1914, 'confirming the optimistic estimates of the United States harvest from the spring of that year'.[10] Weil approved of the German U-boat war as a way of cutting off the Allies' grain supplies. He based his arguments on the assumption that in the event of the country's defeat, Germany would be enslaved, and so he demanded that like be repaid with like: 'We must proceed just as implacably as the English and French intended to treat us; just as ruthlessly we must demand that those who caused this war bear responsibility for its consequences.'[11] He advocated the annexation of whole swathes of France and Belgium and a vast colonial empire in Africa. In the middle of 1917 he fell into line with those who wanted a peace agreement with England. After the war his public loyalties switched and he embarked on a course of extensive philanthropy in Frankfurt, offering generous grants to various institutions associated with the city's university. But, in the event, an initial attempt to establish an institute of social sciences with funds from a Weil foundation came to nothing.

Only when Felix Weil had prepared the ground with other left-wing thinkers, including Karl Korsch and Kurt Gerlach, did it prove possible to set up the Institute for Social Research. Weil had published a piece on 'socialization' after the war and was keen to establish a 'Home for Scientific Socialism'[12] at the university. This time the plan was successful, and the Institute was opened by the Marxist Karl Grünberg on 22 June 1924. Its inner circle was made up of Weil,

Pollock and Horkheimer. 'Weil,' Horkheimer later recalled, 'took his doctorate in Frankfurt in around 1922. My friend Friedrich Pollock . . . and I had got to know Weil as a student. It was within this circle of three young people that the idea of the Institute was born.'[13] Criticism of the Soviet Union was not encouraged. It was not that Weil, Horkheimer, Pollock and their friends were unaware of the Soviet reign of terror. Quite the opposite: they had first-hand information about it. Germaine Krull, who was later to become one of the great female photographers of the twentieth century, had been friendly with Horkheimer and Pollock since their days as students in Munich. An ardent Communist, she had been deported to Russia at the end of the soviet republic in Munich, but, once there, she had soon been imprisoned as a counter-revolutionary. Following her deportation, she wrote to Horkheimer from Riga on 12 January 1922, announcing the fact that she had now become an 'outspoken anti-Bolshevik'.[14] The conditions of her imprisonment were 'appalling' and she had barely escaped with her life. But it was not for personal reasons that she had come to oppose the Soviet system: 'Today I know that it would be a misfortune for the world and above all for the working class if Bolshevism came to the West. – I know that history goes forwards and can only go forwards, but this bloody experiment is an aberration of history – it was branded a crime committed by a handful of criminal geniuses.'[15] Horkheimer no doubt heard the message, but his faith was stronger. He wrote to his girlfriend and later wife, Rosa Riekher, that Germaine Krull's letter spoke only of 'decay' and that the changes in her character were 'terrible'.[16] Anyone who declared their opposition to the Soviet experiment was regarded as morally suspect.

Under Grünberg's leadership, the scholars attached to the Institute initially concentrated on the history of the workers' movement. Its journal, *Grünberg's Archiv für die Geschichte des Sozialismus und der Arbeiterbewegung* [Grünberg's Archives for the History of Socialism and the Workers' Movement], was soon internationally respected. But positivistic historical research was limited and could not appeal to young intellectuals in the longer term. When Horkheimer took over the running of the Institute in 1931, he noted that a gulf had opened up between the new and the old. It was important, therefore, to 'set our sights on new challenges'.[17] The Institute was no longer to pursue merely archival research, which, however labour-intensive, was methodologically undemanding, but was to turn its attention to social philosophy and to do so, moreover, in the spirit of Hegel, which meant examining the whole of the cultural environment, including law, bourgeois society, the state, art and the evolution of world history. Horkheimer realized, of course, that to appeal to Hegel was not entirely plausible and so he advocated a link with empirical research. Above all, political nationalism made it expedient to reject Hegel's doctrine of 'folk spirits' as the agents of history. It was their common aim to 'pursue philosophical questions with the help of the most sophisticated scientific methods, to reformulate and refine questions in the course of work on the object in hand and to devise new methods, while never losing sight of the most general aspect'. For the left-wing intelligentsia of the Weimar Republic, this represented a more attractive definition of the challenges facing the Institute than that of the old Grünberg Institute. An institutional basis for philosophical Marxism had been established, and it opened up the prospect of an academic career within the university system. The Institute distanced itself critically from rival social philosophies, which in Horkheimer's view were concerned only with 'transfiguring' conditions.[18] The euphemistic language that the Institute later elevated to the level of a high art when it no longer described its own doctrine as 'Marxism' but preferred the term 'critical theory', replacing the words 'against the current social order' in one of Walter Benjamin's essays with the more positive phrase 'for a truly humane order', deleting the word 'Fascism' and substituting 'the totalitarian state' and replacing the term 'Communism' by 'the constructive forces of humanity'[19] (Benjamin himself intended the term 'Communism', for all its damaging potential) – this language, which revealed what was meant only to the initiated, began to take shape at this time. Marx is named by Horkheimer only once, and then only in passing – not as his main source of inspiration but as one of several mainstream writers on sociology, including Auguste Comte and Max Weber. From now on, the Institute would refrain from debating its theories in the form of propositions and world-views but would subject them to the scrutiny of empirical research. The Institute's aim, Horkheimer insisted in his inaugural lecture in 1931, was to seek to prove the links between the role of the group in the economic process, the 'change in the psychological structure of its individual members and the thoughts and institutions that affect them as a totality within the whole of society and that are produced by it'.[20] They would begin by investigating qualified workers and white-collar workers in Germany.[21] What was important here was the emphasis on psychology. The research programme amounted to a mixture of Marxism and psychoanalysis that was no longer content to be the handmaid of the workers' movement. The revolution had failed in Germany – this could be put down only to a 'false consciousness' on the part of the actors involved and, as such, it needed to be analyzed. A theory of the revolution became the theory of the failed revolution. For this reason, collaboration with the psychoanalyst Erich Fromm became of crucial importance for the Institute.

In his inaugural lecture, Horkheimer spoke of cooperation between researchers but also of a 'dictatorship on the part of the director' that would make their planned collaboration possible. Even while he was still a young man, Horkheimer had dreamt of enjoying a position of authority when, under the influence of Schopenhauer, he had expressed his indignation at the world's sufferings. His early short stories regularly climax at the point when the philosophizing hero launches into a great speech and is assured of his listeners' attention and emotional involvement. On one occasion, a group of friends travels to England by sea. The narrator begins by expounding the principles of his philosophy of justice and ends: 'I continued in this proud, joyful tone until we arrived in London, and there I continued my narrative until well into the night, then the whole of the next day and the day after that, so that we had long been in Manchester before I had told the others everything that had happened.'[22] Horkheimer's writings show how in this exaggerated account he clearly envisaged the effect that he would later have on the Federal Republic of Germany. From the 'fifties onwards, he made his presence felt above all through the spoken word, with the vast majority of his publications deriving from lectures and speeches, radio talks, discussions, interviews, public readings and seminars. To these may be added the conversations or, rather, 'dictations' that he held every evening with his friend Friedrich Pollack and which the latter minuted under the title 'Shavings': they run to hundreds of pages. 'Listen to me – I'll go mad if you don't listen to me,' says the woman in a 'Dialogue between Two Lovers' that the young thinker wrote.[23] The dream of speaking authoritatively came true for the later Horkheimer. Other motifs in his works are more cryptic. If the main theme of his first philosophical study on the early philosophy of bourgeois history is a question couched in the form of a Machiavellian interpretation, namely, which social groups exercise power, this is motivated not only by a moral concern but above all by a vital interest on Horkheimer's part. In much the same way, the socio-philosophical vignettes that make up *Dämmerung* [Twilight] – a collection of writings published in exile but dating back to the final years of the Weimar Republic – all return to the same basic situation in their analyses of the gestures of power: that of the social inequality between man and woman. Scenes in which the female employee finds herself in an embarrassing situation with her distinguished friend, or a peer of the realm marries a chambermaid – it is these that Horkheimer discusses in every detail as they are his criteria for tact and morality. The emphasis shifted during the 1950s. The oppression of women was not denied but was hesitantly turned into something positive: 'Is the sweetness of love, its form and content, conceivable in any other guise?'[24] Horkheimer, who married his father's secretary, incurring years of conflict with his parents, had an erotic liaison with social inequality. Man found his supreme happiness, he believed, 'in the arms of the slave he worshipped'. The frequency with which he speaks in his letters of his staff and servants marks him out as the last seigneur in every sense of the term. He conceived the role of the intellectual by reference to Voltaire, whose sense of freedom he interpreted on the basis of the sovereignty of the absolute monarch: majesty was preserved and maintained in Voltaire's victory over absolutism.

Horkheimer was Cornelius's assistant in Frankfurt, and it was here, during his studies, that Adorno first met him: 'When I first saw you in Adhémar Gelb's psychology seminar,' Adorno wrote to his friend on the latter's seventieth birthday, 'you scarcely struck me as a student; my elder by eight years, you seemed more like a young man from a well-to-do household who takes a certain distant interest in science.'[25]

> You were unharmed by the professional deformation of the academic who far too easily confuses a concern for learned things with reality. But what you said was so sensible, so perceptive and above all so independent that I soon enough felt you to be superior to the sphere from which you had imperceptibly cut yourself off. At another seminar you read a truly brilliant paper, I think it was on Husserl, with whom you had studied for a couple of semesters. I went over to you quite spontaneously and introduced myself. Since then we have always been together.[26]

The Institute's psychoanalyst was Erich Fromm, who was a member of the circle surrounding Franz Rosenzweig at the Free House of Jewish Learning in Frankfurt and the subject of a witticism transmitted by Gershom Scholem: 'Lieber Gott / mach mich wie den Erich fromm / daß ich in den Himmel komm.' (The pun is lost in English but derives from the secondary meaning of Fromm's surname as 'pious'. Literally, the lines mean: 'Dear God, make me, like Erich, pious that I may enter Heaven.') Certainly, Fromm introduced an Old Testament element into psychoanalysis. In his lectures on 'Psychoanalysis and Religion', he describes three case histories from his analytic practice. According to one of them, a gifted writer consults the analyst and complains about headaches and attacks of dizziness for which the doctor treating him can find no organic cause. The writer's case notes reveal the following picture: two years earlier he had accepted a post that was particularly tempting in terms of its income, prestige and security and, as Fromm records, he had enjoyed tremendous success in the conventional sense of the term. But his work consisted in writing things that flew in the face of his own convictions and that he himself did not believe. The man appeases his conscience by means of a series of rationalizations, in other words, with intellectual constructs aimed at talking himself round. It is at this point that his physical problems begin. Fromm diagnoses an unresolved conflict between, on the one hand, the man's desire for money and respect and, on the other, his moral dilemma.

Fromm developed two possible lines of assistance: a psychoanalytical approach that aims at social integration would regard the man's acceptance of the post as a sign of his healthy conformity with the prevailing culture. But a different analyst – and here Fromm speaks of his own line of intervention – would address the man's intellectual and moral integrity, arguing that otherwise his whole personality would suffer. From this standpoint, Fromm believed, the problem lay in the writer's difficulty in heeding the voice of conscience, and he would be cured if he gave up his present job and could lead a life that gave him back his old self-respect. The basic structure of this particular case history is repeated in the two other biographical sketches quoted by Fromm: one deals with an intelligent and energetic businessman whose entire life is given over to earning money and competing with others and who in the absence of any meaning or fulfilment seeks refuge in alcohol, while the third case is that of a young man with an academic degree who vegetates in his father's firm. Common to all three cases is the poor light in which a working life appears: a career is the most powerful adversary of human development.

This common factor replicates the situation in Fromm's own parental home. In an interview shortly before his death, he explained that his forebears on both sides were rabbis, whereas his father was a businessman. 'He was ashamed of this, because he too should really have wanted to be a rabbi. As a young lad, I felt whenever someone said "I'm a businessman", I felt very ashamed for them because I thought, "God, how ashamed he must be to admit that he spends his whole life earning money".'[27] Fromm's father had destroyed a hallowed system of values that had been valid for generations. The answer was the son's neurosis in God's name, and this neurosis was associated with capitalism: earning money was on one side of the dividing line, while on the other was intellectually worthwhile employment, whether it be the study of the Torah in the traditional world or science and literature in the modern world. It was this childhood conflict that Fromm passed on to his patients. He first formulated it in his dissertation on Jewish law and on the nation of the diaspora. Here he undertook an anti-capitalist reinterpretation of the Jewish laws in life, taking particular issue with Max Weber's professional ethics of Protestantism. Here he examines the rabbinical sources on the world of work and a professional career, arguing that the law aims to 'bring peace to the individual and hence create the possibility for contemplation and reli- gious work'.[28] The religious and ethical meaning of the word 'profession' (*Beruf*) in the sense of a calling or task appointed by God (*Berufung*) had gained acceptance in Germany from Luther's day, Fromm went on, but was alien to Judaism. Weber's puritan capitalist sought 'to find proof of God's mercy in the haste of his daily labours and in the success of his work. Work itself was God's absolute commandment. It was hallowed and became an end in itself.'[29] But the opposite system of values applied to Judaism: 'In Judaism the supreme and unique goal of life is insight. Just as the world is subordinate to God, so work is subordinate to understanding. The idea that work is hal- lowed is unique to Puritanism and is missing entirely from rabbinical Judaism. The highest aim in life is insight, and work is necessary only to sus- tain life, it is a necessary evil. It should be pursued only to meet our needs, not to accumulate possessions.'[30] Within the context not only of the longing for a sense of community in post-war Germany but also of the German youth movement and an anti-capitalism projected on to East European Jews, Fromm conceived an ethical approach to life which he then used as a yardstick on which to base his analyses.

Fromm's picture of society was influenced by his view of an idealized com- munity: 'From the common features of meaningful form we can also explain the characteristics of the mass that is bound together by form. Where the mass is not connected by any form or only by inessential forms, it is very much the trivial and inferior that is common to it. The individual may be valuable and moral within it, but the mass of many such individuals is immoral.'[31] Fromm's critical motif was dismay at a social world that had left behind it the model of the community. By evading the law, humanity became prey to the triviality of the market. No doubt the same is true of the problem of the authority-fixated individual: inasmuch as Fromm set out from the normative premiss of the stateless Jewish nation, which he saw as religiously regulated but not as consti- tuted by any church, he could explain existing authoritarian structures and ter- ritorial associations only as a masochistic or regressively incestuous deformity of character: it was a perverse delight in submission, he believed, that guaran- teed the survival of existing society. All who subscribed to order had failed to overcome their oedipal relationship with their mother. Fromm saw life's prac- tical pursuit from the standpoint of his role as Old Testament prophet: 'The central issue of the teachings of the Prophets is the fight against this incestuous worship. They preach instead the basic values common to all mankind: those of truth, love, and justice. They attack the state and those secular powers which fail to realize these norms.'[32]

The intellectual atmosphere of the Institute for Social Research was thus a medley of motifs associated with the Jewish prophets, coupled with a desire to grasp the whole in the spirit of Hegel, Marxist class theory and a resolute dash of philosophico-cultural modernity. Seen from the outside, the group might well have appeared pro-Soviet, in spite of many reservations on points of detail. But its members refused to hear about Stalinism and the disastrous famine in the Ukraine. In the course of a discussion held at the Institute in the early 1930s, Adorno noted that intellectual freedom was greater in Russia than was generally believed. It was at precisely this time that the exiled Russian journalist Fedor Stepun was desperately trying 'to make clear to leading intellectuals in Berlin and Frankfurt what is happening in Russia'.[33] Stepun spoke of a left-wing snobbery that he had observed at first hand: the feeling that European culture was in decline and that intellectuals preferred to undertake emotional and ideological journeys to utopian worlds. This wish to break free from Europe was driving those who were 'uprooted' further to the left. It was with positive glee that these people claimed that German culture was played out:

> Wagner unbearable, a tasteless and mendacious props manager. His pupil Bruckner is equally intolerable in their eyes, an all-too-typical German. Not to mention the fact that these people cannot bear the 'political eloquence of the banal Schiller' or the 'rhythmicized profundity of a Hebbel or Kleist'. They simply cannot tolerate German profundity in general: it gives them stomach ache. On the basis of this rejection of their own ancient culture, these people have developed a taste for all that is new and exotic, and for reasons best known to themselves, they have also developed a penchant for Soviet Russia. If you are invited to a highly cultured house, where your hosts are interested in politics, philosophy and art, you can reckon that at least with the torchbearers there will be much talk of Russia and of great understanding for the Bolsheviks. But all counter-arguments will be shot down.[34]

Stepun's account clearly contains a grain of truth, as must have been obvious to readers of the *Journal for Social Research*: the first issue, for example, included an article by Leo Löwenthal, criticizing Theodor Storm's 'petty bourgeois soul',[35] while the second issue featured Fromm's diagnosis of the 'bourgeois mind', which was said to be distinguished by 'the typical features of the anal character', especially thrift and rational 'neatness'.[36] This impression would have been confirmed when readers stumbled upon Adorno's contribution, with its thesis that the link between the 'Russian émigré Stravinsky' and 'Fascism' was 'beyond question'.[37]

The first issue appeared in 1932 and was intended to introduce its readers to the new spirit at the Institute. It concentrated on the present. Horkheimer wrote the introductory essay on economics and crisis, while the economist Henryk Grossmann contributed an article on the problem of the crisis in Marx and Pollock wrote about the chances of a planned economic restructuring. Fromm produced a piece dealing with points of principle concerning the methods and challenges facing 'analytic social psychology', and Löwenthal and Adorno contributed two parallel articles on 'The Social Situation of Literature' and 'The Social Situation of Music'. In this way the whole range of the Institute was documented: not only sociology was to be practised here as an academic discipline, the goal was a theory of society as a whole, a theory that included both 'basis' and 'superstructure'. Both would be built on Marxist foundations. Fromm and Löwenthal specifically professed their allegiance to 'historical materialism', a sentiment with which Adorno concurred.

In his own essay, Adorno projected music on to the field of tension associated with the class struggle. His starting point was the role of music in a commodity-producing society. This, he claimed, had resulted in two types of composition, one of which stuck to the side of society and strove for commercial success, while the other essentially turned its back on the market and took its place 'on the side of music'.[38] Although this typology might appear to coincide with the distinction between light and serious music, this was not in fact the case. Among serious works of music, there had long been those that were geared to the market. In this, Adorno was thinking in particular of Richard Strauss: *Salome* and *Elektra* were acceptable to Adorno, but with these two operas Strauss had reached the outer limits of bourgeois taste and from then on was satisfied with compromise: 'Of all the composers of the bourgeoisie, he was perhaps the most class conscious; *Der Rosenkavalier* was his greatest success and in it the dialectic of material is invalidated from without. The diatonic is cleansed of all danger-ous enzymes. . . . With this intellectual sacrifice to consumer consciousness, Strauss's productive power is extinguished: everything that follows *Rosenkava-lier* is either applied or commercial art.'[39] Schoenberg is presented as the main representative of progressive music. For all its isolation from social contingen-cies, the 'composed-out' dissonance is a pointer to 'social antinomies' and hence to a critique of society.[40] Adorno saw a twofold movement or dialectic revolution in Schoenberg's music. On the one hand the composer had succumbed to the drive towards 'undisguised and uninhibited expression of the psyche',[41] thereby bringing his early works into close proximity with psychoanalysis. All links with musical norms were abandoned. Schoenberg's music had freed itself from the 'reflection of an "agreement" of bourgeois society with the psyche of the individual which is now renounced by the sufferings of the individual'.[42] On the other hand, and as a counterweight to individual expression, the technique of twelve-note composition signified such a 'perfected and rational total organization' of the material that it 'cannot possibly be compatible with the present social constitution'. To that extent, Schoenberg had brought music close to 'rational transparence by means of a historical process'.[43] In this, his music resembled a planned economy.

Facing Schoenberg was the 'musical objectivism' that wore the masks of bygone styles and either played cynical games or sought to return to a pre-scriptive order. By applying the theory of the influence of the economic basis to the cultural superstructure, as taught by Marx, Adorno was able to ascribe this trend to the period during which the Weimar Republic had sought to achieve economic stability. Hindemith, above all, had 'decontaminated' Stravinsky's music[44] and in that way expressed his 'principal reconciliation with social conditions'.[45] The despair and destructive potential that can be found in a work like *The Soldier's Tale* were toned down by Hindemith and turned into a 'naturalistic, unresolved, but still undialectic, melancholy, which looks upon death as an eternal state of affairs similar to numerous intentions of contemporary philosophy, evading concrete social contradictions under the banner of "existentialism" and thus subordinating itself willingly to the anthropological super-historical ideals of objectivism'.[46] While the collaborative ventures between Brecht and Kurt Weill – *The Threepenny Opera* and *Mahagonny* – are positively assessed as examples of surrealism in music and as critical reworkings of tradition, communal music and *Gebrauchsmusik* – 'utilitarian music' – are roundly condemned: the sense of commonality that they demand had long been undermined, in Adorno's view, by the 'capitalist production process'. Only Hanns Eisler's Communist battle songs find favour in this context, whereas the same composer's other music, by virtue of the demand that it should be utilitarian, ran the risk of conforming to the masses' state of consciousness, rather than transforming that state. Eisler had adopted an existing proletarian class consciousness: 'In the process it is overlooked that precisely the demands according to which production should orient itself in these cases – singability, simplicity, collective effectiveness per se – are necessarily dependent upon a state of consciousness suppressed and enchained through class domination – no one has formulated this more exactly and extremely than Marx himself – which results in fetters placed upon musically productive forces.'[47] The practical usefulness and 'agitatory value and therewith the political correctness'[48] of Eisler's works was undeniable, but whenever they sought to establish themselves as independent musical forms, they proved to be a 'questionable mixture' of outdated styles – one could almost take this comment as a presentiment of the national anthem that Eisler wrote for the German Democratic Republic, *Auferstanden aus Ruinen*. 'It is, nevertheless, worthy of notice that in the figure of the proletarian composer most consequent for the present, Eisler, the Schoenberg School, from which he came forth, comes into contact with efforts seemingly contrary to the School itself.'[49] This is the penultimate position adopted by Adorno's article, which culminates in a final section envisaging a type of music that 'does not take instructions from the passive, one-sided position of the consciousness of the user – including the proletariat' but 'intervenes actively in consciousness through its own forms'. Adorno was determined to see a link between music and the class struggle in which the rights of both parties would be preserved. Music should follow its own artistic logic and at the same time express 'the exigency of the social condition and call for change through the coded language of suffering'.[50] The objective goal of progressive music was 'the overcoming of class domination. This music must do even where this development takes place in social isolation, confined to the cells of music during the period of class domination.'[51]

During the final phase of the Weimar Republic, the Institute for Social Research had thus advanced a comprehensive claim to revolutionizing bourgeois society on a social, political, psychological and cultural level. At the same time, it was a claim to power on the part of the left-wing intelligentsia, who thought that they had found a key to understanding the basic problems of human existence in Marxist and psychoanalytical theory. But this also indicates the limits of their thinking. However critical this thinking may have been, it meant that all problems were reduced to the level where they could be solved as a point of principle, be it in the class struggle, in a planned economy or in the therapeutic explanations of psychoanalysis. And in the process it revealed a remarkable naïvety. By describing itself as critical theory, philosophy burdened itself with the limitations of its potential questions and began to list towards rationalism. Although the future form of society was not to be spelt out in detail, it none the less implied a solution to all the world's mysteries. 'Reason' was to 'rule' – and with this definition of its task, it fell into a trap of its own making.

5   Kitsch, Death and Crisis

'At the start of my association with Adorno,' Ernst Krenek reports, 'I was particularly struck by his frequent praise of Surrealism, and that was something that fascinated me greatly.'[1] When four 'Surrealist Plays for Reading' appeared in the *Frankfurter Zeitung* on 17 November 1931, few people can have known the true identity of the pseudonymous Castor Zwieback, whose name is a comically incongruous combination of the mythical Castor and the everyday German word for 'biscuit'. Not until the final volume of Adorno's writings was published in 1986 was the mystery solved. Today we know that during the early 1930s Adorno wrote eighteen such pieces with his friend Carl Dreyfus. Walter Benjamin and Ernst Bloch similarly wrote short stories, and Horkheimer also went through a phase of prolific literary activity during his adolescence. Few of Adorno's short stories have survived. We know only the title of his tales of Rabbi Misje Schmah, who must have been a devotee of critical theory. According to Peter von Haselberg, 'The emotionalism of Buber's Hasidic legends was travestied here in the form of jokes lacking in any punchline – tales that were located somewhere between Peter Altenberg, Robert Walser and Martin Buber but which left behind them the field of religion in order to satirize the style of the contemporary Berlin of Ullstein or, rather, the Kurfürstendamm with its innocent bonhomie.'[2] Unfinished narratives are a recurrent feature of Adorno's writings, which reveal a remarkable range of stultified and brutalized characters, extending from elaborately constructed types such as the authoritarian figure and the regressive listener to the veritable inferno of *Minima moralia*. All are evoked with a frenzy worthy of Honoré Daumier: car drivers, bibliophiles and doctors; brutal Junkers as well as sensitive intellectuals ('horn-rimmed spectacles with plain glass before an ordinary face'); social democrats ('the Bebels', a reference to the early German socialist leader, August Bebel, 1840–1913) and a reactionary 'band of noblemen'. It is Adorno the sociologist who tames and conquers these nightmare-like figures. Their prototype may be found in the very first of his surrealist plays, its title, 'Return Visit',[3] referring to a basic social obligation and thereby pointing to social theory in general. The piece is, indeed, nothing less than a gloss on society. A business associate travels to his late friend's burial; the mourners are moved. But wrongly so, as it turns out, for the man has acted according to business principles only for consistency's sake: 'The dead man came in person to Pirmasens for my late father's burial, and so I too have to pay him my last respects.'[4] Basic to social obligation, in Adorno's view, was the law of commodity exchange. The hardened individual whose emotions are clearly calculated and who drifts into madness while acting perfectly rationally is the negative prototype from the world of critical theory. At the same time, the problems of critical theory are already apparent here: for Adorno, commodity exchange became the all-purpose key that could be used to explain everything from behaviour at Hollywood parties to military strategy in the Second World War. The history of critical theory may be summed up as follows: the more the assumptions of Marxism came to seem implausible, the more its shrinking body of ideas was believed capable of explaining an ever increasing number of social phenomena. The history of critical theory is the history of a theory that has come to be seen as increasingly hollow.

Adorno's co-author, Carl Dreyfus (originally Dreyfuß), was born in Frankfurt in 1898 and died in Munich in 1969. He saw active service in the First World War, before embarking on a business career in his father's firm. But he then went back to school and in 1923 took his doctorate with a dissertation on 'Relation and Will'. His supervisor was Hans Driesch in Cologne. Thus qualified, he joined the staff of the Institute for Social Research in 1930. His friends included not only Adorno and Horkheimer but also Siegfried Kracauer, Alfred Sohn-Rethel and, above all, the actress Marianne Hoppe, with whom he cohabited from the early 1930s and who helped him in 1963 when he returned to Germany from exile in Argentina. She told her biographer, Petra Kohse, that her long-term lover was

a sociologist, a Jew, heir to a paint factory, a real ladies' man, very experienced. That's how he ran his factory. He was a kind of private scholar and also wrote prose. He had great charm, that's undeniable. In Berlin I more or less drifted around. I never felt the urge to go to lectures or read. It was Dreyfuß who taught me how to read properly. In this way I began to understand things a bit more. It was Dreyfuß who showed me all this, everything about art and books and how to deal with people in general. Basically, too, it's he whom I have to thank for protecting me during the whole of the following period.[5]

Dreyfus worked in industry during the 1920s and initially planned to write a novel about the life of white-collar workers, but during his time at the Institute for Social Research he produced a sociological study on *The Profession and Ideology of White-Collar Workers*, which he was able to see into print just before the National Socialist takeover in 1933. A social scientist who had studied Marx and Kafka, he examined the new reality of white-collar workers, including their profession and the subtle shadings in their consciousness of their status, their ideologies and, finally, their media, especially the cinema. There is no doubt that Dreyfus was a snob, but it could be argued that a snob is in the best position to examine social differences as he misses none of the signs that convey information about the individual's social position. In 1931, at the height of his professional collaboration with Dreyfus, Adorno certainly believed in a 'mysterious sympathy between snobbery and the avant-garde'.[6]

White-collar workers were a topic of contemporary criticism. Among the authors who wrote novels set in this kind of environment are Joseph Breitbach, Hans Fallada and Irmgard Keun. Meanwhile, sociological and professional studies, including Kracauer's famous monograph, examined the growing social stratum between the bourgeoisie and the working class. But Dreyfus, who had reviewed the relevant literature in the pages of the *Zeitschrift für Sozialforschung* (frequently using the pseudonym Ludwig Carl), went his own way. He published two chapters of his draft novel, first in 1930, then in 1931, describing a company outing and a *thé dansant*, both evoked in a language that recalls brochures, official speeches and announcements,[7] an elaborate literary technique which avails itself of set phrases that have only to be taken literally to be exposed as untrue. Even before his conversion to Marxism, Dreyfus had planned something similar using the language of theology: a glance at his dissertation shows that he envisaged a programme of redemption through understanding at the interface between religion and enlightenment. People were said to 'live in a state of blindness and a lack of freedom' and to be 'fleeing from self-knowledge', but as early as 1923 Dreyfus was able to offer them help: 'The road to salvation lies through the gateway of understanding.'

Adorno had reached a similar conclusion at about the same time in his writings on the aesthetics of music, although in his case it was the French Surrealists who inspired these ideas. The schema of progress and reaction that he was later to apply to music with radical single-mindedness was still capable of subtle distinctions in the years around 1930. True, his views on Schoenberg on the one hand and neoclassicism on the other were already fixed, but between these two extremes Adorno accorded a systematic role to 'musical surrealism' as 'a style based upon montage, which abrogates the "organic" surface structure of neoclassicism and moves together rubble and fragment or by adding wrong notes constructs actual compositions out of the falsehood and illusion that nowadays finds expression in the form of nineteenth-century harmonies'.[8] Here Adorno was thinking of *The Threepenny Opera* and *Mahagonny* by Bertolt Brecht and Kurt Weill, as well as works by Stravinsky such as *The Soldier's Tale, Ragtime* and *The Fairy's Kiss*. Colourless sounds, excessive sweetness, eerily revenant salon music, tangos and marches rendered unrecognizable – in all of these Adorno saw the legitimate material for music that revealed its underlying meaning by means of quotations. From here it was but a short step to Dreyfus's experiments with the 'false' resonances of language. Adorno argued along identical lines in a contemporary speech on Wedekind, whom he hailed as the German precursor of Surrealism and as the man who had discovered 'authentically genuine rubbish'.[9] From Wedekind, one could learn 'to remove, as it were, the elements of composition from the rubbish tip of aesthetics'.[10] Surrealism, under whose aegis Adorno and Dreyfus met in 1931, was mediated by critical theory and as a result had little to do with the classic devices of the French Surrealists, namely, automatic writing and séances. Their concern, rather, was to make their readers aware of the ingratiating element that renders ideologies so attractive. For Adorno and Dreyfus, the Surrealist component was not synonymous with the production of an oneirically wondrous element, as it was for the French Surrealists, but implied an ideologically critical reading and interpretation. And there was another way in which their approach differed from that of the Surrealists: in their 'plays for reading', life seems to have been worn down between production and consumption, between capitalism and the culture industry, leaving it empty and banal, torpid and devoid of meaning. But it was easier to discover this by reading the novels of Julien Green, which appeared during the late twenties and left a deep impression on Adorno: *Adrienne Mesurat*, the novel that made Green famous, describes the life of an ageing woman who lives an uneventful life in the French provinces and slowly goes mad.

By the years around 1930 the lines of communication between philosophy and literature were more intense than at any time since the days of the early German Romantics. Walter Benjamin, Ernst Bloch and Siegfried Kracauer all experimented with small-scale forms between theory and prose, hoping that, having bade farewell to their dreams of systems, they might finally capture reality. They homed in on smaller details in an attempt to improve the focus. The feuilleton set out on the road to modernity. For all their independent and distinctive tone, the plays by Adorno and Dreyfus are part of this movement.

These scenes from social life are peopled by marionettes: white-collar workers, board members, students, young professional women who are often involved in brief relationships while attending meetings or as part of a group of tourists. Their strings are pulled by kitsch, death, crisis and rationalization. The last gasp of the Weimar Republic seems like a grinning vacuum. All these texts presuppose the worldwide economic crisis that hit Germany particularly badly, even though it is never referred to as such but generally described in euphemistic terms. Only once do they mention the 'difficult circumstances'. The characters that appear here are linked above all by one thing: they are all fleeing from the need to think and are unbeatable when it comes to avoiding understanding. A board member of a company that is in difficulty is confronted with the successes of a Hamburg-based enterprise and immediately responds with the ready-made jargon of essentiality: 'The fundamental principles are totally different. In Hamburg the possibilities are still far from being exhausted as they are with us. There they are far more basic.'[11]

These are fine words, but if they fail to acknowledge the true economic situation, they offer instead a new insight into the way in which individuals assert their demonstrative membership of a group that is already agreed that in future 'basicness' will matter. In terms of linguistic criticism, Adorno's achievement lay in turning aesthetic reactions to set phrases to sociological advantage. He recognized the functional importance of the set phrase as a means of holding together society, a device to bridge the gaps in it. Clichés are stimulants that create a sense of unity between strangers, much as good liqueurs contribute towards 'a good mood' in another of these plays.[12] And it is here that we see the best example of how to say literally nothing in an elegant and contemporary way, when the representative of a large concern describes an amorous adventure: 'The days slipped past like hours. Neither of us asked the other's name or sought to find out more about the other's character. When we parted, we knew nothing about each other. In this way the incident became a pleasant memory and so it has remained.'[13]

The country's economic crisis was also a time when people were officially urged to be happy. In his study on white-collar workers Dreyfus reports on a case heard by an industrial tribunal and won by a major department store, which argued that it had the right to dismiss one of its female employees on the grounds of unsuitability: she was too serious and never smiled. The publishing house of Ullstein-Verlag organized a competition under the title 'Berliners, smile!' And at around the same time the film *The Man With a Heart* was released in Germany. It tells how the daughter of a bank's president arranges for herself to be employed incognito as a secretary in her father's company in order to be able to work for the bank employee whom she secretly loves. The loyal employee prevents the bank from making a huge loss and is rewarded by its president. He receives the hand of his lover, who is revealed as the president's daughter.

The play *Nothing but Laughter* is little more than a montage of all this:

> When the farce was over, a theatre employee came into the dressing room in search of one of the performers. She had played the part of a wealthy young woman from a genteel house who was working in her future husband's firm in order to observe him. She was now called into the director's office. The director asked her to take a seat and said: 'My dear child, why aren't you happier? In a farce in summer your first priority is to be cheerful. Is something the matter? Why don't you laugh more loudly? Why don't you move more? It's a delightful role. Also, why don't you speak in a livelier manner? The best lines are going to waste. It can't be difficult for someone as young and beautiful as you are. You'll doubtless be better tomorrow.'[14]

The last of these pieces is called 'Pronunciation' and describes the grand finale of the culture industry. Here utter madness reigns, with the material made up of scraps of illustrated novels, filmscripts, the words of popular hits and concepts from the world of contemporary design. Everything is wonderful: the house on the tree-lined avenue and the 'cigarette box made of jade'. The company that meets for dinner at Professor Georgi's is positively radiant. But at the same time it is all terribly embarrassing. Is it the fault of Frau Hegemann, who lives in a luxury apartment and whom we see reclining on a couch in a flimsy light-blue dress? Two gentlemen arrive and make a long-winded attempt to discuss 'something very serious' with her: it seems that Frau Hegemann has been unfaithful to her lover. The two gentlemen make so bold as to recall a whispered conversation during a car journey, to say nothing of a letter to a certain Gladys that they would prefer not to talk about. And did not Frau Hegemann once tell one of the two gentlemen that she was having an affair with Dr Tsian – it was on the afternoon that she played him some dance records? In a word, it was impossible to avoid the suspicion that her friend was a figure of fun to her. 'Even a marble ashtray falling on his head while he was moving seemed to you only a pretext for laughter. You described the injury to me on the telephone. "Do you deny all this?" Frau Hegemann was incapable of lying. "No," she said. Her face had regained its calm. She leant against the window and looked out on to the tree-lined avenue whose trees retained the final traces of light. "That's enough," the older friend said as he got up. The two gentlemen kissed her hand in turn and left together.'[15]

When Dreyfus was forced to leave Europe at the end of the 1930s (his residence permit allowing him to stay in England had not been extended), he applied to join the staff at the Institute for Social Research, which was now based in America, and also to work for Paramount. The story of Frau Hegemann is set at this very point of intersection between sociological Marxism and the world of dreams. It requires only a slight shift of emphasis to find ourselves in one of the screwball comedies of the 1930s and films such as *Bringing Up Baby*, with a type of woman embodied in Germany by Marianne Hoppe in some of her finest roles and in America by Katharine Hepburn. Walter Benjamin wrote to Gretel Adorno on 20 July 1938: 'I recently saw Katharine Hepburn for the first time. She's magnificent and reminds me very much of you. Has no one ever told you that?'[16]

6 Stargazing

If there was anything that attracted intellectuals of a philosophical bent to Marxist theory during the 1920s, it was not just its account of social injustice, the exploitation of the working class and the claim that capitalism was inevitably leading to a state of ultimate crisis, with only socialism as a way out. To pass critical comment on these ideas would have required an expert understanding of economic processes that few intellectuals could muster. It was not Marx the economist who appealed to the writers who theorized about consciousness and culture but the chapter on 'The Festishism of the Commodity and Its Secret' in the first volume of *Capital*. Here capitalism is interpreted as a cultural phenomenon: it is not only an unjust system beset by crisis, it is also one that produces its own semblance of transfiguration. Marx believed that as the result of a kind of optical illusion the capitalist system must strike the observer as something entirely natural. History, Marx argued, rigged itself out as nature. The exchange value of a commodity seemed to be its natural quality rather than the expression of a social relationship. Hence his use of the term 'fetish', a man-made object on to which mysterious forces are projected. In this way the commodity became a subject for philosophy. In *Capital*, Marx calls it a 'very strange thing, abounding in metaphysical subtleties and theological niceties'.[1] For it is something with specific natural qualities and at the same time a sign of social relationships, but these relationships are concealed, as it were, in nature. 'If commodities could speak, they would say this: our use-value may interest men, but it does not belong to us as objects. What does belong to us as objects, however, is our value. Our own intercourse as commodities proves it. We relate to each other merely as exchange-values.'[2] Marx thought that in proposing this definition he had found the key to the way in which ideologies are formed:

> The religious reflections of the real world can, in any case, vanish only when
> the practical relations of everyday life between man and man, and man and

nature, generally present themselves to him in a transparent and rational form. The veil is not removed from the countenance of the social life-process, i.e. the process of material production, until it becomes production by freely associated men, and stands under their conscious and planned control.[3]

This was a grandiose programme that gave enormous impetus to critical self-consciousness. Criticism was no longer just literary criticism, as it had been for the Romantics and the Schlegel brothers. It now affected the whole constitution of society, at least to the extent that society could be decoded as a world of appearances and the fetishism of the relations governing capital:

It is nothing but the definite social relation between men themselves which assumes here, for them, the fantastic form of a relation between things. In order, therefore, to find an analogy we must take flight into the misty realm of religion. There the products of the human brain appear as autonomous figures endowed with a life of their own, which enter into relations both with each other and with the human race. So it is in the world of commodities with the products of men's hands. I call this the fetishism which attaches itself to the products of labour as soon as they are produced as commodities, and is therefore inseparable from the production of commodities.[4]

During the 1930s Adorno was not alone in working to implement this programme. Walter Benjamin, for example, drew up a plan for a major work on the Paris arcades – the covered shopping streets that date from the nineteenth century and, in Benjamin's eyes, the locus classicus, aesthetically and socially, of the fetishism of the commodity, with what he termed its 'sex appeal'. The phantasmagorias of the commodity were quite literally the basis for the remote and imaginary worlds of fashionably pseudo-oriental music and the draperies of the nineteenth century. Benjamin toyed with images and concepts but, much to the annoyance of Adorno, who from the outset was involved in discussions for the project, he thought along poetic rather than Hegelian lines. Another writer who was friendly with Adorno and who developed an obsession with the fetishistic character of the commodity was the philosopher Alfred Sohn-Rethel. Indeed, Sohn-Rethel even attempted to derive the origins of philosophy and abstract thinking from the development of a commodity and money economy among the ancient Greeks. Even the somewhat playful analyses of popular hits that Adorno occasionally undertook drew on the emotional language of critical theory and were more than mere reviews, being designed, rather, to expose the world of social appearances. In order to distinguish between appearance and essence, it was necessary to go back not only to Marx but also to Hegel, whose *Science of Logic* provided the philosophical basis for their discussions.

Marx's theory of the fetishistic character of the commodity was a lucky find for Adorno as it was well suited to giving a socio-critical dimension to the relation between history and nature that had interested him long before his reflections on the concept of landscape in Schubert's music. History could appear as nature, and nature in turn could be conceived of in historical terms. Adorno's subsequent endeavours could be described as a kind of universalized Marxism that pointed out the relations between the different elements: that which is nature was to reveal itself as society, as history, while history for its part was close to nature, at least to the extent that it signified transience. On 15 July 1932 Adorno addressed the Frankfurt branch of the Kant Society, delivering a paper entitled 'The Idea of Natural History'.[5] It was his first attempt to do systematic justice to the process of seeing nature and history reflected in a reciprocal mirror, something that had exercised him for some time – if his late reminiscences of Amorbach are genuine, nature and the most recent civilization had already thrown light on each other during his childhood. His lecture attempted to provide a more detailed account of this procedure. The opposites were to be seen as dialectically interlinked, with history, pursuing its unconscious course, being interpreted as pure 'nature' in capitalism. Needless to say, Adorno did not mean nature in the sense of natural science but in the sense of human experience, namely, myth. The usual 'antithesis of nature and history', he wrote, was to be 'sublated'.[6] The two entities should not drift apart but should be brought closer together.

It was on this point that Adorno found himself in closest agreement with Walter Benjamin. He had been introduced to Benjamin by Siegfried Kracauer in 1923, at a time when Benjamin was hoping to receive his postdoctoral teaching qualification in Frankfurt: 'I saw Benjamin very often, I would say at least once a week, probably more frequently during the whole of the time that he was living in Frankfurt,'[7] we read in Adorno's reminiscences of Benjamin:

> It is really quite difficult to speak of a 'purpose' in our spending time together. We spent time together in the way that forty years ago intellectuals used to meet, simply in order to talk and in that way to tug a little at the theoretical bones that they were currently gnawing. That is how it was with Benjamin and me. I was then very young, eleven years younger than he, and of the two of us I saw myself entirely as the one who took rather than gave. I know that I listened to him with tremendous fascination and would then sometimes ask him to explain things in greater detail.[8]

For both men, this was one of the most important relationships in their lives, and it was not free from tension. Benjamin, who was never able to teach at a university, found a pupil in Adorno – his only pupil, if we may believe Hannah Arendt – and it was Adorno who then introduced a rationalized version of his ideas into academic philosophy. The frequency with which Benjamin enquired after Adorno in the letters that he wrote to Kracauer during the 1920s suggests how interested he was in the younger man. On the other hand, there was always a danger in Adorno getting too close to philosophy. He had emulated his mentor Hans Cornelius to such an extent that he seemed a mere copy of the original, and anyone who examines any of Adorno's later writings such as *Minima moralia* will not fail to notice Benjamin's conceptual and stylistic influence. In this case we may speak of a continuing conversation that not even Benjamin's death could terminate. But we could also speak, as Sigrid Weigel has done, of a melancholy ingestion of the absent Other.

Be that as it may, the close contacts between Adorno and Benjamin were not without their dangers. Never at a loss for a derogatory remark, Soma Morgenstern describes a scene that is probably pure invention but that may well be close to the truth:

> We were sitting in Kracauer's room while he was out. Walter Benjamin, who was still thinking about our extended conversations on the subject of Karl Kraus, came back to them. 'I dreamt about Kraus last night,' he said. 'He was sitting in a room in front of a large table. Everything was flat, there was no perspective.' 'As in medieval pictures,' Wiesengrund interjected. Benjamin said nothing and looked at me for some time. But I did not understand what his expression meant. He then went on with his narrative: 'On the table behind which Kraus was sitting were several revolvers of various sizes. Karl Kraus argued briefly with everyone who passed, then shot them.' – 'Shot each of them with a different revolver,' Teddy interposed. Benjamin looked at me again, and again I did not understand why. He then went on with his dream: 'A long line of people passed in front of Kraus, and he disposed of them all in the same way. He then got up with a jolt. I woke up, terrified.'

Morgenstern reports that he then left with Benjamin. While they were eating, he came back to the earlier scene and said that he assumed that Benjamin had already discussed his dream with Adorno. 'Not a bit of it,' Benjamin replied. 'I'd told him nothing. He pursues me even in my dreams.'[9]

Benjamin and Adorno defined the standards by which the intellectual was judged, not only in their own day but for later generations, too. They were philosophers who encapsulated their age in thoughts and yet who were not really members of a philosophy faculty in a university department with its traditional division of labour. At the same time, they thought about language; they were thinkers capable of giving appropriate linguistic form to every valid insight. Convinced as they were that style and thought are not external to each other but are able to enhance and challenge one another, they were able to devise an appropriate form for their writings. The real subject of their discussions was, therefore, the constant question as to the demands that can be made of intellectuals. What intuitive force, what argumentational reworking may be expected of them? And, above all, what demands on their thinking were made by the historical and biographical caesura of their exile? Their thinking was characterized by an extreme tension that finds expression in their correspondence in the interrelationship between solidarity and criticism. Their relationship was based almost entirely on their work together. If it survived the tensions to which it was exposed, this was entirely thanks to Gretel Adorno, as is clear from Benjamin's letters to her. Here he was able to communicate his true feelings without being directly responsible for each and every thought. Whether he was describing an opium-induced high in the Red Room of the art historian Jean Selz, his reaction to the natural beauty of southern Europe or the unfathomable depths of his relations with Brecht, in every case Gretel Adorno maintained a benevolent response. Benjamin used the familiar 'Du' form in his letters to her, while retaining the more formal 'Sie' when writing to his friend.

The most striking aspect of their reciprocal and often rigorous and sometimes even enthusiastic discussions of their work together is the emergence of a theory of art involving intellectual effort, a technique developed by intellectuals and seen from the perspective of a laboratory. Throughout all this, it was Adorno who was the more argumentative of the two men, with his interest in Husserl's philosophy permeating almost their entire correspondence during the 1930s. His writings were the result of a more powerful process of rationalization, and so they generally made 'good' or 'solid' progress, while Benjamin became bogged down in an endless struggle with the material on which he made notes in the Bibliothèque nationale in Paris. When compared with Adorno's contribution, his own work resembles nothing so much as a series of outlines, studies, drafts, copies, revisions, chapter divisions and lists. His unpublished papers are full of mysterious drawings: circles, triangles, crosses, fields, compass cards and coloured symbols all give his ideas a cabbalistic dimension. The placing of an idea was as important to him as its logical consistency within a particular argument. His contribution to the intellectual theory of art had less to do with arguments in the strict sense of the term than with a taste for paradox and the sort of intuition more often associated with detectives. On one occasion he drew Adorno's attention to a book by G. K. Chesterton, which he described as 'an extraordinary work with the irresistible music of healthy common sense',[10] and on another informed him of one of the maxims of Hérault de Séchelles: 'The ideas which are important to an individual should be coordinated with his ten fingers and their individual joints.'[11]

In his recollections of Benjamin, Adorno reports that everything that Benjamin said sounded 'as though it came from a secret world'.[12] The problems discussed in their correspondence are the result of their different theoretical concepts: Benjamin's idea was 'philosophical observation', Adorno's 'philosophical interpretation', and both followed different rhythms. Observation implies a passive element, it abandons itself to the matter in hand, and it is unending. Central to Benjamin's work is the long, intoxicated, almost addicted look filled with desire. His study of the Parisian arcades took as its starting point the shop windows of the glass-covered arcades and as such was his attempt to write the history of this look. His last major study of Baudelaire was the negative counterpart to this, an unanswered gaze into the eye of a camera to which no aura responds. Interpretation, conversely, signifies a conscious act. Here the dream of merging with the object under observation is over. The interpreter abandons himself to no sense of intoxication or ecstasy but seeks to collect all his powers of concentration. The interpreter's task is always complete, the observer's never – this was the law governing their philosophical debates. Adorno's perpetual reproach that there were things in Benjamin's writings that were 'not fully explained', 'not yet raised to the level of a concept', 'not yet fully dialectical' and still in need of interpretation applies to Benjamin's equally insistent reference to the category of 'experience', a category developed above all in his essay on the Russian novelist Nikolay Leskov. Experiences derive from long, intimate and practical dealings with others and are not always communicable to all. Only when experience is properly articulated, Benjamin believed, does interpretation have any point. If the postulates of experience and argumentational analysis wore each other down in their correspondence, the two men none the less agreed that the demands made of intellectuals were thereby increased. This signals a rejection of hectic bustle. But we need to go further than this: if Adorno was the true intellectual who found his goal in 'interpretation', it is tempting to call Benjamin the man of intellectual experience. True, Adorno promised intellectual experience in the finest passages from his writings (it is this that constitutes his appeal), but his greater rationality also involved a loss when compared with Benjamin's puzzling figures.

Adorno's postdoctoral thesis on Søren Kierkegaard was written at the crossroads between his own natural historical philosophy and the influence of Walter Benjamin. There may well have been external reasons for his decision to choose the Danish theologian, philosopher and writer as the subject for his dissertation inasmuch as his supervisor was the left-wing Protestant theologian Paul Tillich, who taught social philosophy in Frankfurt and for whom a Christian writer must have been an obvious choice. In Kierkegaard, Adorno could find a connection between philosophical thinking and literary reflection, two categories that were bound to appeal to him as being related. Moreover, Kierkegaard had been alone in seeing the beginnings of modern faceless society. Finally, Kierkegaard, like Schopenhauer, Nietzsche and Marx, was one of those nineteenth-century thinkers who had opened up Hegel's system. It was no longer necessary to assume a purely logical development that produced from within itself everything that the world contained. Rather, individual experience and the individual him- or herself were now given greater philosophical importance. And Adorno must also have been attracted by Kierkegaard's engagement with music: a long section of *Either/Or* is devoted to Mozart's opera *Don Giovanni*. Kierkegaard assumed that human existence was modelled on a series of spheres, where the aesthetic sphere was broken by the ethical, which in turn was relativized by the religious sphere.

This was a literary and philosophical model that would repay critical examination. Above all, Kierkegaard had adopted an extreme position vis-à-vis the official Christianity of the Church and brought religion to a point of extreme tension with bourgeois society. Like Schoenberg, Kierkegaard was someone who refused to compromise and whom Adorno duly took as his guide. 'Kierkegaard had no wish to play along,' he noted laconically in an essay that he wrote decades later and dedicated to Paul Tillich.[13] The non-conformist radical intellectual who adopts a position that can no longer be shared with the majority – this was a figure already adumbrated in Kierkegaard in the pupal nineteenth century.

What was Adorno's thesis? The first surprise to confront the reader is the fact that the Christianity that was central to Kierkegaard's thinking is given a wide berth here and only implicitly criticized. What Adorno discovered instead were, on the one hand, mythical features, including direct allusions to Nordic myth, and, on the other, Kierkegaard's world of images, in which Adorno saw the Danish philosopher's principal contribution inasmuch as it spoke in passing of reconciliation. The result was a 'dialectical picture' whose model he had learnt from Benjamin: it was not a self-contained type of thinking or personality that was posited here, but a sense of movement in which the darker features of the beginning brighten up, as it were, at the end and even acquire a utopian dimension. The very form of the book reflects the course that it is hoped that history will take. Even the outward form of the study's seven chapters was influenced by Benjamin's disquisition on *The Origin of German Tragedy*. The early chapters are given over to a critique of Kierkegaard, who, it is claimed, fell prey to the bourgeois interior, while his concept of paradox meant that the intellect was sacrificed. Above all, however, Christianity was brought closer to myth – to quote from the later *Dialectic of Enlightenment*, Christology was 'the monotheistic disguise of myth'.[14] And just as in psychoanalysis, the seemingly unimportant – slips of the tongue, dreams and Freudian slips – may be a key to the unconscious, which can complement or refute conscious statements, so Adorno interprets Kierkegaard's images and narratives in exactly the same way. Christian spiritualism – the conscious content – is in fact 'hostility to nature':

> Spirit posits itself as free and autonomous in opposition to nature because it considers nature demonic as much in external reality as in itself. In that, however, autonomous spirit appears corporally, nature takes possession of it where it occurs most historically: in objectless interiority. Spirit's natural content must be investigated if in Kierkegaard the being of subjectivity itself is to be explicated. The natural content of mere spirit, 'historical' in itself, may be called mythical.[15]

Here we find the category of the 'victim'. Within the context of the early 'thirties, this no doubt meant above all the victims of a war that was still fresh in people's memories. But it also implied the question as to the meaning that their sacrifice could have had and, by implication, the meaning of Christ's sacrifice. But Adorno wanted nothing to do with sacrifice: 'For sacrifice indeed wants to absolve nature, and nature has its determining power at Kierkegaard's historical moment and even for his knowledge in the spirit of the isolated individual.'[16] The sacrifice was replaced by the concept of 'sacrificeless fulfilment', 'sacrificeless reconciliation', the 'reconciling redemption of sacrifice'[17] – in short, a private world of myth in contrast to the sufferings of Christ, a concept of sensual happiness and the longing for that happiness.

Adorno's idea may be seen as a desire to bid farewell to a childhood that had been marked by Christian beliefs. But it also reflects the philosophy of socialism, with its view of a world at peace, a world that has left behind it wars and sacrifices and that meets its citizens' demands for happiness. Adorno had discovered his own philosophy by interpreting Christianity as part of a process of Hegelian sublation. At the same time, however, this meant that his philosophy included a trace of theology that repeatedly demanded reflection. At virtually every stage in his development we find a point at which he was able to formulate his own ideas only by distancing himself from Christianity: in his youth it was the promise held out by Catholicism to offer an objective order that prompted him to decide in favour of radical subjectivity. In his postdoctoral dissertation it was Christ's self-sacrificial death that was to be offset by the happiness of the inner world. And for a long time – virtually throughout the whole of his maturity – he was to be exercised by the music of Beethoven, whose *Missa solemnis* demanded an answer to the question whether and in what way sacred music was possible in the modern age.

The state of Utopia was to be governed by aesthetics. Adorno believed that in Kierkegaard he had discovered a world of images that pointed in this direction. This world is 'not eternal, but historical-dialectical; it does not lie in perfect transcendence beyond nature, but dissolves darkly into nature'.[18] 'Where, however, nature – free of resignation – perseveres as desirous instinct and eloquent consciousness, it is able to survive, whereas in sacrifice nature succumbs to itself; nature, which truly cannot be driven out with a pitchfork and returns until genius is reconciled with it.'[19]

The idea of reconciled nature and a world of sensual fulfilment was combined with a Dickensian romanticism about the poor. Adorno had recently read *The Old Curiosity Shop*, and traces of this interest may be seen in his study of Kierkegaard:

> Do you think that it is almost a kind of childishness in me to persist in seeking this quality among the poor and the suffering? Or maybe you have degraded yourself by adopting the shocking division that assigns the aesthetic to the distinguished, the rich, the mighty, the highly educated, and at the most assigns religion to the poor? Well, it seems to me that the poor do not come out badly in this division. And do you not see that the poor in having the religious have also the aesthetic, and that the rich, in so far as they have not the religious, have not the aesthetic either?[20]

It is impossible to strike a more lyrical or esoteric note in praising the class struggle. Beauty, Adorno believed, could be systematically justified only in the Utopia of reconciliation: 'Every aesthetic form is directed toward truth and disappears in it.'[21] Aesthetics was the governor of the revolution – for the present at least. But the time might come when it replaced revolution. On 21 August 1930 Adorno was able to write to Alban Berg from Pontresina in the Engadine and report that his book on Kierkegaard was 'almost finished'. He had invested all his energy in the work and overtaxed himself: he had 'collapsed and fled into the mountains' and rediscovered himself 'in their beauty'[22] – a recurring pattern in Adorno's life: there was never a time when he did not seek a rhythmic balance between the work ethic of conscious exertion and the relaxation of the 'man of the mountains' in the unconscious world of nature.

Contrary to expectations, the book did not sink without trace in National Socialist Germany. Between its date of publication and the mid-'thirties there were reviewers who were deeply impressed by Adorno's account, even if there were also voices raised in dissent. 'Would the author have not at the very least formulated his views in a different way if he had seen Kierkegaard as more of a "religious person"?' Heinrich Fels asked in 1935 in the *Philosophisches Jahrbuch der Görresgesellschaft*.[23] A more critical review appeared in the *Kant-Studien*, with the reviewer, Franz-Josef Brecht, taking issue with Adorno's associative thinking. 'None the less, the literature on Kierkegaard has been enriched by a book whose intellectual level, sensitive adroitness and subtle way with words are virtually unique in their field.'[24] Criticism and admiration were also counterbalanced among Adorno's friends, so that on 15 January 1933 we find Benjamin writing to Gershom Scholem to report that he had found much in *Kierkegaard* that was 'very good', before continuing: 'But the writer's case is so complex that I cannot begin to describe it in a letter. If I tell you that during the second term, following on from his previous seminar, he is lecturing on my book on tragedy without making this clear in the lecture timetable, you have an idea of what I mean, a miniature *pars pro toto*. But quite apart from this you should definitely take note of his book.'[25] Scholem did not reply until the following October, but when he did so he did not mince his words:

> I've so far read about two thirds of Wiesengrund's book on Kierkegaard – I read his name with fifty others in the official list of those who have been dismissed in Frankfurt. In my own view, it combines an eloquent plagiarism of your thinking with an unusual degree of chutzpah and, in complete contrast to your analysis of tragedy, it will have little impact in future on objective accounts of K. . . . You would not have taken pleasure in certain 'revelations' that this author seems to find particularly delightful. Of course, there is a lot that is very good, but there are other things that, not to put too fine a point on it, I have simply not understood.[26]

The esoteric style to which Scholem took exception was the outward sign of a philosophical wish to compete with the coded riddles on the surface of society. This vaguely old-fashioned desire to alienate even extended to Adorno's physical appearance, for, as Peter von Haselberg reports, Adorno currently referred to himself, jokingly, as Dapsul von Zabelthau, an astrologer in E. T. A. Hoffmann's *Die Serapionsbrüder* who reads people's future in the stars. The analogy captures the slightly magical tone of Adorno's interpretations. Hoffmann describes the character mysteriously encountering others: 'But while you are thinking about it, he has already gently brushed your forehead with a "With your permission, Sir!" and peered at the palm of your hand. "May Heaven bless you, Sir, the stars are looking good for you!" he says in as hollow and lachrymose a tone as before, and goes on his way. – This strange man was none other than Herr Dapsul von Zabelthau.' It was very much the concept of the constellation that Adorno had arrogated as an alternative to the philosophical system in his inaugural lecture in Frankfurt. Philosophy had the task of 'placing its elements, which it receives from the sciences, in changing constellations or, to use a less astrological and scientifically more up-to-date expression, in changing experimental arrangements until they produce the figure that may be read as the answer.'[27] Again: 'In using philosophy to deal with the conceptual material I am consciously speaking of grouping and experimental arrangement, constellation and construction.'[28] In his inaugural lecture, Adorno was careful to avoid referring openly to the concepts of dialectical and historical materialism. The 'enclosed space of understanding'[29] should be abandoned in favour of 'praxis' and even 'materialistic praxis'. Thinking 'compelled' praxis, and the solution to philosophical problems could be found only in a transformed reality: 'The interpretation of existing reality and its supersession are interrelated. True, reality is not superseded as a concept; but the construct of the figure of the real is always immediately followed by the demand for its actual change.'[30]

Others regarded this mystification of the class struggle as merely a flight from reality. The political climate at Frankfurt University is described by Adorno's pupil Kurt Mautz, then a member of the Group of Socialist Students. His roman-à-clef, *Der Urfreund*, depicts the final phase of the Weimar Republic:

> The political tension became dramatic when the Nazi students tried to enter the University buildings in their brown shirts, thereby violating the ban on uniforms that had been issued by the vice-principal. The Red Students' Group set up a series of checkpoints and kept an eye on all entrances and exits to the University. If anyone turned up in a brown shirt, we agreed to throw him out. In the air well by the side entrance, vicious scuffles would occasionally break out, with our opponents writhing on the ground, until the vice-principal appeared with the University porter and separated us.[31]

The students knew that in the wake of the world economic crisis they would form the new academic proletariat – always assuming the situation did not take a turn for the worse. Mautz reports that barely a third of those who wanted to become teachers could reckon on finding a job once they had completed their studies. The students also became more radical. While the right-wing students celebrated 'Bismarck Day', their left-wing counterparts organized a demonstration that inevitably included the sort of procession with *Martinstrompeten* that was typical of marches by members of the workers' movement. (The *Martinstrompete* is a type of mouth-blown free-reed instrument made up of a number of conical brass horns, each containing a free reed that sounds at a certain pitch and that can be selected by a piston valve placed between the horns and the mouthpiece.) As Mautz reports, they produced 'a peculiarly strident, provocative and at the same time mournful sound'.[32] The demonstration organized by the socialist students passed through the Westend district of Berlin to the main station, then along the Kaiserstraße to the Hauptwache, thence over the Opernplatz through the Westend district and back to the University:

> In the Beethovenstraße we go past the villa in which Amorelli is living. I can see him standing by the first-floor window and I say to Kreifeld: 'Amorelli is looking our way. Do you think he can see us?' 'Of course he can see us. He's just pretending not to. He lives in a villa and so he can't show that he sympathizes with the have-nots.' 'So what's he interested in? Surely not the banner.' 'What else?' 'The brass-band music. He's simply listening to it and then he'll write an essay on it.'[33]

Amorelli is none other than Adorno, the University's 'new, unknown star', as he is described in Mautz's novel. True, Mautz oversimplifies the link between aesthetics and music on the one hand and social change on the other, but his description, veering as it does between sympathy and caricature, touches on a point that the left-wing student movement of 1968 was also to criticize about Adorno: 'In his thinking, he struck us as more logically consistent, more critical and more radical than Paulus' – Paulus is Mautz's fictional name for Paul Tillich, Adorno's supervisor – 'and everything he said was polished to a fault, every sentence sounded as though it could not be otherwise. We were enthusiastic about him, even if we also made fun of his semi-feudal, middle-class manners.'[34] Among the students who took part in Adorno's seminars on aesthetics at this time were a number who later made a name for themselves, including the Germanist Oskar Seidlin and the sociologist Heinz Maus. Another of his students was Wilhelm Emrich, who was an eager participant in his seminar on Benjamin's study of tragedy and who later taught at the Free University in Berlin – not that this prevented him from publishing some extremely anti-Semitic texts during the war before causing a furore with a major study of Kafka that appeared during the early years of the Federal Republic.

Adorno's seminars on aesthetics were attended by only a few students. Again, it is Mautz whose account provides us with a satirical view of Adorno: 'The round head with curly black hair, the first signs of baldness and the large dark eyes behind dark horn-rimmed spectacles had something of a frog about it. Sometimes he arrived in the company of a young lady with golden blond hair, golden brown eyes and a pink complexion. She would sit next to him like the princess in the fairytale about the frog prince, not saying a word all evening.'[35]

7 Twilight

'No one', wrote Adorno in *Minima moralia*,

> who observed the first months of National Socialism in Berlin in 1933 could fail
> to perceive the moment of mortal sadness, of half-knowing self-surrender to
> perdition, that accompanied the manipulated intoxication, the torchlight
> processions and the drum-beating. How disconsolate sounded the favourite
> German song of those months, *Nation to Arms*, along the Unter den Linden.
> The saving of the Fatherland, fixed from one day to the next, bore from the first
> moment the expression of catastrophe that was rehearsed in the concentration
> camps while the triumph in the streets drowned all forebodings.[1]

During the winter of 1932/3 it had still been possible to hope for an alternative
to Hitler in the form of a government under Kurt von Schleicher – it too,
admittedly, was authoritarian, but it was not totalitarian, and in its links with
the unions it tended, rather, to be socialist. And at the very least it envisaged a
planned economy. In a conversation with Peter von Haselberg in which the two
men looked back on the National Socialists' seizure of power, Adorno advanced
the view that the cardinal political mistake had been the Jewish upper middle
class's failure to 'insist on the unity of the working class and to finance it. In this
way the previous government of General Schleicher could have been kept and
would have been forced to continue its cautious attempts to forge a link with
the unions. It was still not too late for this' – the conversation between the two
men took place in the autumn of 1933 – 'because Hitler's amateurish approach
to economics would soon spell his end.'[2] It may be added here that Adorno's
initial explanation of Hitler's success sounds like a classic example of the
economic materialism that seeks to derive the 'superstructure' from the 'basis'.
In conversation with Haselberg, he explained that 'the invitation that Hitler
received to form a government could be directly attributed to the division of
power within the German economy, namely, to a desperate concentration of

those parts of it that were heavily in debt and no longer competitive in the international markets.'[3]

When Hitler seized power, the situation was still far from clear. The National Socialists in the cabinet were hemmed in by conservative ministers, while the regime had a parliamentary majority made up of the NSDAP (Nazi Party) and the German National People's Party. The Germans still hoped that Hitler would be tamed or that he would soon be got rid of. It quickly became clear that the left had suffered a historic defeat, but it was not until the Reichstag was burnt down on the night of 27/8 February – the fire was started by Marinus van der Lubbe, a confused left-wing Communist from the Netherlands – and the Enabling Act passed on 23 March that the way was opened for a dictatorship. Even the Social Democrats were initially in some doubt about the character of the regime. During the early weeks of its existence, the leaders of the German Socialist Party regarded Hitler's government as entirely 'constitutional', with a 'parliamentary basis'. Not even the Social Democrats could know what was in store. As a result, there was a general desire to compromise not only on the part of the middle-class parties but on the left as well. When its newspapers were banned and Goering demanded that 'the witchhunt in foreign Social Democratic newspapers' be stopped before he would relicense them, the party resigned from the Socialist Workers' Internationale. Shortly afterwards the SPD supported Hitler's foreign policy statement in the Reichstag, a move described in pamphlets of the time as a declaration in favour of a peaceful foreign policy rather than a vote of confidence in Hitler. Otto Wels, the legendary Social Democrat whose refusal to back the Enabling Act had turned him into a symbol of steadfastness, none the less spoke out in the Reichstag against the reports on the Nazi reign of terror in the foreign press, which he claimed were 'an exaggeration'. On 19 June 1933 those members of the committee of the SPD who had remained in Germany voted its Jewish members out of office. It was a desperate, opportunistic measure, but it was insufficient to stop the party from being banned.

The anti-Semitic character of the new government did not remain hidden for long from the outside world. In March 1933 Jewish organizations in the capitals of the Western world went on the offensive and demanded an economic boycott of German goods. And in New York's synagogues prayers were said for the persecuted German Jews. For their own part, the National Socialists organized a boycott of Jewish businesses on 1 April, shameful images of which are still all too familiar to us today. A week later the Reichstag passed a law reinstating the professional civil service and announcing the dismissal of civil servants 'of non-Aryan descent'. In Frankfurt the university dismissed fifty-two Jewish scholars, including the expert on international law Hermann Heller, the economist Adolf Löwe (a childhood friend of Horkheimer who later changed his name to Adolph Lowe), the psychologist Max Wertheimer, the sociologist Karl Mannheim and the historian Ernst Kantorowicz, who was a member of the group associated with Stefan George. Adorno, too, lost his right to teach – it was withdrawn on 11 September 1933, his thirtieth birthday. In November he wrote to Berg, 'As for my own work, things are not going too well at the moment. My right to teach has now been withdrawn, after all, on the strength of the Aryan paragraph and I'm wasting a lot of time and energy looking for a new lectureship.'[4]

The reign of terror began to spread. Left-wing thinkers had fled the country or were incarcerated in concentration camps. Brecht, Ernst Bloch and Walter Benjamin had escaped abroad to Denmark, Prague and Paris. And the Institute for Social Research had sensibly and presciently transferred its money abroad, having set up a branch in Geneva even before Hitler had come to power. Contact between Adorno and the Institute was broken. On 3 April 1933, Horkheimer wrote to Benjamin from Geneva, expressing his relief at the latter's lucky escape and adding: 'We are still uneasy about Wiesengrund. I wrote to him briefly in a business capacity around two weeks ago but haven't done so again, because in no circumstances did I want to compromise him from here. Whether he is justified in thinking that he will be able to continue his academic work unimpeded, I do not know. Perhaps you could inform him of our concern in one of your letters – without naming me, of course, and in the most circumspect form.'[5] Paul Tillich had lost his professorship in Frankfurt on political grounds and was preparing to emigrate. The *Neue Blätter für den Sozialismus* for which Tillich used to write and to which Adorno had once contributed had been the organ of the young, unorthodox socialists of the Weimar Republic who had adopted a critical attitude to the dogmas of the old social democracy. Members of the group included the two resistance fighters Theo Haubach and Carlo Mierendorff. The final issue appeared in the spring of 1933 and expressed the hope that in the longer term the new regime would be socialist rather than nationalist, after which the journal was banned.

Adorno not only lost his right to teach at Frankfurt University. In the summer of 1933 the police searched his apartment. Some three decades later, in a lecture that he gave on 17 November 1964, he recalled the ill-defined sense of terror that was inevitably caused by such an incident at a time when there were rumours that people were being dragged away and tortured:

If it had been nothing more than two relatively harmless officials from the old police force turning up and if the visit had not simultaneously implied the knowledge that the entire form of political rule was changing, this experience would not have been what it was, just as one cannot, conversely, imagine the terror of a totalitarian regime unless one has first-hand experience of a fact like the fatal ring of a team of policemen at your door.[6]

All who remained in Germany in 1933 sought to conform as best they could and to find niches in which to survive. Among the opposition there was a widespread belief that Hitler would be unable to hold out for long. In the arts, too, not everything seemed to be lost: there were still National Socialist students who tried to forge a link with Expressionist modernism, and Kurt Schwitters, Max Beckmann and Mies van der Rohe were still living in Germany. Works by Hindemith and Bartók continued to be played, and even pieces by Berg were performed under the direction of Erich Kleiber.

In November 1933, Adorno wrote to Berg from Berlin to report on the emigration of his friends and colleagues from the world of new music. But he also announced that his main reason for being in Berlin was to ensure his acceptance as a member of the Reichskulturkammer, 'on which depends the possibility of being published – and which it seems as if I shall be granted. At all events, Stuckenschmidt told me today that the chances of modern music being performed here are improving. In general, there are certain signs that non-Aryan intellectuals will retain the chance to work.'[7] Meanwhile, Walter Benjamin was still writing pseudonymously for German newspapers from his exile in Ibiza and Paris. The world had changed, but as yet no one knew how deep and how lasting the changes would be. This was true not least of human contacts. In looking back on the Germany of the 1930s, Sebastian Haffner painted a double portrait of a country that he likened to Dr Jekyll and Mr Hyde. Others must have felt the same. Benjamin read Stevenson's novel of the physician with a split personality, part bourgeois, part monster, in the spring of 1933, and was no doubt prompted to do so by contemporary events. In the political twilight of the time it was important to learn to see with new eyes. While in Ibiza, Benjamin himself befriended a young man who shortly afterwards joined the SS.

Solidarity was not guaranteed even among the outlawed and persecuted: every group that was under attack from the National Socialists may well have had interests of its own, interests that were not necessarily the same as those of other persecuted minorities. In a letter to Soma Morgenstern, Berg complained about his position between two battle fronts – he evidently expressed himself in similar terms to Adorno:

To add to all the misfortune that Hitler's regime has caused me is the fact that I am not Jewish & that people like me do not have to attempt, therefore, to make good from the *other side* any wrong caused to us by the Nazi side & in that way obtain satisfaction. How many words and actions for the martyrs Bruno Walter, Huberman[n] &c – & what silence at the fact that not a note by me and Webern & *also* by Hindemith is heard in a German studio or concert hall.[8]

Adorno could report on similar experiences of his own, allowing him to confirm his friend's thinking in a letter of November 1933 in which he wrote to say that he

could not see why you should profess solidarity with a Jewry to which you do not belong and which certainly does not profess solidarity with you and over which one should ultimately have as few illusions as over other things. In this context it may interest you to know that the League for Jewish Culture that has been set up with such a to-do refuses to work with me in Frankfurt because I am a Christian by denomination and by race only half-Jewish.[9]

Adorno continued to review concerts and to write about new music, occasionally publishing his reports in the *Frankfurter Zeitung* and the *Vossische Zeitung*. He also read Ludwig Klages' writings on the 'mind' as the enemy of the 'soul', an idea that he planned to subject to his critical scrutiny as a prelude to penning his own critique of man's domination of nature. And he continued to work away at a children's Singspiel based on Mark Twain's *Tom Sawyer*, which he had begun in 1932. It was called 'The Treasure of Indian Joe'. He spent the summer of 1933 on the island of Rügen, where he also met Paul Tillich, who told him about the reopened Institute for Social Research in Geneva, while adding the disappointing news that there was no prospect of a paid post for Adorno there. He saw a production of *The Merry Widow* at the spa theatre in Binz that he enjoyed more than the one he had to review only a short time later in Frankfurt: it was 'thrown together without a proper orchestra, but I have to say that I preferred it; undemanding, cursory and with the patina of an amateur stage that is so well suited to the antiquated modernity of *The Merry Widow*'.[10] He spent the autumn with Gretel Karplus in Berlin, where Peter von Haselberg visited him. The couple pretended to be relaxed and claimed to be convinced that the new regime 'could not last'.[11]

They, and many like them, thought it unlikely that Jewish lives would be seriously threatened, at least to the extent that they were not civil servants or lawyers. In one conversation he developed the theory that the 'purification of the body of the German folk' would peter out in clearing-up operations:

after 'clearing out' the attics there would presumably be a propaganda campaign against rats, followed by the slogan 'A War on Rust'. In general, the economic situation was far too precarious for the government to be able to
intervene in any drastic way, not least because of the impression that this
would have abroad and the resultant withdrawal of credit facilities. 'That is
exactly how I imagine it,' he concluded his prognosis.[12]

But the moments of relaxation became increasingly rare. Adorno could speak
only codedly of the new situation, describing it as 'serious', a word that now
begins to appear in his reviews, too. In general, they are marked by a new tone
far removed from the jauntily dogmatic and glib modernism of his earlier
years. In 1928 he had been sure of both himself and his cause when declaring
war on 'musical reactionism', a war that would not be suspended 'out of consideration for its prominent names': 'A tortuous approach to the works of the
late Strauss, for example, which can only be treated polemically, or to Pfitzner
can no longer be reconciled with the new attitude on the part of the *Anbruch*.
In particular, it is necessary to keep a close eye on provincial critics who repeatedly fantasize about the purity of *Palestrina*.'[13] But in a review of a performance
of *Palestrina* in Frankfurt in March 1933, Adorno had begun to have his doubts.
For him, too, something had changed, for in Pfitzner's opera on the subject of
the artist he now heard a different note – one, moreover, that was by no means
old-fashioned:

> In this melismatically sparing, contrapuntally undeveloped music, with its
> audibly archaic harmonies, it is invariably the idea of sonority that provides
> the driving force: a sound that is admittedly unadorned but that is heard and
> realized in the most highly concrete manner, summoning every instrumental
> group into life from its dark ground; not a single note is 'instrumented'; in
> this compelling and noiseless instrumental – and also vocal-instrumental –
> view, all the material for Pfitzner's future lies concealed.[14]

Adorno's positive response was limited, in fact, to the first act of the opera, and
even here he was not slow to express his objections. If he conceded that the piece
had a considerable suggestive power and acknowledged the 'demonic nature of
its desperate entreaty', then there is no doubt that this implied a certain criticism, but this critical note then gives way to one of greater solemnity, recalling the
tone that he generally adopted only when speaking of Mahler and Schoenberg.
At the end of the opening act, 'at the vision of the bells, this demonism
continues to sweep us along into a realm of sounds that have genuinely never
been heard before'.[15] Adorno thought that he had finished with Pfitzner (he was

later to return to this belief), but here he admitted, albeit only briefly, that there was something in Pfitzner's music that he had previously missed.

Arabella – the last collaboration between Hofmannsthal and Strauss – likewise struck him in a new light. He now saw it as coming close to the sort of piece in which composers adopted a critical stance by treating anachronistic material, an approach that had temporarily fascinated him in the case of Stravinsky and which he now conceded had a truth of its own:

> The precision with which the Romantic folklorism of the Viennese Hofmannsthal allows his own bygone Vienna to speak; the wan weariness with which the memory of the nineteenth century clothes the music of the almost seventy-year-old composer: it is very much this defenceless, distanceless return by both men to that period that takes them beyond it. *Arabella* is imbued by a pale transparency: we hear its music as if through the lens of those magic lanterns through which the world was captured in a camera obscura eighty years ago and that prepared the way for photography. This dull transparency, this tone, one might also say this tone of faded wallpapers and old plush is unprecedented in Strauss and must be described as inspired; the result is the strangest affinity with the Stravinsky of *The Fairy's Kiss*.[16]

The music was thinner in the following acts, but it was still possible to sense a substance 'that may continue to present us with its riddles for a long time to come'.[17] In February 1934 Adorno praised Humperdinck's *Königskinder* and its 'thoroughly assured and critically worked-out craftsmanship'.[18] It was a 'profound instinct' that had led the composer to undertake an 'independent and thorough reworking of the German folk tradition'.[19] 'The production of this important and original work can be recommended without reservations, a work that could help lend a note of seriousness and contemplation to the lively appropriation of folk material in much contemporary music.'[20]

All of these were attempts to retain something of the old spirit and its critical standards under the new dispensation, while at the same time revising points of detail. Part and parcel of this ambiguous approach is the fact that in 1934 Adorno praised Herbert Müntzel's choral songs *The Flag of the Persecuted*, to words by Baldur von Schirach – the leader of the Hitler Youth Movement. In Adorno's eyes and ears these songs were in a different class from similar pieces. 'Not simply because as a result of the choice of Schirach's poems the work is consciously marked by National Socialism but also because of one particular quality: an unusual structural will. It is concerned not with a patriotic mood or vague enthusiasm. Rather, the question as to the possibility of new folk music is raised by this work as a matter for serious consideration.'[21] Musically convincing was the return to the older German folksong of the sixteenth century, while the late Romantic material added a sense of 'freedom'. Most important of all was a device that Schoenberg, too, admired: 'recitative-like speech-song'. Strange though it may seem, Adorno must have felt a particular affinity with this aspect of the work. It is to Peter von Haselberg that we owe an observation concerning Adorno's own way of singing that points in this direction: as the son of a professional singer, Adorno had learnt the technique of good breathing. According to Haselberg, his voice 'sometimes seemed almost to produce the effect of two-part writing, having come to rest on the transition between a boyish timbre and one more sonorously youthful, with the result that it never slipped down into the self-complacent, oleaginously croaking timbre that is normal among Germans. But he had learnt in Vienna that the time for singing was over, and so the transition from bel canto to speech-song was all to the good in his view, representing as it did the "new departure" [Anbruch] promised by the Viennese journal that he helped to edit.'[22] The confusing adoption of the most modern aesthetic resources by the art of National Socialism, which flew in the face of all the rhetoric concerning the regime's backward-looking character, was bound to cloud Adorno's judgement, too. 'There is a demand for the picture of a new Romanticism,' we read in his review of Müntzel's The Flag of the Persecuted; 'perhaps of the kind that Goebbels has defined as "Romantic realism".'[23]

While praising the National Socialist choral song, Adorno offered a cool, cynical account of the proscribed genre of jazz in the conservative Europäische Rundschau: 'The regulation that forbids the radio from broadcasting "Negro jazz" may have created a new legal situation, but artistically it only confirms by its drastic verdict what was long ago decided in fact: the end of jazz music itself.'[24] This brief essay represented another tightrope walk for Adorno, for, unlike the National Socialist propagandists, he claims here that the 'dissolution' of jazz was nothing to write home about: jazz had long since abandoned 'big-city degeneration, deracinated exoticism and . . . the bizarre quality of stimulating or clashing asphalt harmonies' and had aligned itself with military marches. New music had nothing to learn from jazz.

The music that really still meant something to Adorno was that of melancholy late forms of modernism. In the arts reviews that he wrote at this time on the subject of background music, the organ and the hurdy-gurdy, the reader already senses something of the pain of parting. To the extent that Adorno was still able to hope that the situation would change, he expressed those hopes in his planned Singspiel based on Mark Twain's Tom Sawyer. There was a wide-spread tendency to write for children among left-wing thinkers and representatives of the New Objectivity at the time of the Weimar Republic. Brecht's *He Who Says Yes*, with music by Kurt Weill, was a work that celebrated the individual's sacrifice to the collective. Another work that praises joint endeavours is Paul Hindemith's children's opera *Let's Build a Town*, a piece still popular in the German-speaking world today. And the radio play *The Stone Heart* that Walter Benjamin and Ernst Schoen based on the fairytale of the same title by Wilhelm Hauff warns its audiences against the demon of capitalism. Two songs from Adorno's Singspiel, one for Tom Sawyer, the other for Huckleberry Finn, are currently available on compact disc, conducted by Gary Bertini. Compared with the far more accessible score to Hindemith's *Let's Build a Town*, Adorno's music sounds extremely complex and dissonant, and it is unlikely that the piece would have been a tremendous success with children even if it had been completed, although it might have been helped by its great theme of the conquest of fear, as envisaged by the composer: Tom and Huck witness a murder and swear that they will never tell anyone what they have seen. But when an innocent man is accused of the crime and threatened with the death penalty, the two friends decide to break their oath. At the end of the story they are rewarded with the treasure that they have found. It is clear from Adorno's choice of subject and from his treatment of it that, unlike Brecht and Hindemith (or even Erich Kästner's *Emil and the Detectives*), his main concern was not collectivist solutions but individual responsibility. But although he had expected Benjamin to show the greatest understanding, the latter reacted coldly, and Adorno, offended by his friend's rejection, abandoned the project.

Adorno's admiration for Marianne Hoppe, to whom he was introduced by Carl Dreyfus, was not affected by contemporary events. The autumn of 1933 found him in contact with Hoppe and Dreyfus, albeit only at a distance. The occasion was the filming of Theodor Storm's short story *The White Horse Rider*, which was released by UFA in 1934, with Hoppe as the female lead. In September 1933 Adorno wrote to Berg to report that Dreyfus was making

> a *very* serious avant-garde film based on Storm's *White Horse Rider*. He asked me about the possibility of writing the music for it, and, mindful of your card [Berg had complained that he was short of money] I mentioned your name, naturally as a chance that can be counted on only if you are extremely lucky. . . . *Artistically* speaking, I am convinced that the matter will be taken entirely *seriously*, and it goes without saying that you will first receive all the documentation. I expect you already know *The White Horse Rider*; it's a wonderful story.[25]

But by November 1933 Dreyfus was no longer involved in the project.[26] In spite of this, the film was completed and although it was later to fall into unjustifiable neglect, it turned out to be a masterpiece of the art of cinematography in terms of both photography and editing. In few other films did Marianne Hoppe radiate such magical youth and beauty, such vitality and intelligence. Adorno's claim that the film was '*very* avant-garde' was perhaps an exaggeration, but even today the viewer is bound to appreciate its genuine artistry. Yet even here the dubious light of the period lies over the finished product: on the one hand, the film is an emphatic plea for modernity (the main character, Hauke Haien, is a working-class dyke-builder who has to force through his rational plans for a new dyke in the face of the superstitiously passive local population), but at the same time the more intelligent National Socialists could see in Hauke Haien a powerful and visionary leader untroubled by traditionalist considerations and capable of inspiring the nation to achieve great things. Ultimately the film appears as contradictory as the age that produced it.

Once Berg had turned down the invitation to write the music for the film, Adorno approached another of Schoenberg's pupils, and this time he was successful. The man in question was Winfried Zillig, who after the war became principal conductor of the Hesse Radio Symphony Orchestra in Frankfurt. Zillig had studied twelve-note composition, but his talents extended beyond this technique, a circumstance that Adorno was happy to accept, encouraging him to speak of the composer's fondness for utility music. And in the tribute to Zillig that he wrote on the latter's death, he returned to the composer's 'masterly film music' for *The White Horse Rider*.[27] Berg, too, was content with this solution, for we find him writing to Adorno just before Christmas 1933: 'In the meantime I have heard from Zillig that you have helped him with *The White Horse Rider*. That is most gratifying & is bound to have turned out splendidly.'[28] Indeed, the very quality that Adorno later singled out for special mention in Zillig's music – the combination of an 'appreciable amount of sinewy tension and a folklike tone without a folk tone'[29] – was tailor-made for the film's north German setting. Even so, Adorno was also responsible for promulgating a few legends in his positive but slightly cool portrait of the composer, claiming, for example, that Zillig's music had been banned 'under Hitler's Reich' and arguing that his setting of poems by Verlaine – they were written in 1940 following the German army's French campaign – 'attested to German resistance'.[30] This may be true, but Zillig's music was far from being 'banned' at this time. In 1940 he was appointed principal musical director of the Reichsgautheater in occupied Poznan and also ran the local composition department, in which capacity he was directly responsible to the Reichsmusikkammer. And he not only set poems by Verlaine and Brecht (two writers whom Adorno personally held in the highest esteem), he also wrote two operas to librettos by Richard Billinger,

Die Windsbraut [The Tempest] and *Rosse* [Horses], that depict the clash between Christianity and paganism among the peasants of southern Germany. Another opera, *Das Opfer* [The Victim], is based on an Expressionist play by Reinhard Goering. In discussing the music itself, Adorno too spoke of its ambivalences and mentions Zillig's willingness to compromise and his natural tendency to be conciliatory. The lessons that he learnt from Schoenberg, he continued, were then integrated into his own predefined musical language. And he also discusses Zillig's naïvety and the 'anachronistic' contents of his works. Zillig, who, like Adorno was born in 1903, is said to have attempted to combine the most modern and austere aesthetic with a regional cultural basis, which in his case meant Würzburg in Franconia. But Adorno was writing about Zillig during the 1960s, when it was impossible to go beyond the complexities of the music and take account of the contradictions within the composer's life and the history of his works. As a result, Adorno retrospectively replaced the ambiguous light of the period with the idea of 'resistance'.

8 Early Years of Exile

Adorno arrived in England in the spring of 1934. Contacts had already been established through his uncle, Bernhard, and in the autumn of that year he was accepted for a second dissertation by Merton College, Oxford. His subject was Husserl. On 7 October 1934 he wrote to Krenek:

> Merton College, which is the oldest and one of the most exclusive in Oxford, has accepted me as a member and advanced student, and I am now living here in a state of indescribable peace and working under conditions that, superficially at least, could hardly be more agreeable; objectively speaking, there are difficulties, of course, as it is impossible to make the English understand my own philosophical things and I am having to ratchet down my work to the level of a child in order to remain intelligible – which means dividing the whole work into academic and actual things, something for which I really consider myself too old – but I now have to shoulder this burden and be glad that I can work undisturbed (in passing, I may add that, materially speaking, I could easily have survived in Germany and would have had no political trouble; it's just that I would have been deprived of the opportunity to have any impact on others, including the possibility of being performed, so that's why I left; I'll spend my vacations at home or in the south[)].[1]

Adorno's beginnings ten years previously had already been marked by his critical engagement with Husserl's philosophy. During the four years that he spent in Oxford, he produced an extensive manuscript, of which he later prepared a shortened version. It was called 'On Husserl's Philosophy'.[2] But neither of these versions have ever been translated into English. His lecture on 'Husserl and the Problem of Idealism' dates from his later period in the United States.[3] Not until the 'fifties did Adorno address the task of working through his papers, which were then published under the title *Zur Metakritik der Erkenntnistheorie: Studien über Husserl und die phänomenologischen Antinomien* [On the Metacriticism of Epistemology: Studies on Husserl and Phenomenological Antinomies].[4]

Adorno had considerable difficulty getting used to life in England. His position as an 'advanced student' meant a palpable loss of status when compared to his lectureship in Frankfurt, a loss about which he complained in numerous letters. And few English philosophers were willing to engage with Adorno's dialectical thinking. A. J. Ayer, for example, wrote in his autobiography that no one really took Adorno seriously but regarded him, rather, as a dandy. The fact that a philosopher took an interest in jazz, even if that interest was critical, encountered only amused incomprehension in the Oxford of the 1930s. But in retrospect Ayer regretted not having discussed aesthetics and Marxism with Adorno.[5] For Adorno, one of the disadvantages of his new position was that he had to take his meals in Merton's communal dining hall, a situation that struck him as 'a nightmare come true': it was 'like having to return to school, in short, an extension of the Third Reich'.[6] He retained his role as an outsider until the very end: between 1934, when he arrived in Oxford, and 1938, when he moved to the United States, none of Oxford's many clubs for intellectuals listed him as a speaker.

The disappointments that Adorno experienced during his early months in Oxford were bound up, in part, with the totally different institutional structures of British and German universities, but also with the fact that academic possibilities were severely limited for German émigrés. Although Adorno hoped that he might become an assistant to Ernst Cassirer, who had arrived in Oxford from Hamburg in 1933, these hopes soon proved to be illusory, while causing a jealous Max Horkheimer to complain about his colleague's lack of loyalty. 'Even so, you prefer to discuss your future with Herr Cassirer than with me,' he wrote accusingly from New York in the autumn of 1934.[7] But Adorno was soon able to reassure Horkheimer on this point, writing to him in May 1935 to inform him that he considered 'Herr Cassirer a complete fool'.[8] His prime concern was now to resume work for the Institute for Social Research.

Adorno's period abroad continued to be interrupted by relatively lengthy visits to Berlin to see Gretel Karplus and to Frankfurt, where he renewed contact with family and friends. According to Peter von Haselberg, 'It was visibly difficult for Wiesengrund to leave Germany for good'.[9] But there were more tangible reasons than mere homesickness for Adorno's visits to Germany, namely, foreign exchange control regulations. 'I simply *have* to return to Germany,' he wrote to Horkheimer from Oxford, 'in order not to count as an émigré and lose the chance to return; and for material reasons I am dependent for the present on being able to return, for what I have at my disposal for term time here is not

'Horses are the survivors of heroes', Adorno wrote in his *Essay on Wagner*. The photograph was taken in Oxford in 1935

sufficient for a full life outside. My return to Germany is always a great strain on my nerves, and may even be dangerous, but for now I have to run this risk.'[10] The concrete danger that Adorno was running consisted above all in being sent to one of the 'training camps' that the regime had set up for returning émigrés. In Frankfurt, he would play piano duets with Haselberg, a pastime that he enjoyed but which Haselberg remembered as an 'adventurous undertaking as he was tremendously moved and would always add passages that were inadequately reproduced in the transcription, doing so from memory, before interrupting our performance to demonstrate how the relevant part was made up and how it should be understood. When we repeated it, he would then expect that with my help, too, it would sound more correct.'[11] But even these idyllic moments were spoilt by political tensions:

Somehow or other I had managed to track down a transcription of Mahler's Seventh Symphony for piano four hands – given the date, this was a stroke of luck. We played it several times, and I was extremely startled when my landlady told me that she thought she had recognized it as a piece by Mahler. . . . It was with some difficulty that I discouraged Wiesengrund from inviting her to attend our next performance, not least because her political views made me uneasy. Even now he thought that this music was more effective than any propaganda and that it produced an indestructible minimum of morality that would prove itself even in the current climate.[12]

As for the general situation, Adorno no longer had any illusions. The regime had gained a certain degree of stability as a result of job creation schemes and had been successful in terms of its foreign policy, while by the summer of 1934 internal rivals such as the leaders of the Storm Troopers no longer posed a threat to Hitler. Ernst Röhm had been liquidated, as had Kurt von Schleicher, on whom conservative circles had pinned their hopes. The Catholic deputy chancellor, Franz von Papen, had been shunted off to an ambassadorial post overseas. In October 1935 Adorno reported on the situation in a letter to Horkheimer: 'In Germany it was grimmer than ever, the country has become a hell on earth on even the most trivial level.'[13] Of the former students at the Institute for Social Research, he was particularly affected by the fate of Liesel Paxmann, who had died in Düsseldorf, ostensibly from pneumonia, but more probably as a result of her arrest and questioning after the political police had learnt about her resistance activities and had arrested her on the German-Czech border. Another of the students working at the Institute, Willi Dörter, had already been sentenced for founding an opposition group. He later succeeded in escaping from the concentration camp at Börgermoor and fled to the United States.

Adorno's supervisor in Oxford was Gilbert Ryle, who was able to help him overcome his concern that 'no one' would understand his work on Husserl. Ryle was an analytical philosopher, who had regularly commented on the development of phenomenology in reviews and who had also known Husserl personally. It may be the case, then, that the two philosophers not only thought along similar lines but enjoyed a lively exchange of ideas. The planned dissertation was intended to expose the contradictions in phenomenology by analyzing Husserl's work and in that way drive it to the point of self-resolution. At the same time it was to make it clear that these contradictions were not due to any personal shortcomings on Husserl's part. Rather, they were 'necessary'. In short, Adorno's approach exactly mirrored Marx's: just as Marx had arrived at his theory of capital by criticizing political economy and analyzing the work of his two predecessors, Adam Smith and David Ricardo, so Adorno wanted his critique of Husserl to provide 'a kind of critico-dialectical prelude' that would lead to a 'materialistic logic', and, as he explained in a letter to Horkheimer, his work would then be 'as closely connected as possible with your own'.[14] In another letter to Horkheimer, he announced his intention of 'turning idealism upside down'.[15]

What Adorno had in mind was a detailed criticism of phenomenology that was intended not only to expose Husserl's conceptual uncertainties, as he had done in his Frankfurt dissertation, but also 'to allow logic to speak' and reveal its social tendencies, which were bound to remain hidden from itself.[16] Husserl's rationalism was emphasized as something positive, but its overall construction was to be exposed as the final manifestation of the falsenesses of bourgeois consciousness. In terms of its execution, this meant drawing a number of parallels between economic and philosophical categories and a search for possible economic and materialist metaphors. 'All of Husserl's regressive features,' wrote Adorno, were dominated by fear, a fear manifest above all in 'the desire not to express a theory that was not completely covered against all eventualities, a theory safe from doubt and not subject to the changing times. The ideal of Husserl's philosophy is that of absolute *security*.'[17] And Husserl was accused of clinging to this ideal 'with the blind naïvety of a belief in property'.[18] His insistence on being guided by 'the given' revealed the 'resigned, late bourgeois character of phenomenology'.[19] Husserl's juridical rhetoric also made it possible 'to justify property conditions'.[20] In this he was helped by the tendency of phenomenology 'to perpetuate existing ideas and "actualities" within the consciousness as if they unquestioningly belonged to the philosopher and at the same time were essential for all time'.[21] True, Adorno acknowledged phenomenology as the 'final serious effort on the part of the bourgeois spirit to break out of its own world, the immanence of consciousness, the sphere of constitutive subjectivity'. But the attempt had failed.[22]

If the 'idealistic system' was 'a self-contained whole', Adorno wrote in his essay on Husserl, this was because it was 'held together by guilt'.[23] This is a formulation that Adorno took over from his friend Alfred Sohn-Rethel and that he mentions in a letter to Horkheimer of May 1937. Here he speaks of a 'formula that appears in Sohn-Rethel's new manuscript ... , idealism's character as a system is an expression of the fact that bourgeois society is held together by guilt (i.e., by exploitation)'.[24] Sohn-Rethel, too, was currently working on a critique of epistemology of a kind envisaged by Adorno's study of Husserl, its aim being to portray bourgeois philosophy as the true expression of false consciousness. Sohn-Rethel had initially studied chemistry, economics and philosophy but had then broken off his studies and between 1924 and 1927 went to live on Capri. A relative of his owned a villa in Anacapri, while his favourite uncle, the painter Karli Sohn-Rethel, lived in Positano. He was in contact not only with Adorno but also with Benjamin, Kracauer and Ernst Bloch, all of whom were exploring the philosophical links between commodity exchange, money and capitalism. None of them, however, devoted himself to the subject with the exclusiveness revealed by Sohn-Rethel. He was born in 1899, at a time when the expansion of the major powers encouraged writers to attack the very concept of 'imperialism' and the growth of production organization along more scientific lines altered the very nature of work. As a result, capitalism became a lifelong subject for him, its basic idea, as he once wrote, coming to him in a moment of inspiration.

His literary works from the 'twenties include a description of his ascent of Vesuvius. With the 'tremendous' crater before him, he noted that 'this sight was not, however, the most powerful or the most immediately crushing aspect of the first impression. It was the sound that rang out from the crater like mountains of molten metal striking against each other in its unfathomable depths. The millions of years that elapsed before life stirred on our planet were present in this sound, acquiring a living presence in the ear that heard it.' Later he noticed the lava that had cooled after pouring from the crater: 'But who would have expected to see the hellish entrails that lay exposed here and in the colours in which they lay there, sulphurous yellow, phosphorescent green and copper-red – unmixed, but interwoven and intertwined?' The idea of molten metal in the depths seemed like a natural and aesthetic model for the research into new methods of producing iron and steel that was undertaken in the early 'thirties within the context of the 'Central European Economic Day'.[25] In their colourfulness, sulphur, phosphorus and copper recall the chemical industry. Sohn-Rethel's family originally intended him for a career with Agfa, which was then run by a distant cousin, Franz Oppenheim.[26] He had spent part of his youth with the steel magnate Ernst Poensgen, who accepted him as his foster son. The conflicts between heavy industry and the chemical industry, and between Stahlverein and IG Farben that he later attempted to show were behind the National Socialists' planned economy, were part of this family novel. Poensgen also helped him obtain a position with the Central European Economic Day, which Sohn-Rethel hoped would provide him with the chance to work as an observer. His publications from the early 1930s admit of multiple readings: on the one hand, they helped the industrial élite to gain greater self-understanding, while on the other they were intended to serve as informational material for the left.

Sohn-Rethel's closeness to the protagonists meant that he often bowed to the logic of their arguments, regarding that logic as inevitable and believing that alternative possibilities of action could be found only in an economy that was anti-capitalist in principle. In early 1936 he was obliged to emigrate when his resistance activities became known. It was a conscious change of sides: from an academic white-collar worker who had formulated German expansionist interests, notably in the direction of south-east Europe, he became adviser to the English journalist Wickham Stead, who was a leading expert on Germany and a decisive opponent of Britain's policy of appeasement. It was for Stead that Sohn-Rethel wrote the analyses that were republished in the 'seventies under the title *Ökonomie und Klassenstruktur des deutschen Faschismus* [Economy and Class Structure of German Fascism]. During the First World War, Stead was in charge of British propaganda in Central Europe. Meanwhile Sohn-Rethel's foster father was advancing his career: in 1934 he took over the running of the country's iron industry and soon became one of the leading figures in Germany's arms policy before being replaced by Albert Speer and Walther Funk in 1942. Among the most striking aspects of Sohn-Rethel's analyses of Fascism are not only his knowledge of information from the economic centres of power to which he had had access from the early 'thirties but also their key concept: the need attributed to every individual development here. National Socialism emerges as the result of a 'predicament' in which German industry was said to have found itself. Immediately after fleeing from Germany, Sohn-Rethel wrote a study entitled 'A Sociological Theory of Knowledge' in which he questioned the validity of science and at the same time discussed the difficulties bound up with his own loyalty. He wanted his development from a collaborator on Germany's programmes of expansion to an adviser on British policy to be regarded not as a journey from error to truth but as a change of viewpoint on the part of a figure who had toppled over. The laws of mathematical science were to be acknowledged as statements of the truth, but the reality that they depicted was reality in the form of the exact opposite of its reality. The fact that Sohn-Rethel's chief concepts – above all, 'affirmative negation' – were all based on paradox is a reflection of the remarkable course that his life took.

For a long time, Adorno tried to help his friend to gain access to the Institute for Social Research but in the end his attempts were largely unsuccessful. Although he received the odd financial contribution that helped to support him for a while, Horkheimer was unable to summon up any real enthusiasm for his highly speculative theory. And Sohn-Rethel himself was a thinker for whom the monologue was a natural vehicle of expression and who found it difficult, therefore, to enter into dialogue with the Institute. He remained an outsider until his books were republished in the 1970s and he suddenly proved successful with those readers who had arrived too late for the student movement of the late 'sixties and who were keen to reexamine the question of the relationship between capitalism and philosophy.

The link between false consciousness on the one hand and a commodity economy, dictatorship and aesthetics on the other was also central to Adorno's exchange of views with Benjamin. Both philosophers hoped to be able to make sense of present-day conditions by gazing into the remote mirror of the nineteenth century, Adorno in the music of Wagner, Benjamin in the Second Empire and the poetry of Baudelaire. In his study of the Paris arcades, which covers the period between the building of the first glass-covered shopping arcades in 1820 and the Paris Commune of 1871, Benjamin adopted a symbolic approach to historical research, an approach geared to meanings rather than to events and methodologically most closely related to Bachofen's studies of antiquity. In this vast unfinished work, we learn less about economic processes than about commercial art, less about industrial development than about the railway poetry of the Saint-Simonists, less about the political actions of Napoléon III and a good deal about the symbols of power associated with the boulevards, less about secret communist societies and a great deal about their ceremonies, rituals and insignia. Benjamin belonged to a generation of historians whose attention was drawn in particular to the symbols of authority and the symbolic staging of politics. Even his study on Baroque drama, *The Origin of German Tragedy*, had included a detailed analysis of the ruler's crown, sceptre and regalia, as well as the processions associated with rulers. As such, it constituted an early contribution to our understanding of the theatrical aspects of power. Capitalism and revolutionary class struggle – the Marxist elements in Benjamin's picture of history – appear in an amoral Nietzschean perspective, with financial capital associated with gambling and prostitution and with the workers' movement seen as a form of revolt that could include hatred, cruelty and suicide. Perhaps news of the Spanish Civil War and the hitherto unknown atrocities committed by both sides had a direct impact on the conception of Benjamin's study. But his figurative and poetic logic, with which he sought to establish links between the 'basis' and the 'superstructure', was repeatedly criticized by Adorno, who had the highest hopes of his colleague's work on the Paris arcades but who insisted on seeing the intermediary steps in the argument spelt out in painstaking detail.

In his study on jazz, which appeared in the same issue of the *Zeitschrift für Sozialforschung* as Benjamin's pioneering essay on 'The Work of Art in the Age of Mechanical Reproduction', Adorno revealed himself as a thinker who set store by critical distance and who held out little hope for mass culture. His intellectual horizon was that of a thinker whose system regarded totalitarianism, democratic façade and a permissive culture industry as essentially synonymous, and for Adorno jazz was the music that was produced by this dystopia. His treatise reads like an initial reaction to the shock of 1933, when it seemed as though the cities' white-collar workers, geared to the New Objectivity and moderately permissive in their lifestyle, could be integrated into a dictatorial system. Adorno's keenly critical approach was already signalled by the martial pseudonym that he adopted in his attempt to evade the scrutiny of the German authorities: Hektor Rottweiler – the name of a fearsome fighting dog. Original though his question was, his attempt to provide an unambiguous answer was bound to be problematical: the thesis that he took over from Benjamin, namely, that jazz was the right sort of music for pogroms, is manifestly absurd. And his attempt to interpret jazz rhythms from a psychoanalytical point of view and to claim that its tendency for the beat to come too early or too late was a musical representation of impotence, failed orgasm, coitus interruptus and the fear of castration and that it was even an unsuccessful 'coition machine',[27] left even Horkheimer feeling unhappy, so that he suggested cutting various passages and rewriting others. But Adorno continued to insist on the castration complex as the study's main idea. Perhaps its most remarkable aspect is his proposed derivation of the word 'jazz' from the German word *Hatz* (hunt) and his argument that it 'suggests the pursuit of a slower person by bloodhounds'.[28] The echo of Adorno's pseudonym at this point is unmistakable and begs any number of questions.

Adorno also analyzed Wagner's music from a politico-psychological standpoint at this time. His concern above all was to revise the Marxist image of the 'rising bourgeoisie' and to contrast it with that of an internal dissection in order to expose the 'focal points of decay in the bourgeois character'.[29] The sociohistorical figure of the bourgeois was to be elucidated by means of psychoanalytical speculations, with both aspects ultimately being related to the music. In this, Adorno was in no doubt about the music's destructive impulses: 'At its peak, bourgeois nihilism is also the wish to annihilate the bourgeois.'[30] Brecht read Adorno's manuscript some years later and noted: 'Wiesengrund-Adorno here. He has become round and fat and offers us an essay on *Richard Wagner*, not uninteresting, but rummaging around exclusively for repressions, complexes, inhibitions in the consciousness of the old myth-maker, in the manner of Lukács, Bloch and Stern, all of whom are merely repressing an old psychoanalysis.'[31] Adorno's interest in psychoanalysis dated back to the 1920s, when he had planned to write a postdoctoral thesis on the philosophical interpretation of Freud's theories in the spirit of Hans Cornelius's teachings on consciousness. The working title of this unrealized project was 'The Concept of the Unconscious in Transcendental Psychology'.[32] But it was an error to include Freud's teachings in social theory, and not only Brecht but other readers such as Arnold Schoenberg and Helmuth Plessner, who were otherwise sympathetic to Adorno's views, remained unconvinced by his use of psychoanalysis: the more he attempted to make the discipline his own, the more he was tempted to abandon his search for the real reasons for social attitudes and opinions, with their basically rational assumptions, and to presuppose irrationality and neurosis instead. In this way Freudianism became a short cut to epistemology and hence an epistemological barrier to social theory – how much easier it was, after all, to see the symptom of a personality disorder in a social disposition or a sequence of actions rather than attempting to fathom its possible meaning. At the same time, however, this journey from critical theory to psychoanalysis was compelling in its socio-theoretical approach: for if, as Adorno was later to write, the 'whole' is 'what is untrue' and if bourgeois society and capitalism are 'irrational', then the parties concerned can no longer be seen as rational beings, and complexes and repressions may be assumed as an a priori element in their interpretation. This explains the curious mixture of perceptiveness and misjudgement that jeopardizes Adorno's work at every point.

'What does a woman want?' Sooner or later, Freud's question is bound to engage every man, including even the members of the exiled Institute for Social Research, who regarded themselves as peculiarly well qualified to answer it. In 1937, while he was working on his *Essay on Wagner* in London, Adorno had a dream that spirited him away into the world of the *Ring*. He even had a title for it: 'Siegfried's Last Adventure' or 'Siegfried's Last Death'. The hero, wearing a costume that is half mythical and half modern, encounters an enemy whom he finds in a recumbent position. The hero is carrying a small dagger, which he keeps in his jacket pocket like a fountain pen – Siegfried appears in this dream as a regular intellectual – and which he plunges into his enemy's breast. When the latter groans, it turns out that he is in fact a woman. She now has to die alone, she explains, and withdraws:

> Siegfried sends his companion after her, with instructions to appropriate her treasures. At this point Brünhilde [*sic*] appears in the background in the form of New York's Statue of Liberty. She calls out in the tone of a nagging housewife: 'I'd like to have a ring, I'd like to have a beautiful ring, don't forget to take the ring from her.' In this way Siegfried acquires the Nibelung's ring.[33]

In a long letter that he wrote to Erich Fromm in November 1937, Adorno addressed the problem raised by his dream and suggested a study of the female character such as he had already mentioned to Horkheimer and Leo Löwenthal during his first visit to New York: 'But the idea preoccupies me to such an extent that I cannot refrain from indicating, at least briefly, what I have in mind here.'[34] Löwenthal had expressed the view that woman, who at this time still played a relatively minor role in the capitalist production process, was less 'reified' than man, an idea that Adorno regarded as 'somewhat romantic'.

Indeed, he believed that women were *more* dominated by the character of the commodity than men: with their 'specific consumer consciousness', they functioned very much as 'an agency for the commodity in society'.[35] Every observation taught us that 'even women who, sexually speaking, are completely uninhibited can reveal the worst features of the bourgeois character'.[36] Did his dream about the ring support this theory? Whatever the answer, he told Fromm that Wagner '*unconsciously* perceived the specifically bourgeois features of women' because Siegfried failed to seize the 'final opportunity' to break free from the curse on the ring when he told the Rhine Maidens that if he wasted his wealth on them, his wife would 'surely chide' him.[37]

Adorno and Margarete Karplus were married on 8 September 1937 – the witnesses were Max Horkheimer and the Oxford economist Redvers Opie. Benjamin must have been deeply disappointed to discover afterwards that he had not been invited. We may assume, therefore, that it was not just Adorno's interest in Wagner that inspired him to ask questions about the character of women but also his entry into a new phase in his life. And Horkheimer knew even more about his friend's theories than Erich Fromm, for Adorno had told him about the 'dialectical point' of his thoughts on the commodity and sexuality: the 'utility value' of sexuality could be rediscovered only in the 'total implementation of the exchange value. Or, to put it another way, the only nostrum to counteract the fetishization of sexuality is sexual fetishism.'[38] Readers of the correspondence between Horkheimer and Adorno will at some point come upon the passages in which the two men use a sort of secret language to discuss the best places in Paris where sex was on offer as a commodity. Although Adorno was repeatedly consumed by passion for other women, his marriage with Gretel, as he called her (among the pet names that had already been common currency in his family were 'Horse' and 'Giraffe-Gazelle'), was none the less more than just a conventional liaison. Evidence for this claim comes above all from the jottings that Adorno made during his first return visit to Germany after the war, when he was separated from his wife for some time: 'Infinite attachment to Gretel, unto death,' we read here. Again: 'Wouldn't like to die without her being present.'[39] Their marriage remained childless. When Bloch wrote to him in 1937 to report on the birth of his son, Jan Robert, Adorno replied to the effect that it was 'beautiful and brave to have a child now, almost a little shaming for us, as we don't dare to have one, not knowing, after all, with whom it will one day have to march'.[40] But this was no more than an attempt to rationalize the situation.

The question of Stalinism slowly entered Adorno's field of vision in his arguments with Benjamin. Former sympathizers with Communism such as André Gide had given public expression to their disillusionment following their return from the Soviet Union. On 4 May 1938, shortly after completing his *Essay on Wagner*, with its treatment of the category of the 'betrayed revolution', Adorno wrote to Benjamin: 'Incidentally, I have learned a good deal from reading Trotsky's book *La Révolution trahie*, and despite your aversion against getting involved in this whole matter, I think you should take a look at it some time.'[41] Above all, the trial of Nikolay Bukharin, in which a confession of guilt was extorted from the accused, had polarized intellectuals, including many of Adorno's closest friends. Bloch and Hanns Eisler declared their opposition to Bukharin and hence their continuing support for the Soviets, whereas Adorno and Horkheimer, in their editorship of the *Zeitschrift für Sozialforschung*, cautiously distanced themselves from the Stalinist system, a process that was barely articulated and impossible for outsiders to see, yet their attitude was to prove decisive for the future course of critical theory. Even then there were already pointers to the later division between those émigrés who returned to the German Democratic Republic and those who chose to return to the Federal Republic. In the mid-thirties Adorno was still projecting an image as an orthodox Leninist and dismissing the sociologist Karl Mannheim as a 'traitor to the working class',[42] but he later sought to divorce the idea of Marxist social theory from socialism and the labour movement. Meanwhile, Benjamin found it more difficult to distance himself from events and reacted with an instinctive blackening of the concept of history: as in the thinking of the radical leader of the labour movement in France, Auguste Blanqui, extreme hope and the vision of cosmic captivity were brought closer together. The later sections of the correspondence between the two men show how narrow had become the scope for thought between the opposing political camps and the pressure on them to conform.

In July 1937, Benjamin complained that they were 'faced here with the inflexibility of an orthodox left intelligentsia crippled by the Russian developments on the one hand, and with the often unconscious fascist sympathies of the more independent writers on the other'.[43] The last of Adorno's writings to overlap with this correspondence provide an echo of Benjamin's complaint: 'It is as though the age of thinkers is past,' he wrote, quoting Kierkegaard, while it was Stefan George whom he cited in the context of the conformism of democracies: 'Everything was sayable – talking a lot of hot air.'[44] In consequence, Benjamin's essays on Baudelaire and on the writer on language, Carl Gustav Jochmann, and Adorno's writings on Wagner, Kierkegaard and George must be seen first and foremost as attempts to assert the autonomy of thought. In this situation, dialectics signified a final refuge of old-style European tact, an unremitting obligation to seek out nuances. The works were meticulously examined in terms of their expression and any possible change of meaning. Benjamin subjected Baudelaire to a political interpretation, initially locating him in the ambiguous and dubious setting of Bohemian bars frequented by conspirators and in contact with police spies and subversive elements, and finally pointing up his proximity to Blanqui and all who had been deprived of their rights. And if Adorno sought to expose Wagner's 'reactionary' aspects, this did not prevent him from seeing a vision of freedom in the composer's works and in the 'black, abrupt, jagged music' of the third act of *Tristan und Isolde*.[45] Their thinking was autonomous, but not unpolitical. In particular, Adorno's essays on Kierkegaard's doctrine of love and on the correspondence between Stefan George and Hugo von Hofmannsthal reveal that on their deepest level his reflections mirrored German resistance – George's strength of resistance struck Adorno as greater than Hofmannsthal's, as it was from the circle surrounding George that Hitler's would-be assassin, Claus von Stauffenberg, later emerged. It was during these years that Adorno and Benjamin founded a tradition of critical theory that may be summed up in the names of Marx, Nietzsche, Jochmann and George. These writers, too, had been 'émigrés', and exile was certainly an integral part of the theories of both Adorno and Benjamin. They were not afraid to see an element of self-deception in the Enlightenment and an element of truth in the Counter-Enlightenment. This was an attitude that had already characterized their immediate predecessors among intellectuals, Karl Kraus and Charles Péguy.[46]

A further subject of debate between Adorno and Benjamin was mass culture, a topic suggested by the propaganda and entertainment machines that acquired new importance during the 1930s: the cinema and radio became the two media that dictatorships were able to use most successfully. Whereas Benjamin had a positive view of the cinema, which he saw as 'devoid of any aura' and as technical and, therefore, remote from myth, so that, if correctly used, it could help the masses to acquire a sense of class consciousness, Adorno had a much more pessimistic attitude to the radio, an attitude that he expressed in his essay 'On the Fetish-Character in Music and the Regression of Listening'.[47] The aesthetic concept of the 'aura' of the work of art had been coined in the years around 1900 and was based on the assumption that a work radiated a quality that was to be mirrored by a cultic and emotional response. The concept came into use at a time when the status of works of art and the cultural tradition in general was being called into question within the field of tension created by historicism, modernity and mass culture. Initially, it seems to have been only clairvoyants and theosophists who used the term 'aura' to describe a subtle emanation of the body that was imagined as having one or more colours and which, it was believed, would provide information about the essence of the individual. The circle of writers associated with Stefan George then began to use the concept of the aura to articulate its disquiet at the way in which the world had lost its mystique, a development that was felt above all as the loss of cultic authority, which ancient artefacts had suffered by being placed in museums. Benjamin took up the concept around 1930 and redefined it: setting out from the works of avant-garde artists, especially Dadaism, glass architecture, Brecht's epic theatre, photomontage and mass culture, he predicted shifts in the concept of art that was to be characterized in future by demythologization, mechanical reproduction, didactic transparency and relaxed reception. In placing his hopes in the 'destruction of the aura', Benjamin, too, had large-scale, historico-philosophical expectations, except that in his case the circumstances were different. Initially he hoped for an art that would promote the cause of anti-Fascism, then a humanity freed from cultic religion. In all this, the cinema, with its montage technique, was to provide the artistic model. Adorno did not share this hope, which he roundly criticized in a letter to Horkheimer, complaining that Benjamin was evidently placing trust in the proletariat 'as in a blind world spirit'[48] and that he was harbouring 'donnishly romantic ideas' about technology: 'He really has something of an insane bird of passage about him and still has a long way to go before he achieves Brecht's level of emancipation.'[49] Instead of the alternatives of auratic and non-auratic art, Adorno proposed a different type of alternative, one that drew a distinction between the products of the culture industry, with their manipulatively manufactured aura, and authentic works of art that even in the modern age should retain an auratic element of remoteness. The aura regained its positive import by retaining an element of remoteness and representing something that is not the same as social being.

The long letters that Adorno wrote to Horkheimer during the 1930s make clear his contribution to the conception of the *Zeitschrift für Sozialforschung* and its political line. Time and again they thought of moving geographically closer together and pursuing their common philosophical goal of a materialistic and dialectical logic. The opportunity for a longer meeting finally presented itself in New York in the summer of 1937: 'I have rarely been as happy as I was during these weeks – certainly not since totalitarianism burst upon us,' Adorno wrote to Horkheimer on his return to London on 6 July 1937:

> And if I may mention only one thing, it is this – that a writer such as myself, someone who has made profound loneliness and the basic impossibility of ever fitting in what he thinks and says an a priori for him, should suddenly see himself fitting in fully and in reality into a good existing collectivity, without his thereby having to 'fit in'; the fact that a man whose basic impulses include resistance to the market should ultimately find the very thing that he has most rigorously had to deny himself but for which he has always yearned most profoundly (because it is here alone that one finds the only binding confirmation of the fact that loneliness has been superseded); and the fact that he can exchange his products – this is an experience that I simply cannot exaggerate.[50]

Plans for Adorno to move to the United States now took on a more concrete aspect. On 20 October 1937 Horkheimer telegraphed: 'Possibility of your imminent move to America now closer Stop In event of agreement set aside time to work on new radio project Princeton University two-year income total four hundred dollars a month guaranteed Stop.'[51] It was the sociologist Paul Lazarsfeld, who had emigrated to America from Austria and who later became one of the pioneers of opinion polling in the United States, who offered Adorno a post which, Horkheimer believed, would also improve the Institute's contacts with the academic world. Adorno cabled back to say that he was 'happy and agreed in principle'.[52] He abandoned his Oxford examination: the prospect of guaranteed work, even if it lasted only two years, and above all the prospect of being in communication with the circle of scholars associated with the Institute weighed more heavily. Before he embarked on the ship that was to take him to New York, Horkheimer wrote to him on 24 December 1937 with clear instructions for the New World:

> On the occasion of your lecture at the Institute of Sociology I would ask you to speak extremely scientifically and not say a word that could be interpreted politically. Even expressions such as 'materialistic' are to be avoided at all costs. . . . Your lecture must on no account give the impression that the brickbats that the Institute has received on account of its materialism are in any way justified. Also try to speak as simply as possible. Complexity is already suspect. On the other hand, you should expound a lot of material. That is always the best.[53]

9   Brave New World

'In the autumn of 1937,' wrote Adorno, when looking back on his experiences of American academia, 'I received a telegram in London from my friend Max Horkheimer, announcing the possibility of a rapid move to America if I were prepared to collaborate on a radio project. After considering the matter briefly, I agreed by telegram. I did not even know what a radio project was: the American use of the word "project", which is nowadays translated into German by the word "Forschungsvorhaben" [research project], was unfamiliar to me.' The Princeton Radio Research Project was run by Paul Lazarsfeld, who specialized in the mass media and pursued an empirical line in his research. It was Adorno's task to examine the field of music. The Princeton Radio Research Project was based in Newark, New Jersey, where its headquarters were located 'in a somewhat improvisatory fashion in an unused brewery. Whenever I travelled there, through the tunnel beneath the Hudson, I imagined myself rather as though I was in Kafka's natural theatre in Oklahoma'.[1] Adorno took the subway every day from New York to Newark, using one of his journeys as the basis of an account – 'No Adventure' – that breathes the melancholy of the émigré.[2] His attention is caught by a young woman, who strikes him as charming, not to say delightful, even if her dress is a little faded. He looks over to her and smiles at her with a mixture of compassion and 'absorbing longing', but instead of responding to his approach, she snubs him, 'making herself unwelcoming and drawing her skirt over her narrow knees'. One might be inclined to dismiss all this as banal and commonplace: a man is given the brush-off. But here the reader observes an unbridled socio-critical imagination that is almost out of control. Adorno supposes that the young woman is an émigré from Europe – in Vienna or Berlin his flirtatious encounter would have led to something, but in America things are different: 'Do you not know, says the gesture, that we are in America, where you are not allowed to accost women? Smiling, too, is out of the question as far as I am concerned. When I travel home, I am travelling home; I amuse myself only when I amuse myself.' The socio-psychological interpretation of the scene becomes increasingly elaborate, and by the end the young woman seems to be part of a much greater picture designed to serve as a façade: 'Without knowing it, she obeyed the coercive constraint of an existence that had turned her beauty into a natural monopoly, the only one that she could use whenever she spoke to powerful bosses, busy relief organizations and impatient relatives.' We recognize in this scene the terrible sadness that must have motivated Adorno's sociological analyses – and we smile at the discrepancy between the philosophical apparatus that he uses and the particular incident that inspired it.

On 2 August 1938, Gretel Adorno wrote to inform Benjamin that she had started to furnish their flat in New York: '3 rooms on the 13th floor with a view of the river. Although the furnishings have not been specially chosen for the place – it is old stuff from Frankfurt and Berlin, which reduces the considerable customs duty – I hope that we will be able to make it nice at least for us and a few friends, if not for larger groups.'³ But the situation in which Adorno's parents found themselves was a cause for worry. In the wake of the events of 9/10 November 1938 – *Kristallnacht* – when German synagogues had been destroyed and Jewish premises vandalized, the situation had become intolerable for those Jews who had remained in Germany. 'I do not know,' Adorno wrote to Benjamin on 1 February 1939, 'whether you are aware how closely my parents have become involved in all the turmoil. We did succeed in getting my father out of prison, but he suffered further injury to his already bad eye during the pogrom; his offices were destroyed, and a short time afterwards he was deprived of all legal control over his property. My mother, who is now 73 years old, also found herself in custody for two days.'⁴ By the skin of their teeth, Oscar Wiesengrund and Maria Wiesengrund-Adorno managed to escape from Germany, and in June 1939 Adorno was reunited with them in Havana, only weeks after they had arrived in Cuba. At the end of 1939 they travelled to Florida, and from there to New York. Even after he had moved to California, Adorno remained in regular contact with them by letter.

Adorno's work in New Jersey meant a mental break with Europe and with purely philosophical speculations. 'At Lazarsfeld's suggestion, I went from room to room and spoke to my colleagues, hearing words such as "Likes and Dislikes Study", "Success or Failure of a Programme" and the like, although to begin with it meant very little to me. But I understood enough to realize that it was a question of collecting data that was to benefit planning positions in the field of mass media.'⁵ As Adorno soon realized, there was little scope for critical socio-philosophy, but in spite of this, he assumed the role of the empirical sociologist and felt very pleased with himself when he conducted his first 'interviews, which were, of course very disorganized and lacking in any system'.[6] Yet the results of his work left him feeling depressed and were well calculated to prepare the way for his concept of the 'culture industry'. For classical music, the radio distorted the listening experience, while for light music it infantilized the listener, who was fed with musical stereotypes, its invitation to witty self-parody representing a fragmentation of the listener's personality. Music on the radio became the model for propaganda in the worst sense of the word. The mobilization of fans, Adorno believed, already pointed the way forward to political alignment. In the ninth volume of the *Zeitschrift für Sozialforschung*, now published under the English title *Studies in Philosophy and Social Science*, Adorno revealed his findings in a piece headed 'On Popular Music'. It was signed 'T. W. Adorno', the name that he had adopted since his move to the United States and under which he was now to become famous.

Adorno's radio studies gave him his first opportunity to develop a sociological approach to different types of music. If in his sociology of music he was later able to propose a typology of listeners that allowed for subtle distinctions between them, it was his experiences in New Jersey that laid the foundations for this. The 'expert', we read in his *Introduction to the Sociology of Music* (1962), listens to music in a fully conscious manner and is able to follow the logical course of the piece: 'Whereas he spontaneously follows the course of even complicated music, he hears all at once the various elements – past, present and future – that occur in the piece in succession, so that a coherent meaning is crystallized out.'[7] The 'good listener' is technically speaking less well-versed in music and understands it in the way that people understand language even if they are unable to explain its grammar. Historically speaking, such listeners are part of the highbrow culture of the nineteenth century, but were already threatened with extinction. A third and more topical type is the consumer who respects music as a 'cultural asset'[8] but who knows more about the lives of the performers than about the music itself. He 'lies in wait for certain passages, ostensibly beautiful tunes, moments of grandeur. In general, his relationship to music has something fetishistic about it.'[9] The 'emotional listener' is less intransigent and superficial than this cultural consumer, for all that he uses music as a means of regressing and 'triggering otherwise repressed instincts that are controlled by civilizational norms'.[10] Russian music is said to be the favourite type of music for this sort of 'emotional' listener: Tchaikovsky and Soviet symphonies come under this heading. This raptly romantic type of listening is contrasted with the 'aggrieved listener', whom Adorno finds above all in Germany among the adherents of 'fidelity to the work', as well as among those listeners who are fond of pre-Bachian music and who belong to the Youth Movement. In Adorno's view, German music teachers were dominated by this type of listener. The jazz fan was another type of listener who was guilty of a misconception by regarding himself as a member of the avant-garde whereas he was actually following simple schemata. But even lower in Adorno's estimation were the people who listened to light music on the radio. At the lowest end of the scale came the type of unmusical and antimusical listener who was lacking in any willingess to resonate with the music: 'I should like to risk the hypothesis that brutal authority has brought out defects in this type.'[11]

It was with the eyes of a Central European émigré that Adorno also saw nature in his new home: 'The shortcoming of the American landscape,' he wrote in *Minima moralia*,

> is not so much, as romantic illusion would have it, the absence of historical memories, as that it bears no trace of the human hand. This applies not only to the lack of arable land, the uncultivated woods often no higher than scrub, but above all to the roads. These are always inserted directly in the landscape, and the more impressively smooth and broad they are, the more unrelated and violent their gleaming track appears against its wild, overgrown surroundings. They are expressionless.[12]

Adorno missed human traces in nature. He missed the paths and trails leading down into the valley as he knew them in Germany: 'It is as if no-one had ever passed their hand over the landscape's hair.'[13] This description, too, captures the pain of the exile, with Germany as the yardstick by which America is judged and found wanting. Also part of this vignette of America is a dream that Adorno had in the early 1940s, and indeed the dream may even have prompted him to write down his observations on the American countryside. The scene is a mountain path similar to those found in the region of Amorbach. Adorno is out walking with his mother and aunt. But at the same time they are on the West Coast of America. 'Below us on our left lay the Pacific Ocean. At one point the path seemed to become steeper or to stop. I set about looking for a better one through the rocks and undergrowth to the right.'[14] The landscape seemed almost trackless and impenetrable and so Adorno, still dreaming, had to turn back, at which point he encountered two blacks whose laughter struck him as a symbol of relaxation – and then, once he had passed through a gate, he found himself standing 'in the square outside the Neue Residenz in Bamberg, shaken by happiness'.[15] But as though to counterbalance the sense of homesickness, the very next piece in *Minima moralia* contains its antithesis, the European's typical reaction to the New World: the beauty of the American countryside, he noted here, consisted in the fact that 'even the smallest of its segments is inscribed, as its expression, with the immensity of the whole country'.[16]

The Second World War broke out on 1 September 1939 with Germany's declaration of war on Poland. Within days, France and Great Britain, both of which had agreed to help Poland, had in turn declared war on Germany. But even after Hitler's rapid defeat of Poland, the situation remained far from clear. The Soviet Union had concluded an alliance with the German Reich, granting it large-scale territorial gains in eastern Poland and enabling it to march into Poland in mid-September while simultaneously fighting its own war with Finland. On Germany's western frontier, meanwhile, all was quiet, encouraging the French to speak of a 'drôle de guerre': although it seemed to have declared war on its eastern neighbour, France appeared reluctant to engage in hostilities. At the end of October 1939 Adorno and Horkheimer met to discuss the draft of a political manifesto. It was intended to justify the 'actuality of Marxism' in the present international situation.[17] As their immediate goal, the two philosophers demanded the overthrow of the German government by the German proletariat and the overthrow of the French government by the French working class – Adorno and Horkheimer regarded the French regime as secretly in league with the National Socialists because of their lack of military engagement. 'It is the task of all proletarians to get rid of the obstacles that stand in the way of a rational world order. The best means of achieving this is war with Germany.'[18] The Soviet Union represented a particular problem. For many left-wing émigrés, the Hitler-Stalin pact had come as a shock. The draft manifesto drawn up by Adorno and Horkheimer seemed anxious to avoid this problem: 'For the present, Russia must be left to one side until we have a rational situation in our own country, when we may be able to use force to impose a better society on Russia, too.'[19] Revolution remained the goal. But there were evident doubts in the proletariat to whom the draft manifesto appealed. 'The prospect is such that, if the world is not struck blind, the proletariat could sort out the matter at once,'[20] Horkheimer believed, whereas Adorno had his misgivings: 'We have to remain outside, we may not be identified with the proletariat.' And so, under Point Nine, they noted: 'Critique of the proletariat.'[21] But even now they still clung to the idea of a Utopia: 'Liberating knowledge is divided from men and women only by a thin partition wall.'[22] They were to return to this thesis in their *Dialectic of Enlightenment*.

Horkheimer moved to the West Coast in 1941, while Adorno initially remained in New York. But their joint work on what was to become their *Dialectic of Enlightenment* demanded personal contact in order for them to discuss its contents. The three parties – Horkheimer ('Mammoth'), Adorno ('Hippopotamus') and Gretel ('Giraffe-Gazelle') – spent the whole of the summer of 1941 exchanging letters on the subject of a move, letters not free from a certain disquiet about the future. 'I've spoken to Fritz [Friedrich Pollock],' Adorno wrote on 2 July 1941, before availing himself of the animal imagery of which he was so fond and that his family had used before him. 'He was extraordinarily warm and open. He shares your view that it is better if the horses are transported by rail, and we tend to think the same. Sad though it is to think that our entry will not take place on a cart, as it says in the folksong, we none the less trust in your generous mammoth prophecy that the problem of a car will solve itself in Hollywood.'[23] And once again, somewhat more insistently: 'And so we should be very happy if you were to make arrangements categorically for us finally to end up in Hollywood.'[24] But in spite of repeated requests, Horkheimer's confirmation failed to arrive. As head of the Institute for Social Research, he had the difficult diplomatic task of ensuring relations with Columbia University, and so for a long time no news of the Adornos' plans to move was allowed to leak out – this required strong nerves. At the same time, serious thought had to be given to the financial situation. It was against this background that Adorno suggested that the three of them – Adorno, Horkheimer and Gretel Adorno – should spend their free time training to become psychoanalysts 'in order to open a sanatorium, perhaps in association with Menninger'.[25] But Horkheimer would hear none of it and wrote back, brusquely opining that psychoanalysis had 'a terribly stultifying influence'.[26] 'You can have little idea how bigoted the doctrines that play a positive role in our own dialectics sound as soon as people take them naïvely.'[27]

On 10 November 1941 a happy Adorno was finally able to write to Horkheimer:

Dear Max, if one could translate the phrase 'alea est iacta' from Caesar's Latin into a more circumspect language, now would perhaps be the right moment to quote it. I am also reminded of the Sedan speech by the Swabian colonel, which you can no doubt speak much better than we can write it: 'Gentlemen, the day has now come when thirty years ago the Prussian eagle trod on the tail of the Gallic cockerel with its iron fist.' If everything goes smoothly, this day will be Saturday. We're travelling to Cleveland, spending the night there, then on to Chicago on Sunday and in the evening to the Wild West. We're due to arrive in Los Angeles on Wednesday at 8.35 in the morning Pacific Time.[28]

'Household horrors': Adorno's name for his animals. The photograph was taken in Los Angeles in the mid-'forties

They could now start work on their philosophical project: 'Ah, Max, we're finally there, we'll do it together.'[29]

The émigrés who settled on the West Coast included the film director Fritz Lang, the composers Arnold Schoenberg and Hanns Eisler, the philosopher Ludwig Marcuse and the writers Thomas and Heinrich Mann, Alfred Döblin, Bruno Frank and Bertolt Brecht. The conditions in which they lived were later described as 'exile in Paradise': although foreign and homeless, they were surrounded by palm trees, and if some of them, especially Heinrich Mann, were not well off financially, their lives and livelihood were never under threat. A number of them, including Fritz Lang and William Dieterle, gained a foothold in Hollywood. United in their opposition to National Socialist Germany, they met, although not always with mutual goodwill. Small communities of exiles, in which everybody knew everyone else, formed their own little coteries. Now and again they worked together because the situation demanded it, only to react a moment later with mistrust or outright envy. On the other hand, they would meet to hold discussions and plan projects together. Brecht wrote filmscripts for Lang, with Eisler composing the music for his film *Hangmen Also Die*. Adorno, too, worked with Thomas Mann and Eisler, while Schoenberg looked on severely from afar. He also set some of Brecht's poems and advised Mann – whom Brecht could not abide – on his novel *Doctor Faustus*. It was the ideal breeding ground for gossip, which duly flourished.

Brecht had already planned a number of satirical stories on intellectuals in the class struggle at the time of the Weimar Republic. Initially they were set in distant China and revolved around a group known as the 'Tuis' – a play on words involving the syllables 'tellec-tual-ins'. Brecht was inclined to see in the politics of these intellectuals the comical contortions to which they subjected themselves in being torn between conformity and resistance. The project offered him a chance to distance himself as a poet from their 'vacillations'. The Social Democrats of the Weimar Republic, the members of the Bauhaus and ultimately the Institute for Social Research were the butts of his capers and Mephistophelean sideswipes. In August 1941 he noted down details of Walter Benjamin's death on the Spanish border. He had received from Günther Anders a copy of Benjamin's *Theses on the Philosophy of History*, which had been sent to the Institute for Social Research, and his reaction had been one of total wonderment. It is impossible to imagine a greater contrast with the tone of the rest of his diary entry:

> And now to the survivors! At a garden party at Rolf Nürnberg's I met the two clowns Horkheimer and Pollock, the two Tuis from the Frankfurt Sociological Institute. Horkheimer is a millionaire, Pollock merely from a good house, so that only Horkheimer can afford to buy a professorship wherever he happens to be staying 'to provide a front for the Institute's revolutionary activities'. This time it's at Columbia, but ever since the great red raids, Horkheimer has lost the desire 'to sell his soul, which more or less happens at every university', and they are moving to the paradisical West. What are academic palms! – With the help of their money, they keep around a dozen intellectuals afloat, and in return the latter have to supply them with all their work without any guarantee that the journal will ever publish them. And so one could claim that 'their main revolutionary duty throughout all these years has been to save the Institute money'.[30]

Brecht's account is certainly entertaining, but it is exaggerated to the point of distortion. The same malicious gaze is also found in his contemporary jottings for his *Tui* novel: 'Pollock gets the women for Felix [Felix Weil], who marries them. He then takes his ten percent. The Institute turns its hand to speculation; it has to survive. The contempt shown by Ho [Max Horkheimer] when he draws his guest's attention to the coffeeshops of the lower Tuis. The Institute requires constant financial help. It is the basis without which revolutionary work is impossible.'[31] Hanns Eisler retained a similar impression, recalling the situation in the early 1940s in conversation with Hans Bunge: 'Horkheimer is the director of the Institute. Pollock is the financial director of the Institute, whose activities had less to do with scientific speculations than with speculating on houses and property.'[32] Eisler called Horkheimer 'gefinkelt', a Viennese word meaning 'cunning' or 'skilful'. Needless to say, the exiled Institute had become a refuge for left-wing intellectuals, who hoped that it would publish their writings and, hence, provide them with fees, no matter how frugal the latter might be. Merely in order to protect itself, the Institute was forced, therefore, to be circumspect in awarding commissions and bursaries.

The Institute and its financial goings-on were not the only source of satire. There were also some curious incidents among the various individuals who hoped for assistance. In the autumn of 1942 Adorno received a desperate letter from Ernst Bloch, begging him for money: 'I've been fired as a dishwasher, as I couldn't keep up with the others. I'm now counting and bundling up papers, tying them up and taking them to a car . . . I have to bundle them up on my own in a black hole, and so I'm not even among proles, even though the work is proletarian. The truth of the matter is that the work is lumpenproletarian.'[33] Adorno reacted to this dismaying announcement from his old friend with an emotionally overblown public appeal 'For Ernst Bloch', in which he begged the other German émigrés not to abandon the philosopher to his fate: 'As an émigré in Boston, the author of *The Spirit of Utopia* and *Thomas Münzer* has lost his job as a dishwasher. He could not keep up with the prescribed speed; the theologian of the revolution could not adapt, and this was no more forgiven by those who hand out jobs than it is by those intellectuals who demand that the world be rebuilt while he is writing about the form of the unconstructable question.'[34] The appeal appeared in the New York *Aufbau* on 27 November 1942. But Bloch, an admirer of Wilhelm Hauff, had been guilty of a gross exaggeration in calling for help and had merely been fuelling his own narrative genius, producing a regular fairytale about capitalism. He had never had to wash dishes or bundle up papers in a dark and stuffy room. He had secretly hoped for a contribution from Adorno, whom he referred to in a letter to a friend as 'well-to-do Herr Wiesengrund' and whom he believed to be one of the 'seven people whom the Lord blessed with worldly goods', and because he could scarcely restrain his envy of Horkheimer, 'who has built a house for himself in California'.[35] In the wake of this débâcle, relations between Adorno and Bloch were poisoned for almost two decades. Only when Bloch moved from the German Democratic Republic to the Federal Republic in the early 'sixties did their friendship recover.

The course of the war was naturally a topic of conversation among the German émigrés. The Institute's economist, Friedrich Pollock, wrote an essay, 'Is National Socialism a New Order?', that appeared in the ninth volume of its journal and that warned against undue optimism. Pollock was of the opinion that the German economy of 'state capitalism' had proved astonishingly efficient, and so it was impossible to pin any hopes on an economic collapse. The military overthrow of National Socialism was desirable, he went on, but the classic Marxist doctrine of unemployment and the crises associated with overproduction no longer applied. Soma Morgenstern noted the situation in 1941: 'Panic had broken out in the émigré colony in Hollywood. The general mood was that the war had been decided and the Nazis had won. The leader of this chorus was Professor Horkheimer and his Institute . . . . Only two and a half optimists clung obstinately to their belief that Hitler would lose the war. They were Bert Brecht, the author of the present lines and half of Hanns Eisler.'³⁶

The pessimists were currently reading Aldous Huxley. *Brave New World* was a roman-à-thèse, which painted the portrait of a negative Utopia with a totalitarian regime managing to stabilize itself by breeding slaves, by using drugs as the basis for entertainment and by exposing the population to a constant stream of produce from the culture industry. The names 'Lenina' and 'Trotsky' are clear references to Soviet totalitarianism, while the world's great saviour is Ford – the very same Henry Ford who had wanted to make capitalism attractive to the man in the street. Crude material needs have been overcome in this new world, as has pain, but its inhabitants have lost their dignity. Was this the state to which the world was inexorably moving, a state in which European totalitarianism would ultimately merge indistinguishably with the American entertainments industry?

The Institute organized a seminar on the theory of needs, in the course of which Huxley's vision of horror was debated. Among the participants were not only Adorno and Horkheimer but also Herbert Marcuse and Friedrich Pollock. Invited guests included Brecht, Eisler, Ludwig Marcuse, Hans Reichenbach, Rolf Nürnberg and the philosopher Günther Anders. The seminar extended over the whole of the summer of 1942 and, according to Günther Anders' recollections, was an attempt to bring together two groups of people 'who were in fact not closely linked but who, it was felt, should be associated with each other on an intellectual level, namely, the Brecht circle and the circle around the Frankfurt School'.³⁷ Would capitalism succeed in meeting the material needs of those who had previously been underprivileged and in that way ultimately cut off the socialist perspective? The participants were confronted not only with Huxley's theses but also with Nietzsche's negative picture of the 'last human being', who forfeits his creative freedom through affluence and by having all his needs taken care of. 'How do things stand with the question of satiety?' Adorno asked at one of the sessions. 'What disgusted Nietzsche about contented faces was the fact that the contentment of the sated is paid for by the senseless suffering of the many and reflects it through malice. He did not believe that it is possible to do away with hunger by means of concessions. I believe that the same is true of the concept of longing. We should try to complete this translation exercise and achieve something that goes beyond short-term materialism.'[38] Adorno's 'Theses on Need' adopted a more concrete approach to hunger: 'Interpreted as a natural category, hunger can be satisfied with locusts and mosquito cakes, which many savages eat. If they are to satisfy their concrete hunger, civilized peoples need to eat things that do not disgust them. In disgust and its opposite, the whole of history is reflected.'[39] A free society would not tolerate Campbell's 'inferior soups'.[40] Adorno and his colleagues spent the whole summer discussing a philosophy of food: 'Culture begins with eating.'[41] Horkheimer noted that Nietzsche's 'last man' was 'not the one who has enough meat to eat. In this way Nietzsche is describing the whole culture of making do with little.'[42] The minutes of one of these meetings record that 'so-called material needs should not be regarded as unworthy. Today they are a means of controlling the masses'.[43] As soon as material needs are met, 'intellectual hunger' will make itself felt. As always, Brecht and Eisler played the part of troublemakers and refused to discuss Huxley at all.

Once the day's great debates on food and the quality of eating were over, they reappeared to Adorno during the night in his dreams. 'Los Angeles, early December 1942. I attended a large, uncommonly lavish banquet.' His dream seemed to be set in the Palmery at Frankfurt:

At one of the tables that I walked past, a violent and highly emotive discussion was taking place between two male members of a famous banking family. It related to a particular kind of very young small lobster that was prepared in such a way that one could also eat the shells – as with American soft crabs. It was explicitly explained that this was done to preserve the taste of the shells, which were a particular delicacy. One of the bankers kept on at the other, adopting the argument as his own, while the other thought about his health and swore at his kinsman for his presumption. I really did not know what to make of the affair in my dream. On the one hand, I found the argument over the meal unworthy, while on the other I could not help feeling a sense of wonderment that such powerful people could admit to their vulgar materialism in so sovereign and inconsiderate a manner.

The most splendid dishes were served, but they were all hors d'oeuvres, and Adorno's pleasure was marred by the fact that his table companion was a self-important woman of his acquaintance. 'Now the actual hors d'oeuvres were brought in. They were different for women and men. The latter were given very large portions of ones that were highly spiced and tasty. I remember that they included some tiny cold cutlets in a red sauce. The women's hors d'oeuvres were vegetarian, albeit of the choicest kind: palm-honey, leek, roast chicory – it seemed to me the height of sophistication.' So did this vision verge on a genuine Utopia? There was, however, a fly in the ointment:

> To my unspeakable horror, my table companion suddenly called out to the waiter, as though in a restaurant, attracting the attention of the whole company, even though it had been agreed that on so lavish an occasion no one should ask for anything. She wanted not only the hors d'oeuvres for the women, but also those for the men. It ill became her to be disadvantaged, she said. Without waiting for the outcome of her complaint, I woke up.[44]

There was not a right way of eating in the midst of a wrong way of eating, even in a dream. Inhumanity would live on as tactlessness.

Adorno continued to discuss the theory of needs with Eisler, and although these discussions produced few results, the friendship between the two men deepened, culminating in 1942 in their joint authorship of *Composing for the Films*, in which Eisler, who was a pupil of Schoenberg, and Adorno, who had studied with another of Schoenberg's pupils, attempted to prove that modern music was better suited to the aims of political enlightenment than traditional film music or, not to put too fine a point on it, that new music, by avoiding esotericism, could be used for propagandist purposes. Eisler, who had been born in Leipzig in 1898, already had experience in this field, having written a number of rousing songs to words by Brecht for the pre-1933 Communist movement. They included a *Solidarity Song* and *The Secret March*, which took as its subject matter the defence of the Soviet Union against 'imperialists'. He also wrote songs for the members of the International Brigades who fought in Spain, songs of great agitational potential that are still capable of fascinating listeners today in the recordings by Ernst Busch. It was while he was working on *Composing for the Films* that Eisler wrote his *Hollywood Songbook*, a more private and lyrical set of songs that is a diary-like collection of settings of poems by Brecht, Hölderlin, Pascal and others. One of the most moving of these songs was inscribed to Gretel Adorno, while the Chamber Symphony (1940) was dedicated to Adorno. During the 1960s, by which date his links with Adorno had loosened, Eisler discussed his *Hollywood Songbook* with Hans

Bunge, assuring the latter that 'the fact of the matter is that Adorno, with whom I was friendly at that time, begged me to allow him to write the foreword in the event of its publication. (Well, I didn't remind him of this the last time I saw him in Frankfurt in order not to embarrass him. He'd scarcely show himself in public with me, let alone lend me his name.)'[45]

Adorno always found it stimulating to meet people with a lively temperament, and this was undoubtedly the case with Eisler, whose caustic wit and impish nature Adorno found appealing. One should not imagine that the ivory tower of critical theory was unduly isolated. For his part, Adorno was inspired by Eisler to set 'Two Propaganda Poems by Brecht: For Voice and Piano'. The first was dated 5 June 1943, the second 16 June 1943. Eisler's Communist tendencies, it may be added, ran in the family: his brother Gerhart spent some years in the United States, spying for the Communist Internationale; and his sister, Ruth Fischer, was chairwoman of the German Communist Party during the early 1920s, when she steered the party towards the extreme left, later coming into conflict with Stalin and criticizing Communism with the same vehemence with which she had earlier advocated it.

The manuscript was finished in 1944. The concept of new music was interpreted in a wider and less dogmatic sense than was otherwise with the case with Adorno: Schoenberg, Bartók and Stravinsky were regarded as the yardstick by which all other composers were judged and enjoyed the same degree of recognition from composer and philosopher alike. In order to show how music can support certain political aims, the two authors proposed 'models', or examples, from the 'thirties and 'forties, beginning with a depiction of the masses. How could music affect our picture of the collective? The first example was *No Man's Land*, a German pacifist film from 1930 but set in the summer of 1914. Here we see a man who, like so many others, refuses to go to war: 'The atmosphere is melancholy, the pace is limp, unrhythmic. Music suggesting a military march is introduced quite softly. As it grows louder, the pace of the men becomes quicker, more rhythmic, more collectively unified.'[46] It is the musical accompaniment that both depicts and criticizes the formation of an orderly mass: 'There follows a triumphant crescendo. Intoxicated by the music, the mobilized men, ready to kill and be killed, march into the barracks. Then, fade-out.'[47] Military heroism is 'alienated' by the music.[48] The opposite example is also a march, this time taken from Eisler's own soundtrack to Fritz Lang's film *Hangmen Also Die*, which describes the assassination attempt on Reinhard Heydrich by members of the Czech resistance and the consequences of their action. A relatively lengthy shot shows a Gestapo chief studying the documents relating to the case:

The episode is quiet and matter-of-fact, but musically it is accompanied by a chorus and orchestra, which contrast sharply with the scene, performing a marching song in an animated tempo that increases dynamically from pianissimo to fortissimo. . . . Here again the music acts as the representative of the collectivity: not the repressive collectivity drunk with its own power, but the oppressed invisible one, which does not figure in the scene. The music expresses this idea paradoxically by its dramatic distance from the scene.[49]

A third example is taken from the 1933 film *La nouvelle terre* by the left-wing Dutch director Joris Ivens. (The film was released in the English-speaking world in 1934 under the title *New Earth*.) In this case we see workmen transporting a huge steel conduit: 'They walk bent under their tremendous burden, their motions almost identical. The pressure and difficulty of their working conditions is transformed into solidarity by the music.' To achieve this, the music should not confine itself to echoing the oppressive mood: 'The score tried to make the incident meaningful by an austere and solemn theme.'[50]

A second series of examples concerns the sort of music that is in conscious contrast to the depicted image, thereby enabling it to achieve a more powerful impact. Once again, it is a piece by Eisler that accompanies images of slums in the film *Kuhle Wampe* by Brecht and Slatan Dudow: 'A slum district of drab, dilapidated suburban houses is shown in all its misery and filth.' The accompanying music is 'brisk, sharp, a polyphonic prelude of a marcato character', producing a shock 'deliberately aimed at arousing resistance rather than sentimental sympathy'.[51] Heydrich's death scene in *Hangmen Also Die* presented the composer with a challenge inasmuch as he needed to avoid any hint of tragedy: 'Because Heydrich is a hangman, the musical formulation is a political issue; a German, fascist picture, by resorting to tragic and heroic music, could have transformed the criminal into a hero.' Eisler's solution to this problem was to 'bring out the significant point by brutal means':[52] 'The music consists of brilliant, strident, almost elegant sequences, in a very high register, suggesting the German colloquial phrase *auf dem letzten Loch pfeifen* (literally, "to blow through the last hole", which corresponds to the English: "To be on one's last legs"). The accompaniment figure is synchronized with the associative motive of the scene: the dripping of the blood is marked by a pizzicato in the strings and a piano figure in a high register.'[53]

In short, the idea underpinning the book was a cinematic link between new music and the anti-Fascism of the class struggle. But here we stumble upon a striking contradiction: in their *Dialectic of Enlightenment*, Horkheimer and Adorno were to argue against the functionalization of thought: 'Propaganda directed at changing the world,' we read here, 'what an absurdity!' And they go on:

> Propaganda turns language into an instrument, a lever, a machine. . . . Propaganda manipulates human beings; when it screams freedom, it contradicts itself. . . . In it even truth becomes a mere means, to the end of gaining adherents; it falsifies truth simply by taking it into its mouth. . . . Propaganda is antihuman. It presupposes that the principle that politics should spring from communal insight is no more than a form of words.[54]

The political aims of *Composing for the Films* coincided only in part with the goals of American politics. Propaganda directed against the country's military enemies was useful to the Allied aims, but once the war was over and in the face of the growing tension with the Soviet Union, the whole idea of the class struggle became suspect in the United States. Even during the forties, when the book was written, Eisler had already attracted the attention of McCarthy's House Un-American Activities Committee, which sought to combat what it saw as the Communist infiltration of the country. Hollywood in particular came in for scrutiny. Richard Nixon, who was later to become President, said at the time that the 'Eisler case' was the most important to have come before him. Even during his first visit to the country in 1935 Eisler had been regarded as a security risk by the FBI, who knew his music for Brecht's *Die Maßnahme*, a passion play on the subject of liquidation, and who knew that his work had been praised in the Soviet press. And if Nixon had seen the manuscript of *Composing for the Films*, it would undoubtedly have been held up as evidence in the prosecution case that Hollywood had been infiltrated by Communists. Eisler was a popular figure in the capital of the film industry. When Chaplin was questioned by McCarthy's committee in 1947, he declared that he, at least, was proud to be able to call himself a friend of Eisler. He was asked whether Eisler was a Communist, prompting the reply that Chaplin saw in him 'a fine artist and a great musician and a very sympathetic friend'. Would it make any difference to him if Eisler were a Communist? 'No,' was Chaplin's unequivocal reply.

It was Eisler's social contacts that briefly brought Adorno and Chaplin together. In a vignette of Chaplin, Adorno later recalled an evening in California in around 1946:

> That I speak of him at all I may perhaps justify by mentioning a privilege that I enjoyed, albeit wholly undeservedly. He once imitated me. I must be one of the few intellectuals to whom this has happened and who can give an account of the moment in question. Together with many others, we had been invited to a villa at Malibu, on the beach outside Los Angeles. One of the guests left early, while Chaplin was standing next to me. Unlike Chaplin, I held out my hand in a slightly absent-minded manner and almost simultaneously started

back. The man who was leaving early was one of the main actors in a film that was very popular after the war, *The Best Years of Our Life* [the correct title is *The Best Years of Our Lives*], he had lost his hand in the war and in its place wore a claw which, although made of iron, had moveable joints. When I shook his right hand and it returned my grip, I started up violently but immediately sensed that on no account should I show this to the handless actor, and so in a fraction of a second I changed my expression of horror into a friendly grimace that must have been even more terrible. The actor had scarcely moved away when Chaplin was already reenacting the scene.[55]

When Eisler was summoned to appear before McCarthy's committee, he could count on the solid support of his fellow artists and composers: Aaron Copland and Leonard Bernstein both spoke out in his defence. Albert Einstein, Picasso and Matisse signed a petition. Stravinsky, whom Adorno had accused in 1932 of having affinities with Fascism, gave a benefit concert for his colleague in Los Angeles. By October 1947, another of Eisler's acquaintances, Thomas Mann, was so worked up at the political consequences of the case that he toyed with the idea of writing a protest similar to Zola's 'J'accuse'. The essay, he noted, 'would have to take the form of a patriotic warning, expressing the concern that America is exposing itself to misunderstandings'.[56] Early notes attempted to take the sting out of the tail of the accusation of Communism: 'E. belongs to an artistic and intellectual world in which powerful socio-critical elements are traditionally found, it is the world of a certain intellectual & musico-sociological radicalism that may look like "Communism" in the eyes of the uneducated. But there is no doubt that in this world (Adorno) there prevails a clear rejection, nay, loathing of the present totalitarian system in Russia.' But it was Adorno who that very day warned Mann against intervening on Eisler's behalf: 'To tea at Adorno's request to talk about Eisler. Brought down to earth by his remarks about E.'s character and situation. Praise of the musician. No doubt that the case lies on the line of the fascisization of the country. But unsuited to a J'accuse. Also possible that E. would welcome deportation.'[57]

By the beginning of 1948, the pressure on Eisler had indeed become so great that he voluntarily left the United States for East Berlin. *Composing for the Films* had appeared the previous year under the New York imprint of Oxford University Press, but with only Eisler's name on the title-page, Adorno having withdrawn his name as co-author: it had now become clear that if it was to return to Germany, the Institute for Social Research could count only on the goodwill of the American occupying power, with whom all conflict was therefore to be avoided. In the introduction that he wrote for the 1969 West German edition,

Adorno spoke in veiled terms, therefore, of a book that was 'by no means political'.[58] Were these the confessions of a nonpolitical man? Whatever the answer, Adorno was not being entirely honest, although he may perhaps have been traumatized by the demands for politicization that were placed on him by the student movement. 'Eisler and I,' he went on, 'harboured no illusions about our differences of political opinion. We did not want to jeopardize our old friendship, which dated back to 1925, and so we avoided discussing politics. I had no reason to become the martyr of a cause that was not mine and that *is* not mine.'[59]

Following his return to Germany, Eisler wrote a new national anthem for the Democratic Republic, to words by Johannes R. Becher. In a television broadcast, Adorno later offered a wittily apt critique of the work, recalling the fear that he had expressed in 1932, namely, that proletarian music could ultimately end up restoring old material to circulation. As soon as the anthem started, listeners felt 'Haha, a national anthem,' he argued. And the words, 'Auferstanden aus Ruinen' [literally, 'Risen from ruins'] were wrongly stressed on the first and fifth syllables. Eisler got his own back in conversation with Hans Bunge, commenting that 'These Frankfurturists, as Brecht called them, lacked a genuine battle position against the bourgeoisie.'[60]

10 'Dialectic of Enlightenment'

There are two definitions of the word 'enlightenment', one of them socio-political, the other scientific. The two may overlap and may even coincide within a single individual, as they did in the case of the German adventurer Georg Forster (1754–94), who accompanied Captain Cook on his third voyage round the world and who later become a supporter of the French Revolution. Yet the two terms need to be distinguished if we are not to fall into the mistaken belief that we are dealing with a single concept and that social change can ultimately be scientifically justified.

One of the word's two meanings stems from the history of the revolution and is an idealizing construct that sees emancipation as a continuous process. Ever since the emancipation of humanity had begun in America in 1776, continuing in the great French Revolution and reasserting itself in the twentieth century in the Russian Revolution, it had been directed against monarchies, or so the humanitarian revolutionary ideologists maintained. The doctrine of the divine right of kings was abolished, the Holy Roman Empire destroyed, and in 1918 the monarchies of Central Europe were overthrown in the wake of the overthrow of tsarism. This is a revolutionary idea that is rationalist, republican, universalist and, in its socialist sequel, egalitarian. It is indebted to deism or atheism, its highest goal, besides social justice, being the desacralization of politics. As such, this idea was bound to assume that all that opposed it was authoritarian and arbitrary. Ultimately, the pure idea of emancipation finds itself facing the pure principle of power – and this last-named principle embraces both political and economic inequality. To the extent that it revolves around the concept of power, *Dialectic of Enlightenment* was likewise indebted to this ideology and, as such, is a philosophical manifesto of anti-authoritarian and egalitarian politics.

This concept of enlightenment may be contrasted with a second one derived from the history of modern science. The philosophy of this second type of enlightenment was a response to modern Europe and to the age of discoveries, beginning with Columbus and continuing with the development of scientific and technological instruments such as the telescope, compass and microscope, clocks and the sextant, Galileo's discovery of the principle of the isochronism of the pendulum, the theory of the vacuum and, hence, a scientific understanding of the position of the earth within the cosmos and, finally, the discovery of the central perspective in painting. In the eighteenth century, European philosophy found the root of all that had been achieved since 1492: where classical antiquity had divined the actions of gods, modern man saw the force of human reason, a force which rationally deciphered the laws of nature. Enlightenment, wrote Kant in 1784, was 'man's leaving his self-caused immaturity'.

Enlightenment started in Europe. The European disaster of the 1940s was bound to lead to a new philosophical attempt to question the whole concept of enlightenment. While culture had produced Fascism in Europe, the culture industry had triumphed in the United States – this, at least, was the thesis proposed by Horkheimer and Adorno. Enlightenment's promise of autonomy had been undermined on both sides of the Atlantic. From this point of view, to risk a backward glance at European history meant taking account of its failure. The possibility of self-eclipse and self-blinding was bound to lie in the very nature of reason and especially in its growth. Adorno and Horkheimer fantasized about recombining the two types of enlightenment, the emancipatory type and the scientific type. First, however, they had to be analyzed separately. The classic thesis of Marxism was that progress of the forces of production had in itself a tendency to break up the old capitalist production conditions. Rosa Luxemburg had formulated a reservation, arguing that socialism was possible, but so, too, was a slide back into barbarism. And this had duly occurred in the 1940s. As a result, Marxist theory was faced with a problem – and *Dialectic of Enlightenment* was an attempt to solve it. A vast gulf had opened up between technological and scientific reason and emancipation. Even worse, the development of one of them turned out to be an obstacle to the other.

'The enslavement to nature of people today,' thus runs one of Horkheimer's and Adorno's core theses, 'cannot be separated from social progress. The increase in economic productivity which creates the conditions for a more just world also affords the technical apparatus and the social groups controlling it a disproportionate advantage over the rest of the population.'[1] That there is such a thing as a 'dialectic of enlightenment' was an insight that Adorno had stumbled upon in Vienna when he had encountered the works of Karl Kraus. Kraus, too, had discovered in his battles with the press that the latest and most modern ideas were not necessarily more humane and had coined the term *Fordschritt*, literally 'Ford step', a play on the word *Fortschritt* meaning 'progress' or 'step forward'. The older socio-democratic doctrine had still been able to trust in the world spirit and believed that the achievements of capitalism would one day be 'inherited' by socialism. During his exile in France, Walter Benjamin had subjected this belief to a radical critique, arguing in his *Theses on the Philosophy of History* that 'capitalism will not die a natural death'. In the face of the failure of the workers' parties to stand up to Fascism, he recalled the active struggle by the anarchist Auguste Blanqui and also the short-lived attempts to foment revolution by the German Spartacists.

Adorno and Horkheimer had nothing but admiration for Benjamin's theses, and *Dialectic of Enlightenment* became their most important philosophical work during their years of exile in America. Human prehistory, classical antiquity, the modern age and the present day were all linked together in their large-scale conception of a fundamental critique of developments in the West. During the 'thirties Adorno had already taken an interest in such writers as Alexis de Tocqueville, Oswald Spengler and Edgar Allan Poe, all of whom had adopted a sceptical view of democracy and shown what the modern age had lost. In his work with Horkheimer, Adorno revealed an even more pronounced tendency to turn to the 'dark' writers of the bourgeois age – Sade and Nietzsche, Hobbes and Machiavelli – rather than to the ideas of the liberal optimists, and to distil from them the truth about the contemporary situation. Marx and Engels had done exactly the same: conservative, not to say reactionary, critics of the modern period such as Carlyle were more important to them than writers who theorized about a free market economy, for here, they believed, the contradictions and problems of society were at least raised. Only the answers had to be different.

Dialectic of Enlightenment was the left-wing response to Spengler's *Decline of the West* and was equally ambitious in its claim to present a comprehensive interpretation of history. Central to the study was the concept of domination or, rather, a whole group of different types of domination and their associated motives. Their concern was not only man's domination over nature but also that of man over woman, that of the factory owner over his workers, that of the culture industry over our free time and, finally, that of the West over colonized nations. Domination is the root phenomenon – the same thesis had already been found in Horkheimer's study of the beginnings of the bourgeois philosophy of history – and now it is very much the way in which man uses his power to safeguard his own survival that is seen as increasingly fatal. By dominating nature, the authors argue, man has secured his immediate survival, but at the same time he has held himself back, mutilated himself and robbed himself of the opportunity for happiness. Not only was the proletariat repressed, so, too, were women, coloured people and, finally, the consumers of mass culture.

And it was very much this culture industry that made sure that the oppressed could no longer be aware of their situation. If readers of *Dialectic of Enlightenment* are bound to take away the impression that the system described here is internally perfect and proof against all resistance, it is above all because of the black anti-theology that they find here in Adorno's analysis of the American entertainment industry, from Hollywood to jazz, and from radio and television to advertising and the American dependence on the automobile. The chapter headed 'The Culture Industry: Enlightenment as Mass Deception' resembles nothing so much as an apocalyptic portrait of a triumphant idol parodying the promised sense of fulfilment. Capitalism and brain-washing seem to be part of this vision. Commercialized mass culture in the United States had already come as a shock to Adorno while he was working on his first radio project, for it went far beyond anything that he had dismissed as infantilization in the Europe of the 1920s. The omnipresence of advertising that he saw all around him had no counterpart in Europe – the closest was Fascist propaganda. As early as 1936 he had already drawn attention to this topic in a letter to Horkheimer:

> One will finally have to tackle the problem of Fascism, although this immediately raises the problem of its socio-psychological 'mediation'. But this can be studied by means of an apparently 'harmless' model, namely, advertising. One can probably achieve the deepest insights into the structure of Fascism by studying advertising, which first comes to the political centre – or, rather, to the political foreground – in Fascism and whose economic preconditions presumably correspond in turn to those of Fascism.[2]

It was not chaos that ruled in the United States and that cultural pessimists in Europe had predicted, but, quite the opposite, the strictest organization and 'systematic ingenuity'.[3] Instead of the differentiated logic of the work of art, one found stereotypical monotony and scenes and melodies that were all entirely predictable. Even American houses struck Adorno as made to be torn down again very quickly. And it was not consumer needs that were responsible for spiritual impoverishment but the 'total power of capital'.[4]

The picture that is drawn here is that of a dictatorship entirely reminiscent of Huxley's *Brave New World*, albeit with the difference that the criticism of capitalism is ever-present: 'Added to this is the agreement, or at least the common determination, of the executive powers to produce or let pass nothing which does not conform to their tables, to their concept of the consumer, or, above all, to themselves.' The 'objective social tendency of the age' is embodied in the 'obscure subjective intentions of board chairmen.'[5] Adorno often described the cultural industry as the genuinely American form of a totalitarian system, speaking of 'purges'[6] and of the 'jazz leader' Benny Goodman. But there is something else that determines the seductive rhetoric of this chapter: it is not only the vision of horror of an unavoidable coercive system, a negative Utopia, but the echo of a theological language of description. When Adorno writes that the culture industry is 'a mocking fulfillment of Wagner's dream of the total art work';[7] when he castigates the 'triumph of invested capital',[8] to which the masses 'unresistingly succumb';[9] and when he denounces the radio as a demonic parody of the omnipresence of the divine spirit and uses a biblical formula to describe the filmstars Mickey Rooney and Victor Mature ('They come to fulfill the very individuality they destroy'[10]), it is no longer the culture industry alone that he can mean here. It is, rather, the golden calf and, even more, the Antichrist that capitalism proves to embody.

Dialectic of Enlightenment was written at a time when the first reports of the annihilation of European Jewry were reaching the outside world. 'Elements of Anti-Semitism: Limits of Enlightenment' is the title of one of the book's six sections. Hatred of the Jews, the authors' thesis may be summed up, is the revenge of those in power on those who uphold the downtrodden idea of happiness. Whatever exercises the individual in the process of civilization is projected on to marginalized groups as a hostile tendency: in the Jew, domination is contrasted with the Other as the epitome of Utopia. But *Dialectic of Enlightenment* was a Jewish book not just in the sense of a critique and analysis of anti-Semitism: it was also a philosophical assertion of Jewishness at a time of its greatest danger. Not a few readers of Horkheimer's later writings and notes of the 'fifties and 'sixties were surprised at the agnostic Marxist's return to religion. But in expressing this surprise, they overlooked the fact that *Dialectic of Enlightenment* had already pointed in this direction, for in passing the whole of history through the mill of their universalist theory, its authors were arguing that ultimately only one spiritual form was justified: the Jewish religion. This, they insisted, was a religion without transfiguration, a religion with no semblance of ideology or myth but at the same time without the self-deceptions of the Enlightenment and without the speechlessness that threatened logical positivism:

> In the Jewish religion, in which the idea of the patriarchy is heightened to the point of annihilating myth, the link between name and essence is still acknowledged in the prohibition on uttering the name of God. The disenchanted

world of Judaism propitiates magic by negating it in the idea of God. The Jewish religion brooks no word which might bring solace to the despair of all mortality. It places all hope in the prohibition on invoking falsity as God, the finite as the infinite, the lie as truth. The pledge of salvation lies in the rejection of any faith which claims to depict it, knowledge in the denunciation of illusion.[11]

Unlike Buddhism and its 'caricature, bourgeois skepticism' and unlike pantheism, the denial of myth was not abstract in Judaism, for even those of its ideas that seemed remote from myth still implied a faith in the universe or in oblivion and, as such, were sublimated, magic practices.[12]

Christianity was subjected to a far more critical appraisal inasmuch as it struck the two authors as the true source of all the doctrines that legitimize power: not only does woman 'bear the stigma of weakness' among Christians,[13] not only does her 'defenselessness legitimize her oppression . . . as with the Jews among Aryans',[14] but the attempt on the part of Christianity 'to compensate the suppression of sexuality ideologically by the veneration of woman, and thus to sublimate the memory of the archaic instead of merely repressing it, is annulled by its rancor against the woman thus elevated and against theoretically emancipated pleasure'.[15] Throughout the centuries of Christianity, the much-touted love of one's neighbour has concealed nothing but 'hatred of the object'.[16] Anti-Jewishness is as intrinsic to Christianity as hatred of women. No less Christian, in the eyes of Adorno and Horkheimer, was the attempt to mediate between the worlds of the divine and the human, to ennoble instinct by sanctifying marriage and to replace the 'crystal-clear law' by the concept of mercy. But it was impossible not to speak of a return to idolatry in this context.[17] With its doctrine of the crucified God, Christianity had sought 'prematurely to purchase' the reconciliation of civilization with nature.[18] In this way, the 'terror of the absolute' had been reduced, but at too high a price:

> To the same degree as the absolute is brought closer to the finite, the finite is made absolute. Christ, the incarnated spirit, is the deified sorcerer. . . . The progress beyond Judaism is paid for with the assertion that the mortal Jesus was God. The harm is done precisely by the reflective moment of Christianity, the spiritualization of magic. A spiritual essence is attributed to something which mind identifies as natural.[19]

With the naïvely credulous believer in particular, Christianity is transformed into a nature religion, that is, a substitute for religion.[20] In this way, *Dialectic of*

Enlightenment became an exercise in settling old scores with Christianity. We may assume that it was Horkheimer, above all, who was responsible for these sections of the book, for in Adorno's case we may speak, rather, of a fragile ambivalence towards Christianity. True, a deleted passage in Adorno's *Negative Dialectics* picks up the old thesis in the 1960s: 'The whole of western culture, including even its highest products, rests on what is untrue, the Christian dogma of the divine nature of a human being; nothing flourished in this culture that was not tainted by this lack of truth.'[21] On the other hand, Adorno had no qualms about dating the prefaces of a number of his writings to Christian holidays – the first edition of *Dissonanzen* was dated 'Whitsuntide 1956',[22] that of *Moments musicaux* 'Christmas 1963'[23] – and this last-named volume, which was written, as it were, under the auspices of Christ's birth, contains an essay on Beethoven's *Missa solemnis* that makes no attempt to sidestep the issue of the work's Christian content but also discusses Beethoven's early sacred works.

Not only Horkheimer, but Herbert Marcuse, too, believed that the Christian origins of anti-Semitism lay not only in the historical Christianity of the Middle Ages and the early modern period but that hatred of the Jews was peculiar to Christianity in terms of its whole structure. Admittedly, the memoranda that Marcuse kept for the American Office of Strategic Services (OSS) contain no explicit reference to the genocide of European Jewry, and one would like to know whether this omission reflects internal guidelines issued by the OSS. But we can still speculate on Marcuse's motives. Writing to Horkheimer in July 1943 in the context of his colleague's research into anti-Semitism, he noted that 'we should again apply ourselves to the task of uncovering the true link between anti-Semitism and Christianity. What is happening is not just a belated protest against Christianity but also its final consummation, at least in its darker aspects. The Jew is of this world, and it is precisely this world that Fascism has to subject to totalitarian terror.'[24] For obvious reasons, this was a thesis that could not find its way into the American propaganda in which Marcuse was actively involved. Whenever it was a question of describing the Institute for the outside world, its members likewise avoided all criticism of Christianity, preferring, rather, to appeal to Judaeo-Christian solidarity.

In a speech that he gave in April 1943, Horkheimer declared that hatred of Christianity was inherent in anti-Semitism, too: 'In Christianity and, even more, in the Jew, they [Fascism and National Socialism] see representatives of the values that they abhor in their heart of hearts, while paying lip service to those same values.'[25] And so here, too, the Institute retained its ambiguity. Just as they once had an internal language that openly argued in Marxist terms and used harmless terminology when addressing the outside world, so their criticism of Christianity was confined to correspondence and esoteric publica-tions on points of theory. It was another émigré from Germany, Leo Strauss, who developed a theory of secret languages available to philosophers at this period: *Persecution and the Art of Writing* was the title that he later gave to the collection of essays that seems like a tailor-made commentary on Horkheimer's strategy.[26] His ambitious aim was to demonstrate that the whole of the philo-sophical tradition, at least since the beginning of the Christian era, could be understood only when measured against a second, more subtle reading – philosophy's tendency to criticize religion was at the forefront of his interest.

But it was only with Adorno's interpretation of Homer in the chapter headed 'Odysseus or Myth and Enlightenment' and with the inclusion of classical antiquity that *Dialectic of Enlightenment* became a comprehensive cultural diagnosis of European civilization that embraced Athens and Jerusalem as well as the present in the form of genocide and the culture industry. For Adorno, Odysseus was the hero who can return home after the war only by dint of repeated acts of cunning. His story 'traces the path of the subject's flight from the mythical powers'.[27] 'The contrast between the single surviving ego and the multiplicity of fate reflects the antithesis between enlightenment and myth.'[28] Odysseus represents a concentrated expression of the history of rationality: he gives names to people and objects and in his navigational skill he anticipates the work of the compass. In the process he survives not only external dangers but also those of inner nature: the 'temptations deflecting the self from the path of its logic'.[29] He escapes from the threat posed by the Sirens' seductive singing by abandoning himself to it in a controlled manner. But by the time he returns to Ithaca, he has become a different man, for in Adorno's eyes he is now 'the implacable judge, avenging the heritage of the very powers he has escaped'.[30] By triumphing over outer nature, he has subjugated his own inner nature. And Adorno assumes that the cunning that the hero uses against the forces of nature prefigures the bourgeois practice of barter or exchange. The sacrifice appears as the first act of barter, exchange as the secularized sacrifice. Particularly impressive and, indeed, inspired about this interpretation of Odysseus is the very thing that sets it apart from the usual science of antiquity, namely, the mixture of concepts and categories which, regardless of the epoch, could see Odysseus as the first 'bourgeois'.

Dialectic of Enlightenment offered a bundle of theories in which the adherents of many later political movements could easily recognize themselves, be they feminists, anti-authoritarian student rebels or media critics, in short, not only all those people who wanted to mobilize the proletariat for the class struggle but also the 'hedonistic left' who latched on to the idea of sensual happiness. It also appealed to internationalists who demanded solidarity with the downtrodden nations of the Third World; to anti-racists concerned that minorities should be recognized; and to all who were sceptical about advances in technology, regarding our domination over nature as a source of disquiet. More than that: the book was an expression of the hope that all those of its aspects that were critical of domination could be combined together, so that its authors could speak with complete justification of a 'message in a bottle'. 'To be continued' are the words that appear in parentheses at the end of the chapter on the culture industry. But when the message in the bottle was deciphered by a new generation of enthusiastic readers in the mid-sixties and later – readers who, if necessary, wanted to write the sequel themselves – the two men who had sent it were no longer the same. *Dialectic of Enlightenment* is a book whose impact has undoubtedly been tremendous, but that very impact constitutes a tragedy of its own.

11   Schoenberg, Faustus and Stravinsky

There is a painting by Paul Klee that depicts a delightful example of the role play associated with bowing: *Two Gentlemen Bowing to One Another, Each Supposing the Other to be in a Higher Position*. It is tempting to see in Adorno's relations with Thomas Mann the diplomatic dealings between two masterly stylists assuring each other of their importance by means of a regular ceremonial. Certainly, anyone who sets out along this road will not go away empty-handed, for there is no end to the different ways in which the praise can be formulated. 'Must I tell you that it was you I was thinking of as the reader of this study?' Adorno asked when Mann expressed a kind word about his essay on Benjamin.[1] And when *Minima moralia* appeared in 1951, Mann stressed the density of the vignettes, adding that 'in order to read you, one should not be tired.'[2]

Their friendship dated back to the early 1940s, when Adorno and Horkheimer were working on *Dialectic of Enlightenment*, with its account of the end game of the bourgeois spirit. Meanwhile, Thomas Mann was working on another end game, *Doctor Faustus*, his novel about a musician that was conceived on the grandest scale as a parable of the German descent into National Socialism, a pact with the devil of a kind that other German writers were fond of depicting, most notably Carl Zuckmayer in his play *The Devil's General*. A great music lover, with a profound knowledge of the subject, Mann projected this subject on to the story of the German composer Adrian Leverkühn as told by his friend, the helpless bourgeois humanist Serenus Zeitblom, who is left with no alternative but to adopt the role of chronicler and accompany Leverkühn on the road to disaster. The intellectuals of the 1920s appear here: Karl Wolfskehl and Oskar Goldberg, both of whom were known to the novelist personally, represent the frivolous trifling with irrationality in the figure of the prophetic Chaim Breisacher. But exiled writers also had a contribution to make: Paul Tillich wrote a long letter to Mann on the Protestant background, while Mann, too, found his way into the book. Reminiscences of Luther and Dürer, whose *Melancholia*, with its magic square recalling not only the magical and mathematical nature of music but at the same time the pall that had been cast over intellectuality, invested *Doctor Faustus* with an echo rising up from the depths of German history. And repeatedly the present day interposes itself, the present being the time when Serenus Zeitblom writes down his recollections of the late composer, pointing up the topicality of Germany's slow, destructive and self-destructive downfall beneath a hail of bombs.

But music was central to the novel. The description of the German myth demanded it. Mann was already knowledgeable enough to write about nineteenth-century composers from Beethoven and Schubert to Schumann, Wagner and even his own contemporary Hans Pfitzner: even in *The Magic Mountain*, he had raised a monument to his love of music in the chapter 'Fullness of Harmony'. But for the compositional techniques of the twentieth century and above all of the Schoenberg School, he needed expert advice, and he found this in Adorno, many of whose ideas found their way into the compositions of Adrian Leverkühn. Adorno provided sketches for Leverkühn's chamber music and his cantata *The Lamentation of Dr Faustus*, which interprets Faust's final meeting with his pupils as a 'negative communion'. The concept of melancholia, which recalls Walter Benjamin's study of German tragedy, plays a major role here, too, describing, as it does, a mental attitude that is grounded in despair and that finds no means of escape through the saving grace of action. Even the uninitiated were soon introduced to Adorno through Mann's account of the novel's genesis, with the philosopher self-consciously asking Mann to give greater emphasis to his 'conceptual and imaginative contribution to Leverkühn's oeuvre and aesthetic outlook than to the factual information' that he had provided.[3] Mann later described Adorno as

one of the finest, keenest and critically profoundest minds that are active today. A creative musician in his own right, he is at the same time gifted with a capacity for linguistic expression whose precision and elucidatory powers are unique, and I know of no one better capable than he of providing the public with more sensible and knowledgeable information about the present situation of music. I know his work very well: he provided me with ideas and instruction for certain parts of my novel about a musician, *Doctor Faustus*, and I very much hope that he will receive the acknowledgement that is his due in the country in whose language it is written.[4]

In *The Story of a Novel: The Genesis of Doctor Faustus*, Mann describes Adorno as a man of a similar mental cast to Benjamin, 'uncompromising, tragically brilliant, operating on the highest level'.[5] It was his concern for the book's technical and musical accuracy that persuaded Mann to seek out an adviser, as the novel was intended to stand up to the scrutiny of musical experts:

> The helper, adviser, and sympathetic instructor was found – one who, through exceptional technical knowledge and intellectual attainments, was precisely the right person. 'Book, *Eingebung im musikalischen Schaffen* [*Inspiration in Musical Creation*]', is recorded for an early date in July 1943. 'Important. Brought by Dr. Adorno.'[6]

Thus runs Mann's account in *The Genesis of Doctor Faustus*. Two weeks later, Mann began to read Adorno's study, *Philosophy of Modern Music*, the first part of which, dealing with the works of Arnold Schoenberg, had been completed by this date.[7] It provided Mann with 'moments of illumination on Adrian's position. The difficulties must reach their highest peak before they can be overcome. The desperate situation of art: the most vital factor. Must not lose sight of the main idea of ill-gotten inspiration, whose ecstasy carries it beyond itself.'[8] The two men discussed Schoenberg and twelve-note music and 'the dire consequences that must flow from the constructive Schoenbergian approach to music. However necessary it may objectively be to subject music to rigorous rational analysis, and however illuminating it may be, the effect is just the converse of rationality. Over the head of the artist, as it were, the art is cast back into a dark, mythological realm'.[9] And they also discussed Beethoven, whom Adorno compared to Rübezahl, the surly mountain spirit in the fairytale. When Mann first read out the episode about Beethoven's op. 111, his guests included both Adorno and Horkheimer. Adorno must have felt particularly flattered to discover his name Wiesengrund transformed as an aide-memoire in the lecture by Wendell Kretzschmar that was to influence Leverkühn's musical development:

> The reading made an extraordinary impression – intensified, it seemed, by the contrast between the strongly German basis and coloration of the book and my own altogether disparate attitude toward the maniacal country of our origin. Adorno, fascinated by the musical material and, moreover, touched by the little tribute to him, came up to me and said: 'I could listen all night!' I kept him close by me henceforth, knowing that I would have need of his aid, of his above all, in the remoter reaches of the novel.[10]

Mann read not only Adorno's study of Schoenberg but also his book on Kierkegaard and his *Essay on Wagner*, whose 'critical dichotomies and somewhat stiff attitude toward the subject, which never entirely passes over to the negative side, give it a certain kinship to my own essay, *Sufferings and Greatness of Richard Wagner*'.[11]

Many writers have pointed out the similarity between Adorno and the modern musical devil around whom the novel revolves. Once the tempter has finished playing his role as a Renaissance German in his conversation with Leverkühn, he turns himself into a contemporary intellectual who occasionally writes music himself. The following portrait is no doubt a composite – Mahler's features are unmistakable – but equally clearly it includes elements of Adorno, too: he

> has a white collar and bow-tie, spectacles rimmed in horn atop his hooked nose, behind which somewhat reddened eyes shine moist and dark; the face a mingling of sharpness and softness; the nose sharp, the lips sharp, but the chin soft, with a dimple in it, and yet another dimple in the cheek above; pale and vaulted the brow, from which the hair indeed retreats upward, whereas that to the sides stands thick, black, and woolly.[12]

As a novel about modern music, *Doctor Faustus* has been admired, whereas its parable of Germany's descent into the abyss has found few friends – and not just because of the resentment felt by the Germans that Adorno mentions in one of his letters. The tone of tormentingly effortful irony with which the narrator, Serenus Zeitblom, describes the 'divine judgment that hangs over us at present'[13] – in other words, the destruction of German towns and cities under a hail of bombs – is something that contemporaries, faced with the grim reality of the situation, must have found almost intolerable. And in the wake of their experiences of the Red Army, much the same is true of Zeitblom's assurance that Bolshevism had never destroyed any works of art.

While the published report on the genesis of *Doctor Faustus* presents an idealized picture of his conversations with Adorno, Mann's private jottings allow us to trace the tension that mounted as the novel drew closer to its completion. Work on it became more effortful. Adorno not only suggested corrections, he also expressed the wish that his famous friend might 'ensure the publication of his writings on music'.[14] On 23 January 1944 Mann noted in his diary: 'With Adorno on the musical problems of the novel. Where is the "breakthrough" leading? He doesn't know either. Promises a piece on Alban Berg, who was born in the same year as Adrian.'[15] And on 12 September 1944 we read: 'To supper with the Adornos. Wonderful wine from the Palatinate. A.'s bad piano playing: Schubert and Chopin.'[16]

From 1945 the indignantly critical remarks increase in number: when Adorno read to him from his *Minima moralia*, Mann noted that it was 'confused intellectual poetry . . . destructive and sad'.[17] And on another occasion he complained about the style of these aphorisms: 'Every thought is broken down and rethought, rolling on formlessly for all its verbal precision.'[18] In a similar vein, he recorded his publisher's dismissal of Adorno's 'super-cleverness', an opinion passed on to him by Gottfried Bermann-Fischer when the latter declined to publish *Minima moralia* following Mann's unsuccessful intercession on its behalf.[19] The friendship between the two men began to cool. On 8 August 1946, after an evening spent in the company of Horkheimer, Adorno and the émigré psychologist Charlotte Bühler, Mann noted in his diary: 'Erudite conversations. Bored.'[20] We find much the same on 5 April 1948: 'Afternoon tea with the Adornos and his pride and joy, the rich baroness, who had little to offer.'[21] Adorno himself added to their growing estrangement when he began to tell third parties about his contribution to *Doctor Faustus*: 'Discovered that Adorno has already compulsively offloaded & unburdened himself to Bibi about his partnership. Am considering measures to calm him,' we read on 8 February 1948.[22] But when Mann came to write down his account of the novel's genesis, he encountered resistance from another quarter. Whereas Adorno insisted on a proper mention, Mann's wife and daughter raised objections: 'Erika's animosity to Adorno, whom she doesn't want to see so acclaimed. But it's necessary to give him a credit,' Mann noted in his diary on 12 September 1948.[23] Two weeks later he complained about 'the problem of the Adorno confessions that are intolerable to the women'.[24]

One might think that Schoenberg would have been the novel's ideal reader, but in the event he reacted with considerable bitterness to it, feeling that he had been misunderstood, robbed of his intellectual property and even denounced as sick – in the novel, Leverkühn dies insane as the result of a syphilitic infection. And he saw Adorno as the main culprit, describing him in a letter as an 'informer'. Mann, Schoenberg complained elsewhere, did not 'know the essentials of composing with twelve notes. All he knows has been told him by Mr. Adorno, who knows only the little I was able to tell my pupils. The real fact will probably remain secret science until there is one who inherits it by virtue of an unsolicited gift.'[25] That he had no direct access to Schoenberg must have been one of the great disappointments of Adorno's years of apprenticeship. A man whom Adorno had declared the key composer of the twentieth century felt only an invincible dislike of the philosopher: 'I could never really stand him,' he wrote in December 1950. 'When he engulfed me with his piercing eyes, advancing on me ever nearer until a wall prevented further escape, . . . And into the bargain: the "grandioso" of his statements, his oily pathos, his bombast, and the affected passion of his admiration.'[26]

Adorno's book on new music was published in 1949. In December of that year, Schoenberg wrote to the critic Hans Heinz Stuckenschmidt: 'So modern music has a philosophy – it would be enough if it had a philosopher. He attacks me quite vehemently in it. Another disloyal person . . . I have never been able to bear the fellow . . . now I know that he has clearly never liked my music.'[27] Adorno, Schoenberg believed, was in fact uncreative from a musical point of view:

> He knows everything about twelve-note music, of course, but he has no idea of the creative process involved. A man who, so I am told, needs an eternity to set a song to music naturally does not suspect how quickly a real composer can write down what he hears in his imagination. He does not know that I wrote both the Third and the Fourth Quartet in six weeks each and *Von heute auf morgen* in ten weeks. And those are just a few examples, for I have always composed quickly. He seems to think that the twelve-note row stops composers, if not from thinking, then at least from inventing – the poor man.[28]

Written during Adorno's years of exile in America, *Philosophy of Modern Music* appeared in Germany in 1949, the first of his books to be published after the war. Far from being a simple apology for Schoenberg's development, it proposed a diagnosis of the situation in which music found itself, hopelessly caught as it was between the 'natural domination' of the rational method and the demand for expression. It was a sharply polarizing work. All that remained of Adorno's 1932 essay on the social situation of music that he had published in the *Zeitschrift für Sozialforschung* was the element of contrast. Eschewing the 'surreal' nuances of the earlier text, he now contrasted the first section, 'Schoenberg and Progress', with the second section, 'Stravinsky and Restoration'. It was a book about decisions, a book about radicalism. Adorno's aim was to prove that in Schoenberg's music the subject came into its own, whereas in Stravinsky's it celebrated its self-extinction. Stravinsky was said to 'renounce the strict self-development of essence in favor of the strict contour of the phenomenon – in favor, that is, of its powers of conversion'.[29] The speculative findings of *Dialectic of Enlightenment* concerning the contradiction between power and happiness, and the empirical findings about the 'authoritarian' and 'unprejudiced' character are now demonstrated by reference to music.

The young Adorno had sought out 'theories' of a potent kind and found them in his lessons with Alban Berg. But what had happened to 'theory' in the meantime? The answer lies in his chapter on Schoenberg in *Philosophy of Modern Music*, and especially in the section headed 'Avant-Garde and Theory'. Of central importance is the thesis concerning the transition from art to understanding: 'The role of the chorus in Schoenberg's recent works is the visible sign of such concession to knowledge. The subject sacrifices the clarity of the work, forces it to become doctrine and epigram, conceiving of itself as the representative of a non-existent fellowship.'[30] But Adorno now appointed himself the school's advocate against both the school and its teacher, arguing, against all expectation, that it was Berg the teacher who had destroyed the teaching – the 'current accomplishments of the school' could not stand comparison with the 'achievements of its early period'. Berg had reversed the radicalism of the Schoenberg School. Adorno's tone is so critical that one is inclined to speak of a betrayal of his teacher.

Schoenberg's works are said to be notable for their brevity: *Erwartung* 'develops the eternity of the second in four hundred bars', while *Die glückliche Hand* depicts life 'before it has a chance to find its place in time'.[31] In contrast to these, Berg's large-scale forms are seen as regressive. *Wozzeck*, writes Adorno, striking a critical note, is a 'great opera':

> The composed tragedy has to pay the price for its extensive depth and contemplative wisdom of its structure. The fleeting sketches of the Expressionist Schoenberg are here in Berg transformed into new pictures of affects. The security of form establishes itself as a medium for shock absorption. The suffering of the helpless soldier Wozzeck in the machinery of injustice attains a composure upon which the style of the opera is based. This suffering is encompassed and assuaged. The erupting anxiety becomes a suitable subject for the music drama and the music which reflects this anxiety finds its way back into the scheme of transfiguration in resigned agreement.[32]

This is the most outspoken criticism that one can imagine from Adorno, and it is continued in his analysis of Berg's Wedekind-based opera, *Lulu*, the libretto of which is said to have been 'idealistically distorted'[33] by the composer: 'Berg's humanism makes the affair of the prostitute his own; in so doing he removes the irritating thorn which the prostitute represents from the flesh of bourgeois society. . . . The decisively final words "O accursed" were eliminated by Berg. Geschwitz dies a death of love, a "*Liebestod*".'[34] In this way, modern music had found its own reformist principle and been reconciled to existing art. But what orthodoxy and radicalism could be summoned up to oppose it? And how would composers set about writing such music?

In the first part of *Philosophy of Modern Music* Adorno analyzed the development of the Schoenberg school, whose character as a school had emerged increasingly clearly with the passage of time:

Just as the twelve-tone technique seems to instruct the composer, so there is a uniquely didactic moment present in twelve-tone works. Many of them – such as the *Woodwind Quintet* and the *Variations for Orchestra* – resemble patterns. The preponderance of doctrinal teaching offers magnificent proof of the manner in which the developmental tendency of the technique leaves the traditional concept of the work far behind.[35]

It turns out that even in its orthodox form, doctrinal teaching was both at an end and not at an end. As Adorno noted, a strict adherence to the rules of twelve-note technique had led to a state of ossification, and it must have been this observation that wounded Schoenberg. But in Adorno's view, music still had to emancipate itself from technique: 'Only from twelve-tone technique alone can music learn to remain responsible for itself; this can be done, however, only if music does not become the victim of the technique.'[36] Its norms were 'the narrow passageway of discipline through which all music must pass, hoping to escape the curse of contingency'.[37] In the strict sense of the term, it is impossible to satisfy the rules, but this very impossibility is the motivating force behind the effort to learn: 'It must fail and the rules, in turn, must be forgotten, if they are to bear fruit.'[38] Adorno speaks of the 'freedom of action' that music must regain:

> It is precisely for this freedom that music is being trained by twelve-tone technique – not so much by means of what the technique determines in compositions, but rather through what is prohibited by it. The didactic justice of twelve-tone technique – its terrible discipline as an instrument of freedom – is revealed in full measure by comparison with any other type of contemporary music which ignores such discipline. Twelve-tone technique is no less polemic than it is didactic.[39]

What Adorno wanted was a paradoxical loyalty to both the school and the theory, and the paradoxes and difficulties increased with the passage of time. He adopted the same line of argument in an essay on Marxist class theory that dates from more or less the same time as his study on Schoenberg. Here he writes that one must 'oneself observe the concept of class from such close quarters that it is both fixed and altered at one and the same time'. Adorno's first attempt to take stock of the paradoxes bound up with pupillage is found in the section headed 'Gaps' in *Minima moralia*:

> Anyone who died old and in the consciousness of seemingly blameless success, would secretly be the model schoolboy who reels off all life's stages

without gaps or omissions, an invisible satchel on his back. Every thought which is not idle, however, bears branded on it the impossibility of its full legitimation, as we know in dreams that there are mathematics lessons, missed for the sake of a blissful morning in bed, which can never be made up. Thought waits to be woken one day by the memory of what it has missed, and to be transformed into teaching.[40]

Here teaching has become a utopian concept that cannot be realized by effort alone.

What are the implications of thinking one's thoughts against a background of schools and theories – in this case, the Freudian school, that of 'Marxist class theory',[41] as Adorno describes it, and the teachings of his mentor, Alban Berg? In the first place, the materials and initial questions already have an extremely rational and binding structure, in which they differ substantially from those of Walter Benjamin, for example. As a result, the individual's own reflections are under constant pressure to answer to his or her teachers and their teachings. The other implication is that readers of Adorno's writings repeatedly stumble upon traces of these teachings, including those that are ossified, atrophied and hollow. It is hard to find a page that does not mention exchange conditions or an overall context designed to blind the observer. But on those occasions where the approach works, the result is an ability on Adorno's part to pursue the inner fate of schools and work away at scholastic dogmas such as Freud's coldness and the ostensible humanism of reconstructed psychoanalysis, Marxist orthodoxy and Marxist revisionism, and all that came after Schoenberg.

Adorno's attempt to come to terms with Stravinsky in *Philosophy of Modern Music* turned into a major confrontation with the avant-garde, which, Adorno claimed, had sought not expression but a cynical and flirtatious concession to reification, pleasure in the alienated masks of subjectivity in the guises of the clown and doll, and a coquettish interest in the baser arts of the fairground and circus. The use of older material, which Adorno had previously seen as a means of obtaining surreal effects, was now subjected to an implacable critique. Indiscriminate sympathy was said to be Stravinsky's principal characteristic: 'Weber, Tchaikovsky, and the entire rhetoric of ballet of the nineteenth century attain grace before the uncompromising ear; even expression is tolerated, so long as it is no longer true expression, but merely the death-mask thereof. Universal necrophilia is the last perversity of style.'[42] Under the terms of Adorno's diagnosis, Stravinsky's music is declared objectively mad, with the discussion dominated by concepts from clinical psychiatry such as neurosis, psychosis, schizophrenia, catatonia and perversion. And it was his social theory that led him to adopt this extreme position, for in both cases all that lay beyond normative demands were mental disorders or at least – as with Stravinsky – their artistic echo. Even the early avant-garde's recourse to prehistory, including Carl Einstein's aesthetic study of African sculpture, now seemed to Adorno to amount to no more than a reaction to what had gone before it. By admitting to only a crude alternative between 'freedom' and 'destruction', *Philosophy of Modern Music* was a product of the war and its immediate aftermath: such was the catastrophe that the world had just witnessed that nuances seemed merely frivolous. The book is innocent of any sense of historical relativism. Stravinsky's machine-like rhythms, which could suit the Russian Futurists' enthusiasm for technology as much as American cartoons, were something that Adorno could interpret only as a concession to enemy forces, just as the description of the ecstatic human sacrifice in *The Rite of Spring* struck him as a crime against life. For his criticism of Stravinsky amounted to the charge of necrophilia and a betrayal of life itself: 'The basic phenomenon in the spiritual movement perfected by Stravinsky is his substitution of the hand organ for the Bach organ. In doing so, the metaphysical joke is supported by the similarity of the two instruments. This joke actually concerns the price of life, which sound is forced to pay for its purification from intentions.'[43] This was more than a psychoanalysis of music. Adorno went beyond his earlier claim that jazz was the expression of a castration complex and took over into music theory concepts from psychiatry, implying a severe mental disorder. On reading *Philosophy of Modern Music*, Schoenberg was unable to restrain his dismay: 'It is disgusting how he treats Stravinsky. I am certainly no admirer of Stravinsky, although I like a piece of his here and there very much – but one should not write like that.'[44]

12 Authoritarian Personality and Pathologization of the Centre

As the war entered its final stages, so it became increasingly important to investigate the enemy both sociologically and psychologically, with the victorious Allies planning to follow up their military defeat of Japan and Germany with a thoroughgoing re-education programme that was to extend as far as the mental roots of their enemies' political systems, which had developed along such disastrous lines. It was against this background that Siegfried Kracauer wrote his book *From Caligari to Hitler,* in which he traced the history of the German cinema from its origins to 1933 in order to point out the reflexes of the political and ideological changes that had culminated in the triumph of National Socialism. Mostly, however, Kracauer was content to draw the shortest possible line between a film and National Socialist ideology, his basic premise being his belief that the German revolution of 1918/19 had not gone far enough in the direction of socialism. The reader may none the less be surprised at the puritanical tone that the author adopts in discussing the wave of erotic films of the revolutionary period: in Kracauer's view, it indicated the public's reluctance to countenance any radical upheaval that would otherwise have absorbed their passions. He criticized the films of the early 'twenties for portraying the revolutions of world history as the result of private passions rather than of economic and ideological forces, as a more didactic approach demanded. In a film by Ernst Lubitsch (a director who, like Kracauer himself, was later obliged to leave Germany), masses threaten the individual, which for Kracauer was evidence of emotions hostile to democracy. Films with exotic settings such as islands were regarded as evidence of a continuing love of world conquest, while a film about schoolchildren was seen as symbolic of the German reluctance to engage in responsible, adult actions. Much the same is true of his interpretation of a scene in which a man collapses in despair and buries his head in his wife's consoling bosom: resistance to emancipation from the mother's womb is said to be a typically German trait. But even a film that dealt critically with the laws on abortion was poorly received, with Kracauer claiming that it distracted from more important social concerns and drained the energy out of the protest – a similar reproach was levelled at a documentary on the universe and its end through 'heat death'. Why were American comedies so popular with German audiences of the 'twenties? Kracauer, who had recently settled in the United States, knew the answer: the Germans lacked any sense of the right to happiness that was enshrined in the American constitution, with the result that for this particular type of film they were thrown back on imports. While acknowledging that the silent film *The Cabinet of Dr Caligari* was organized along internally plausible lines, he also drew attention to the German capacity for organization, which in his view was notoriously paid for by a loss of autonomy. Kracauer's study was part of the great complex of post-war interpretations of history in which the disaster that overtook Germany in the 'thirties and 'forties was extended backwards into the past, to Bismarck, Frederick the Great and Luther. As such, it belonged to the literary genre of the 'genealogy of evil'.

Commentators were naturally bound to ask themselves whether this evil could one day gain political power in the United States. Certainly it was a question that exercised Adorno as a sociologist. The fear that Fascism and anti-Semitism might flare up in the United States persuaded the American Jewish Committee in 1943 to lend its financial support to a series of investigations into prejudice. One of these studies was *The Authoritarian Personality*, which was written jointly by Adorno, the Austrian émigré Else Frenkel-Brunswik, Daniel J. Levinson and R. Nevitt Sanford. It was an attempt to provide empirical confirmation of the theses of *Dialectic of Enlightenment*: if, on that occasion, domination had emerged as a central concept that could be used to decipher the course of world history, it was now a question of identifying the actual features of domination in the individual, namely, the degree and type of 'authoritarian' behaviour. The '*potentially fascistic* individual' was to be identified using the methods of empirical social research.[1] According to the introduction, 'The research to be reported in this volume was guided by the following major hypothesis: that the political, economic, and social convictions of an individual often form a broad and coherent pattern, as if bound together by a "mentality" or "spirit," and that this pattern is an expression of deep-lying trends in his personality.'[2]

An indirect method was used: the sentences for which agreement or disagreement could be signalled were chosen in such a way that prejudices – especially anti-Semitism – were rarely openly touched upon. The authoritarian personality could be described in greater detail from various points of view, including 'conventionalism' (an unyielding commitment to the traditional values of the middle class), 'authoritarian submission' and 'authoritarian aggression'. The term 'anti-intraception' was intended to convey the idea of hostility to feelings and subjective fantasies. 'Superstition and Stereotypy' were diagnosed in the case of those individuals who thought that their lives were determined by fate. Other points of reference were 'Power and "Toughness"', 'Destructiveness and Cynicism', 'Projectivity' and, finally, 'Sex', by which the authors meant an 'exaggerated concern with sexual "goings-on"'.[3] Questionnaires and open interviews were used interchangeably. The research was conducted on the West Coast of America, largely among members of the white middle class, although a group of inmates from San Quentin was also included: there was a particular reason for this inasmuch as it was hoped that symptoms of a 'Fascist character' would be found with greater frequency among this group than among the population at large. Nothing could have provided better proof of the antisocial, morbid nature of anti-Semitism or been more useful from a propagandist point of view.[4] The basic idea behind the research was to examine the understandable and instinctive dislike of irrationality and destructiveness and steer it in particular political directions.

Adorno informed Brecht of his planned research, prompting the playwright to comment on it in a letter to his son Stefan. His letter, dated 18 December 1944, is typically sarcastic and mistrustful, with even a trace of Mephistophelean humour: 'The Frankfurt Sociological Institute (which inspired me to write my *Tui* novel) has now consolidated what had been its fragile financial basis – New York's Jews are financing a wide-ranging project to conduct research into anti-Semitism. Horkheimer and Adorno have already produced some questionnaires that are intended to establish the "fascist type", methodically and strictly on a scientific basis. This is the type of person who is potentially an anti-Semite, and from now on he can be diagnosed in the non-virulent phase (and if necessary treated).' Unlike Adorno, Brecht seems to have been clear in his mind about the sinister nature of this potential treatment, which very much recalls Orwell's *1984* and whose legal basis was left entirely open. He goes on:

Individual questions: 'Do you think that natural disasters – epidemics, earthquakes etc. – follow on from world war?' – 'Do you consider syphilis to be incurable?' I brought the discussion round to Karl Marx's little essay on the Jewish question and once again was told that it is out of date (and, moreover, that it is by the *young* Marx). Marx is said to have been taken in by Goebbels' distinction between creative and money-raking capital. My malicious question whether, in his view, the New Yorkers would finance the Marxist standpoint if

Marx had not been wrong or if the Institute could prove that he had been right after all fell on deaf ears. (I am almost certain that Adorno won't take this over into his questionnaire.)[5]

Marx's 1844 essay links the 'Jewish question' to liberation from capitalism: once the social conditions for the economic dominance of one particular group had been removed, Marx believed that religion, too, would vanish as a cause of conflict. Then the Jews would be emancipated not only politically and legally but on a human level, too. Brecht's view undoubtedly tended to be short-sighted in its economic materialism, but it none the less offered an optimistic prospect for the future: in a communal life of Communism, the conflicts that had raged for thousands of years would at last be resolved. According to Marx,

> An organisation of society which would abolish the presuppositions, and thus the possibility of haggling, would make the Jew impossible. His religious consciousness would dissolve like a stale vapour in the actually living atmosphere of society. On the other hand: if the Jew recognises his *practical* essence to be nullified and works towards its supersession, he will overcome his previous development, will contribute to *human emancipation* in general and will turn against the *supreme practical* expression of human self-estrangement.[6]

But, as Brecht rightly suspected, it was impossible for the Institute and especially for its paymasters to appeal directly for the overthrow of capitalism. His note continues:

> Marx took the Jew as he already existed historically, shaped by persecution and resistance, in his economic specialization, his dependence on available money (his need to buy his way out of or into something), his cultivation of ancient superstition etc. etc. And Marx advised him to emancipate himself (and also set an example for him). Adorno's face *can't* fall, a situation that suits him as a theorist. So I had to move on a little. I suggested that he should attack capitalism because it has *liquidated* haggling and in this way eradicated from trade all the imagination, all the humour, all the amusing struggle, in a word, all the spirit. I told Adorno about the contempt that the Chinese, who are far superior to the Jews in terms of their ability to haggle, feel for the western dealer who simply pays the price and goes away with his booty, with no human process, no battle of wits, first having taken place. If the presence of the seller is *so* superfluous, why not simply cave in?[7]

It was impossible for the Institute to take up Brecht's Marxist proposal, not least because anti-Semitism was seen as a projection, even as an illness. Actual reasons for such a prejudice were excluded from the field of the enquiry as they would have signified a weakening of its position and, given the reports about the National Socialists' policy of extermination, might have struck the Institute as irresponsibly frivolous.

Adorno's team developed what it called the F scale, which was designed to measure a Fascist potential. The people interviewed were divided into two basic groups, the high scorers, whose Fascist tendencies were judged to be high, and the low scorers, where the potential was found to be much lower. The team began its research at a time when Franklin D. Roosevelt was in office and the alliance with the Soviet Union was still intact. As a result, the climate of opinion in the United States was comparatively left-wing. Roosevelt's New Deal had introduced social democratic ideas to America for the first time, bringing with them state intervention in economics. In the left-wing camp, the Soviet Union was regarded not just as an ally in the war but as a land of socialist experiments, even if this last-named view was often accompanied by reservations. Anyone who drew attention even now to Stalin's crimes was a dangerous and unreliable member of the anti-Hitler coalition. This is the basic position that the study's judgments reflect.

The problem was that it sought to harness psychology to social research and political debate, so that it is impossible to absolve Adorno of the charge of being partly responsible for the fashionable 'psycho-history' that attempted, for example, to explain Japanese militarism in terms of cleanliness training – generally it was 'reactionary' positions that were analyzed by the researchers. Among the examples in *The Authoritarian Personality* are those people who declare their opposition to the power of the unions, with Adorno formulating a particular psychoanalytical hypothesis about this group. Their ideas, he believed, dated back

> to the lack of an adequately internalized identification with paternal authority during the Oedipus situation. It is our general assumption that the typical high scorers [those deemed to have a greater fascist potential] fear the father and try to side with him in order to participate in his power. The 'racketeers' are those who by demanding too much (though the subject wants as much himself) run the risk of arousing the father's anger – and hence the subject's castration anxiety.[8]

And there was not only an Oedipus complex but an 'anti-utopia complex'[9] for political realists and a 'usurpation complex' for Roosevelt's enemies – in other words, even political attitudes within the framework of the American constitution could be interpreted as mental disorders. The research that was carried out here into conservative and progressive views and preferences was no longer neutral. Rather, Freud's theory was used to interpret certain opinions as involuntary symptoms analogous to Freudian slips and dreams – with the underlying idea that they would reveal a hidden meaning to the expert. Psychoanalysis became an apparently scientific means of saying something about the normatively desirable and the pathological in politics. In future, people were not only to be simply reactionary but were also to have mental problems. The result was a kind of twentieth-century Inquisition.

The Authoritarian Personality may be seen as an attempt to gain cultural power by defining the enemy. And the enemy was the social middle ground that was now suspected of pathological tendencies. From now on, the patriotic and anti-Communist average American was to be regarded as a potential fascist. The sentence 'There will always be wars and conflicts, people are like that' figures here as one of the central indicators of the authoritarian personality who is motivated by prejudice. Anyone who agreed with it had little chance of being classed as 'low' on the F scale. For Adorno and his colleagues, the remark was a sign of a cynical affirmation of violence, as if anyone who agreed with the sentence was already identified as a bloodthirsty individual keen on fomenting war. Naturally the contemporary situation played a part here: the United Nations had only recently been founded, and the idea of 'one world' found a sympathetic echo among left-wing liberal Americans and those who had elected Roosevelt. Roosevelt's successor, Harry S. Truman, saw the end of the Second World War as the end of all wars. But this example shows that what was investigated by the study was not deep layers of the personality but momentary expressions of the *Zeitgeist*, statements of public opinion from which conclusions were intuitively drawn.

As an experiment, present readers are invited to take the test themselves and measure their own personality on the F scale: the result might be a salutary surprise. Few would escape entirely blameless from this sociological experiment. Take the statement: 'One should avoid doing things in public which appear wrong to others, even though one knows that these things are really all right.' Anyone who agrees with this would be classed as 'conventional'. 'Sciences like chemistry, physics and medicine have carried men very far, but there are many important things that can never possibly be understood by the human mind.' Agreement with this counts as a sign of 'authoritarian submission'. And if we agree with the statement that 'although leisure is a fine thing, it is good hard work that makes life interesting and worthwhile', we disqualify ourselves from being seen as sensitive, caring individuals.[10]

The picture is completed when we examine not only the questionnaire but also the statements made at interviews and Adorno's interpretation of them. A sailor, for example, declares: 'We have a good basis for our political system. The majority of people are not interested or equipped enough to understand politics, so that the biggest proportion of U.S. politics is governed by the capitalistic system.' The researchers dismissed the man as 'semi-educated' and 'confused'. For him, scoffed Adorno, 'the existence or nonexistence of capitalism in this country is simply a matter of "education".'[11] Another interviewee was asked whether he could imagine a legal limit on salaries preventing them from rising above 25,000 dollars: 'I don't believe in that,' was his simple answer, prompting Adorno to accuse him of 'a general pattern of reactionism'.[12] The same was true of a dislike of state intervention in the economy, a dislike that was – and is – by no means uncommon in the United States but which was deemed a symptom of the individual's Fascist values,[13] behind which presumably lay the older theory of the left wing, namely, that National Socialism was a type of rule popular with big business. Should the technology involved in producing the atom bomb be kept a secret from the Soviet Union? 'As is to be expected,' opined Adorno, 'also for psychological reasons, the high scorers are all out for secrecy. Here, as elsewhere, "they want to keep what they have".'[14]

Asked what was the greatest problem currently facing the United States, one of the participants replied: 'I think Russia.' Adorno saw in this dismissal of Russia an affinity with anti-Semitic stereotypes. It then turned out that the man in question was married to a Jewish woman, but this made no difference as Adorno now saw in his anti-Russian remarks a 'phenomenon of displacement'.[15] A woman declared her opposition to both Communists and Fascists: 'In Russia nothing is private, everything goes to one man. They have violent ways of doing things.' Adorno countered with superior irony: 'To the mind of this woman, the idea of political dictatorship has turned into the bogy of a kind of economic supra-individualism, just as if Stalin claimed ownership of her typewriter.'[16]

If the study dealt so extensively with the Soviet Union, it was because there was a suspicion that there were points in common between anti-Semitism and anti-Communism. This may, of course, have been true, but it should not have led to the conclusion that we find in *The Authoritarian Personality*, with its indirect whitewash of the Soviet system explicable only in terms of Stalin's role in the war's system of allegiances. Even Adorno's analysis of the rhetoric used by the popular radio broadcaster Martin Luther Thomas is notable for his invective against the speaker's anti-Communism: Thomas is said to have told 'horror stories' about Communism, to have delivered 'anti-Soviet tirades' and 'filled people with alarm at the vision of their imminent annihilation'.[17] In Adorno's study on *The Authoritarian Personality*, one interviewee declared that Communism may perhaps be useful in poorer countries, but not in America:

> The subject is not struck by the idea that a collectivistic economy might be easier in an industrially highly advanced, mature country, rather than more difficult. To him, communism is simply identified with enhancement of material productive powers through more efficient organization. He seems to be afraid of overproduction as if his concept would still make sense in an economy no longer dependent upon the contingencies of the market.[18]

On some occasions, anti-Communism is equated with sheer stupidity: 'High scorers who make less intellectual effort simply find communism not individualistic enough.'[19]

Adorno was engaged here in politically orchestrated sociological research in which certain opinions, all of which lay entirely within the democratic spectrum of the United States and which included criticism of Roosevelt and the unions, were branded as anti-democratic. The study bears all the hallmarks of its age: it was produced during the brief, anxious period between the left-wing Roosevelt era and the Cold War that broke out under Truman's presidency. By 1951 – the date of his study on 'Guilt and Defence' – Adorno, too, had changed his mind and now regarded the decision to arm against the Soviet Union as a sign of democratic dependability and maturity. Character defects were a question of the right moment.

13 'Perhaps we should go to Germany'

One of the first proponents of critical theory in post-war Germany was the sociologist Heinz Maus, a pupil of Adorno, Horkheimer and Karl Mannheim from the years before 1933, who later continued his studies with Hans Freyer. He was the first of the non-émigrés to make contact with Horkheimer even before the Institute for Social Research had returned to Germany and who as a result received the Institute's publications. He wrote to Horkheimer from the French zone on 27 July 1947, 'Benjamin's observations on the concept of history, Wiesengrund's remarks on enlightenment, your own work on the authoritarian state . . . have unsettled me, a state which from the outside shows itself as criticism, while isolating me, at least for the present.'[1] As the editor of *Umschau*, a cultural journal published in the French-occupied part of Germany, Maus was able to create an early forum for critical theory in post-war Germany. Among the articles that he published were pieces by Friedrich Pollock and Horkheimer, as well as Adorno's 'Philosophy and the Division of Labour' from *Dialectic of Enlightenment*. But Maus had no influence on the institutional aspects of the émigrés' return. Quite the opposite, in fact, as he had come under scrutiny by French counter-intelligence because of his contacts with a Russian officer, the national Bolshevist Ernst Niekisch, with whom he ran courses in imperialist theory at the Humboldt University in Berlin. Not until 1951, when he began to find the atmosphere in the East unduly oppressive, did he return to the West and become an assistant at the Institute. Conversely, Horkheimer's and Adorno's return to Europe was always intended to be a return to West Germany. The vice-chancellor of the Johann Wolfgang Goethe University, Walter Hallstein, who later gave his name to the Hallstein Doctrine that stated the Federal Republic's claim to represent all Germans, wrote to Felix Weil and Friedrich Pollock on 17 October 1946, stating that it was hoped to bring back to Frankfurt the Society for Sociology, which was responsible for running the Institute for Social Research as a foundation, and adding that he had been 'asked by the University to express the hope that in re-establishing its severed association it might see one of the most fundamental means of enabling our University to play its rightful part in the cultural tasks that are set us in Germany today'.[2] This invitation was compelling because the Institute, as we have seen, was a foundation that Felix Weil's father had established for the University. A month later Horkheimer thanked the 'infamously cunning man', as he called Hallstein in another letter,[3] for the 'kind invitation to resume our interrupted work'.[4] And he promised to look carefully into the question, at the same time asking for concrete information. In particular he raised the possibility of a return of three members of the Institute who had previously taught at the University: Pollock, Adorno and Horkheimer himself. A first step, wrote Horkheimer, might be guest lectures by the three of them in Frankfurt.

Almost a year later Horkheimer raised the question of a possible return in a letter to Paul Massing, a letter that is one of the most interesting of all those under discussion in that it reveals the American reactions to what was now a violent debate about the Germans' collective guilt and political responsibility. Massing's study of the prehistory of political anti-Semitism had appeared under Horkheimer's editorship in the series Studies in Prejudice. He had also written an article entitled 'Is Every German Guilty?' that had been published in the magazine *Commentary*. Horkheimer considered the debate on collective guilt to be fundamentally flawed and at the same time spoke out against Massing's 'sophistries in favour of his fellow countrymen and women', as he confided in Leo Löwenthal.[5] True, Horkheimer also dismissed the professions of guilt on the part of Karl Jaspers and Martin Niemöller as 'breast-beating contests', but only because he saw in them an expression of negative nationalism, a preventative form of self-defence. In general, Horkheimer refrained from apportioning guilt in any concrete sense: the 'social dynamic' in general was responsible, he argued, and there was only one way of overcoming the logical shortcomings of the abstract way of judging things, 'that of critical theory'. Massing's attitude, which Horkheimer described with gentle irony as 'the male championship of his compatriots', could not play a decisive role in critical theory, he concluded.[6]

There follows the decisive sentence: 'Perhaps we should go to Germany and work there amidst privations, but is it necessary to solicit understanding in view of what has happened?'[7] For Horkheimer, what had happened was evidently first and foremost the experiments conducted on human guinea pigs by German doctors, on which he planned to write an essay in October 1947. In February 1948 he announced his first reconnaissance trip to Germany in order to examine all the problems on the spot. These involved not only sorting out the legal situation but also rebuilding the Institute, which had been destroyed in the war, and seeing to its library. At the same time, an honorary professor-ship awaited him in Frankfurt. 'I was greeted respectfully by the vice-chancel-lor, the two deans and various others, saccharine, slippery as eels and hypo-critical,' he reported back to America.[8] 'They still don't know whether to see in me a relatively influential visitor from America or the brother of their victims, a brother whose thought is memory. They must decide in favour of the latter.'[9] During the summer of 1948, following his first concrete experiences of teach-ing, Horkheimer initially spoke of his wish to set up a 'branch' of the Institute. Once the objective possibility of a return had been raised, Horkheimer and his closest confidant, Friedrich Pollock, then began to discuss the matter in greater detail, discussions that can only be described as dramatic. In the first memo-randum that passed between them – and it was to be followed by many more – the two friends spoke of their 'decision to turn down the invitation from Frank-furt University'.[10] In spite of all the advantages listed here – a European setting and the material and professional recognition bound up with a professorship in Germany – there were also disadvantages, principal among which was the weight of teaching obligations. Behind this lay the idea of a vast study that would offer a summation of critical theory and that Horkheimer proposed to write. The memorandum also notes that a veto would be used if Adorno were to accept a position that prevented him from working for the Institute in future.[11] Nine days later a second memorandum came to the opposite decision: if they refused to return to Germany, they would have lost their chance entirely. At the same time they now had 'further dramatic proof of T.'s unreliability'[12] – 'T.' is Teddie, who evidently tended to support the idea of a return. By the next day a third memorandum was discussing the 'decision finally to abandon the professorship in Germany' and declaring the earlier resolve as the product of a passing mood. But that same day, the two writers decided 'to travel to Frank-furt for the summer term',[13] a resolve motivated by their wish to examine for themselves the possibilities of working fruitfully in Germany. This decision was then followed up in a further memorandum of 30 April 1949: 'In line with our pessimistic attitude towards the *extérieur* we are entirely reckoning on the pos-sibility that our visit will be a failure. We are already resolved to see this not as a defeat but to take it as an opportunity to begin a new life in L.A. with all the greater *courage et gaieté*, as we have planned.'[14] At this decisive stage in their dis-cussions, it was now only a question of examining the practical questions affecting their own livelihoods. Not until the summer of 1949, when an invita-tion was sent out to internationally acknowledged scholars, asking them to sign an appeal to re-establish the Frankfurt Institute, did Adolph Lowe, who had lost his professorship in Frankfurt in 1933, mention the political context in giving the reasons for his refusal: 'The institution that actually profits from the appeal is the University of Frankfurt am Main. And here I have to be categorical: not until this infamous institution has cleaned itself up shall I stand up and speak out in its favour.'[15] But in Frankfurt everything was going according to plan: Horkheimer, Pollock and Adorno were invited back, the Institute opened its new premises in 1951 – and Horkheimer was appointed vice-chancellor of the University.

There was really no alternative. Quite the opposite: enormous problems made it difficult for the Institute to continue its work in the United States, so that a return to Frankfurt seemed to be the best solution. A committee at Columbia University chaired by Arthur W. MacMahon had examined the Institute's work and on the basis of its evaluation the University's Department of Sociology recommended in March 1946 that the Institute, in the persons of Löwenthal, Massing, Marcuse, Neumann and Pollock, should be reorganized as a department of Paul Lazarsfeld's Bureau of Applied Social Research.[16] In this way the Institute's autonomy would be sacrificed to the favourite friends and enemies of empirical social research. Horkheimer reacted by severing his connections with Columbia. The alternative would have been simply to sustain a small circle of independent scholars using the foundation's funds and to publish a journal. But its recognition would have been uncertain without an institutional network and the natural circle of disseminators represented by a body of students.

If Horkheimer was able to tolerate life among the Germans – in other words, in the country to whose criminal policies one of his cousins had fallen victim – there were reasons for this that could be explained within the socio-philosophical framework of his theory, which was barely concerned with states and nations. Rather, the history of National Socialism was overshadowed by the concept of Fascism, and Fascism in turn was eclipsed by global diagnoses of modernity, the administered world and the end of the individual as the result of the end of the world of circulation. Horkheimer's writings reveal a curious abstraction of the National Socialist past within the wider fate of the world, even though Horkheimer himself repeatedly wrote against it. Once National Socialism had been defeated by military means, it was no longer in his view a specifically German period in history but a universal threat. When he spoke about Julius Streicher's anti-Semitic *Der Stürmer* in the 1950s, it was in connection with Soviet caricatures; and when he mentioned the Führer principle, it was in the context of psychoanalysis. And whenever he spoke about the camps, as he did in his essay 'Recollection', it was in connection with his indignation at experiments on animals.

Horkheimer's writings extend the meaning of the term 'Fascism' in a non-specific way, an extension that commentators often claim is first observable at the time of the student revolt. Above all, anti-Fascism was conceived in such a way that it could pass seamlessly into anti-Communism. Only as a result of this was Horkheimer able to gain his bearings in the Germany of Konrad Adenauer, whom he began to respect, increasingly so with the passing years. The Institute's attitude to former National Socialists is mentioned by Monika Plessner, the wife of the philosopher Helmuth Plessner, in her memoirs: 'A little man with a grey face bowed and looked at me silently with eyes that betrayed no interest. Horkheimer, who was by no means lacking in an instinct for power, had followed a famous example and appointed an administrative official with a dubious political past to act as his chief clerk.'[17]

We can carry out a crosscheck on the post-war Institute's decisive links with the West by recalling Herbert Marcuse's contemporary theses. Marcuse had no institute to run, and so he was able to speak of new revolutionary movements immediately after the war. His expert knowledge of Germany that he placed at the disposal of the American Office of Strategic Services had set out from the premise that he was producing propaganda for a specific class of people, a premise that suggested itself to him as a former member of the soldiers' soviet of November 1918. When he wrote his thirty-three theses for a new journal in 1947, Churchill had already delivered his speech in Fulton, in which he first spoke of the Iron Curtain, and George Kennan had advocated a policy of containing the Soviet Union. Marcuse saw the world divided into a neo-Fascist and a Soviet camp. Although the Soviet Union's foreign policy interests dominated Western Communist parties, he felt that it was possible to set out from the idea of an independent Communism in Germany. And it was here that 'theory' had a chance – as with Adorno, this invariably meant the Institute and its version of Marxism.

The theory, Marcuse went on,

> is allied to no anti-Communist group or line-up. The Communist parties are and remain the only anti-Fascist force. Its denunciation must be a purely theoretical one. It knows that the realization of the theory is possible only through the Communist parties and that it needs the help of the Soviet Union. This awareness must be contained in each of its concepts. More than that: in each of its concepts the denunciation of neo-Fascism and social democracy must predominate over that of the Communist parties.[18]

Horkheimer knew these theses and assured their author that he found them very interesting, but never wasted another word on them.[19] For in the era of the

Cold War this was not the way to rebuild an institute in West Germany. The fact that the Institute for Social Research had in the meantime performed a complete about-turn became clear by 1950 at the latest, when Adorno and Horkheimer spoke out against the manifesto of a 'peace committee' at the University: 'The appeal for peace and the outlawing of atomic weapons are a piece of Soviet propaganda that is everywhere aimed at misusing human emotions so that resistance is broken to the violence that emanates from the Soviet Union and that will not hesitate to unleash war if the tyrants in Moscow believe that they can win it.'[20] Anyone who used the language of pacificism and naïvely appealed for war to be proscribed was 'silently excluding the Red Army and its bemedalled generals; anyone who imagines the horrors of atomic war is knowingly or unknowingly covering up for the stewards and torturers who keep untold millions of slave labourers in concentration camps'.[21]

When the German Democratic Republic's cultural journal *Sinn und Form* published excerpts from *Dialectic of Enlightenment* in its inaugural issue in 1949 without troubling itself about questions of copyright, Adorno and Horkheimer wrote a letter of protest, distancing themselves from the publication in order not to jeopardize their return to the Federal Republic: 'At a time when the Institute for Social Research is being re-established at the University of Frankfurt, which we represent, we see ourselves obliged by the reappearance of the Institute's work in the eastern zone to declare explicitly that our research and our writings are in the sharpest possible contrast to the politics and doctrine that emanate from the Soviet Union.'[22] Marcuse's ideas about revolution and the conditions obtaining at the Frankfurt Institute could no longer be reconciled. But the conflict was merely postponed and broke out again in 1969, when Adorno became the butt of attacks on the part of student demonstrators who had chosen Marcuse as their idol.

Horkheimer gave his first lectures in Frankfurt during the summer term in 1949, but by the following winter he had invited Adorno to take his place.[23] A melancholy Teddie set off from Los Angeles on 11 October 1949, unsure what awaited him in Europe and how he would react to it. 'I'm sad to be travelling,' he wrote at this time. He had the feeling that he was 'the object of constellations, not really in control of myself'.[24] He broke his journey in Chicago, which struck him as 'the most inhuman of cities. At the same time there is the remarkably desolate aspect of the streets because the hundreds and thousands of white-collar workers who are concentrated in this quarter are all now confined in their skyscraper offices. Indescribable filth that blacks occasionally sweep from one corner into another.'[25] In New York he saw his mother again and was shocked to note how much she had aged. One sentence in particular stands out, the importance of which can scarcely be overstated: 'At the same time the knowledge of my mother's genius; that I have to thank her for everything in nature but do not feel it as such.'²⁶ He met not only Kracauer and Leo Löwenthal but also Paul Lazarsfeld and Eduard Steuermann and noted that Steuermann, like Schoenberg, was critical of *Doctor Faustus* and, above all, of *Philosophy of Modern Music*, which was said to be 'too nihilistic and too soon'.²⁷ Adorno crossed the Atlantic on the *Queen Elizabeth*. While on board he became friendly with a Norwegian diplomat and an art student by the name of Magda Brunner, 'who clearly preferred my Norwegian attaché to me', he noted in his disappointment: 'She was no doubt sleeping with him, but without causing me the least pain, just as I can feel no resentment for things that are simply bound up with the fact that I am middle aged [last two words in English in the original].'²⁸

But as soon as Adorno took his first step on French soil he felt his spirits rise and succumbed to a mood of euphoria that drove away all melancholy and sense of resignation. His journey through Brittany brought him back into contact with the sort of European countryside that he had so missed in the United States: 'The tall old eloquent trees, including birches. Villages, stone-built churches. Pathways with edges, not tarmacked. Lively, intelligent horses. A cow with the head of a comic. Conversation with the intelligent waiter.'²⁹ On his arrival in Paris he was able to identify with the spirit of the place in a way that had been impossible in Chicago, and so his return to Europe was also a voyage of rediscovery: 'The typical gesture in Paris – beyond all inefficiency, to dismiss every stupidity by means of the gesture of intelligence, in fact through language. Very much like myself. Finally, I don't need to be embarrassed to be as polite as I am.'³⁰ But he was shocked to discover in Paris just how much he missed Walter Benjamin. Even here, in a country that was relatively but pleasantly backward when compared with the advanced capitalism of the United States, he saw 'helpless and moving attempts to fraternize with America',³¹ but tradition remained steadfast: 'Before 12 o'clock Notre-Dame, through the people streaming out of the church. Mighty organ, incomparable light through the coloured windows, impression of an almost sombre historical greatness.'³²

Adorno travelled to Germany on an American military train and was surprised to note that he felt none of the expected emotion when setting foot in the country and seeing his place of birth again. 'During the journey to the guest house, of course, at dead of night, a terrible view of the west end of the city, parts of which were destroyed, while other parts were completely burnt out.'³³ Frankfurt's old town had been turned into a 'nightmare' – Adorno used the English word: Saint Catherine's Church, where he had been confirmed, had been destroyed, 'as had Agathe's Church of Our Lady'.[34] In the Bockenheimer Landstraße that led to the University, every second house lay in ruins – 'for Frankfurt, intact'.[35] The people he met seemed marked by 'servility and excessive zeal',[36] but were 'lackeys of the great powers rather than Nazis'.[37] On his first weekend back in Germany, he visited his beloved Amorbach, then made an arrangement to meet 'the very pretty Frau Otty Schultz' and spend 'a weekend in the Taunus. . . . Will it work out?'[38] An inhabitant of Frankfurt assured him that 'anyone who did not know about Auschwitz did not want to know about it,'[39] a thesis that Adorno very soon used as the basis of his investigation into the German mentality in his study of 'Guilt and Defence'. But among the earliest impressions of his ravaged homeland were also ones that completely unexpectedly attested to the survival of something older: 'The world has ended, but as in my childhood I recognized the differences between tram lines 1 and 4 by the fact that the former has two green lights, while the latter has one green and one white one. That has remained.'[40] Finally one notes that at the time of Adorno's return the economic upturn that had begun with the currency reform of June 1948 was already making itself felt: 'Frankfurt doesn't exist any longer, but life gives the impression of being *normal*,' he commented. 'Indescribable strength and energy of the German population.'[41]

Adorno's lectures on social theory during the winter term were an attempt to sketch out a new programme that brought together social philosophy and empirical research, a programme already implied by Horkheimer's directorship. It was enhanced by the experiences of his American radio study and his investigations into the authoritarian personality.[42] The first empirical and sociological study by the newly established Institute for Social Research, 'Group Experiment', tended in the same direction. Horkheimer, Monika Plessner recalled, wanted to know 'how people in Germany felt about National Socialism seven years after the war. And so students from the Institute, armed with the latest methods of empirical social research imported from America, including an ingenious "stimulus", were asked to conduct conversations with formal groups in Frankfurt and the surrounding area. These groups included societies and loose groupings, such as drinkers in a pub, and were chosen in such a way that it resulted in a more or less representative cross-section of the population.'[43] The approach was methodologically novel when compared to that of *The Authoritarian Personality*: opinions and attitudes were no longer established through individual interviews and questionnaires but in group discussions. The research took place in 1950 and 1951. Among the team involved in the exercise, the reader will find such famous names as the art philosopher and intendant Ivan Nagel and Ludwig von Friedeburg, who later became Minister of Culture for Hesse, the son of the Admiral Hans-Georg von Friedeburg who, together with Field Marshal Wilhelm Keitel, signed Germany's capitulation in the presence of the Soviet marshal Georgi Zhukov on 8 May 1945, and who took his own life shortly afterwards.

The range of themes covered by the study was extensive, but central to it was the question of the attitude to democracy on the part of the German population. The research was financed by the Office of the US High Commissioner for Germany. Anyone reading the study will see that its findings are entirely consonant with the interests of its sponsors. Indeed, its basic error is systematically to confuse the question of attitudes to National Socialism with that of attitudes to the Americans. Subjects of the experiment who wanted to substantiate their opposition to National Socialism were obliged at the same time to attest to their sympathy with the victors. Or, looked at another way, it seemed obvious to the researchers involved in the project that criticism of the Allies was synonymous with nostalgia for National Socialism. That this was a spectacularly false conclusion should have been clear from a glance at the attitude of Kurt Schumacher's Social Democratic Party, which certainly did not hanker after a return to dictatorship but which had not been slow to criticize such Allied measures as the dismantling of German industry and the catastrophic food shortages of 1947 and 1948. And it was not necessary to be a crypto-Fascist to reject the bureaucratic forms of de-Nazification – in his 1951 novel *The Questionnaire*, Ernst von Salomon enjoyed a huge success by making this very point. Salomon had been a member of the volunteer corps and had taken part in the attempt on the life of Walther Rathenau, the Weimar Republic's foreign minister. Although he leaned to the right, he had maintained his distance from the National Socialist regime and at the same time protected his Jewish wife. The majority of Germans could identify with him when he hit out at the absurdities of the re-education process.

But for Horkheimer and Adorno, any turn of phrase that was directed against the American post-war measures fuelled their suspicion that the person concerned was ill disposed to democracy as such. Adorno's contribution to the project was a qualitative analysis of the subject of 'Guilt and Defence'. 'The aim of the whole,' we read in the introduction, 'may be described as a contribution to research into "public opinion".'[44] The study took its place 'in the tradition of the American investigations that have used Freud's categories to throw so much light on social phenomena.'[45] On this occasion, too, Adorno believed that psychoanalytical statements had been empirically confirmed: 'Not only have we afforded individual proof of mechanisms such as projection, reaction-formation and repressed guilt feelings, all of which belong in the zone of the unconscious's defence by the ego, but we constantly came across examples of subjective opinion and the formation of opinion that very much demanded the use of such concepts by virtue of their irrational character and the fact that they flew in the face of objective reality. They require a psychoanalytical interpretation by dint of their very existence.'[46]

This group experiment was based on an idea of Horkheimer, with the discussions based on a fictional letter by a member of the American occupying forces, the so-called 'Colburn Letter', in which the soldier in question commented on the situation in Germany and the opinions and characteristics of the Germans. But the enquiry was anything but open in terms of its findings. As with *The Authoritarian Personality*, the authors divorced certain opinions from their real-life context in order to be able to interpret them as symptoms of a psychopathology. Once again psychoanalysis was used as a complementary science in the political struggle, its aim being not to interpret statements as part of a process of transference and countertransference but to provide snap judgments. Moreover, the younger members of the team of social scientists were all complete amateurs where Freud's theories were concerned, prompting Monika Plessner to comment on her experiences of her time in Frankfurt and to distance herself from events with a note of evident irony: 'Until very recently, psychoanalysis was a terra incognita for them, just as it was for me, not that this prevented them from peppering our conversations with a powerful dose of Freudian terminology. But when I admitted that words for colour in the scale of brown in statements by the participants in our conversations did not convince me of their anally based anti-Semitic personality structure, we all had a good laugh together.'[47]

Within the confines of the Institute it was believed that democracy in Germany was bound up with statements about 'guilt' that were narrowly circumscribed in terms of their contents. 'Guilt' was a very fluid term and was never more accurately defined in interpretations of the material but could embrace meanings as diverse as the German Reich's war guilt, the guilt of those who had carried out its policies of extermination and the day-to-day behaviour of the civilian population, in other words, their 'looking the other way', their acknowledged or disputed knowledge of the policies of extermination or their failure to offer any resistance. It was very much this vagueness that made it possible to raise the pressure at any given moment by drawing on the concept of guilt, with the result that every Allied measure both during the war and afterwards, as part of the occupying powers' policy, could be justified, if need be, in terms of blame. As a result, the researchers regarded as ideal the statement by a woman who declared: 'I at all times take my bombed-out house upon myself as penance for the great wrong that was done to innocent people.'[48] The interviewers themselves may not have been entirely blameless when it came to the ideological keenness of the climate in the group discussions: after all, they first had to prove that they had learnt their lesson and deserved forgiveness. It is again Monika Plessner who indicates the connections when reporting on her experiences with the students in Frankfurt:

> They spoke about Gretel Adorno with the greatest reverence. She had clearly been everyone's mother confessor. It was she, rather than Horkheimer or Adorno, who had granted them absolution from their venial political sins. It was never clear to me what criteria were used in selecting the young men to work on the group study. They had been in the Hitler Youth Movement and its junior version, they had also been Storm Troopers, one of them had even been in the SS, and they had then become soldiers. They knew other nations only from the perspective of conquerors or the defeated, they had returned to a ruined Germany from hospitals and prisoner-of-war camps, some of them lightly wounded, others more seriously so.[49]

One of the controversial issues raised by the experiment was the Treaty of Versailles of 1919, which had declared Germany uniquely guilty for the outbreak of the First World War. It was by no means only extremists who, following the signing of the treaty, felt that, in Thomas Mann's words, the Allies were attempting to foist 'the fate of Carthage on a respected and civilized nation of seventy million people'.[50] This was a sentiment shared by Germany's middle classes, too. Max Weber, who was one of the advisers to the German delegation, commented on the economic conditions attached to the treaty, describing them as 'so terrible and so cunning that, even if only half of them are accepted, it is like looking into a black hole with no ray of light, however remote'.[51] Ultimately even a witness as impartial as Sebastian Haffner came to the conclusion that the Germans would have been entirely right to feel the treaty as an insult and a diktat, 'and it would not even have needed the countless defamatory, discriminatory and bullying individual regulations with which the treaty was full to confirm them in their resolve "to shake off the fetters of Versailles". This resolve determined the whole of Germany's foreign policy between 1919 and 1939, under Weimar as under Hitler.'[52] And this was very much the sore point: every admission of a historical injustice or even of a political error in the Treaty of Versailles would have given a certain legitimacy to German attempts to revise it, including those made under the terms of Hitler's foreign policy, and this had

to be avoided at all costs in a study that was financed by the American occupying forces. Any reference to the injustice of Versailles was bound to be interpreted as a 'defence' against 'guilt', with the result that Adorno assumed that
statements critical of the treaty 'continued to reflect the cliché that was used
after 1918 by the whole of the nationalist reaction, not just by Hitler alone. The
fact that Hitler came to power is something for which the "shameful peace of
Versailles" is said to be to blame'.[53] Even earlier, when the Treaty of Versailles was
raised by Americans in interviews for *The Authoritarian Personality* ('The
treaty of Versailles was obviously unfair to them,' one interviewee claimed[54]),
Adorno speculated that the 'legend of the "unjust" treaty of Versailles' must
'feed on tremendous psychological resources' in non-German countries:
'unconscious guilt feelings against the established symbol of prowess . . . otherwise it could not have survived the Hitlerian war.'[55]

'In the defeated Germany,' Adorno began the section on 'The Period of
Famine', 'hunger reigned. Without American help it would have turned into a
disaster. This help is often forgotten, and in its place the "Yanks" are accused of
real or invented episodes of the early period of occupation.'[56] In this way the
actual content of any remarks made by interviewees who reported to contrary
experiences was relativized from the outset. One participant in the group
experiment interjected that 'the whole period of famine – thank God it lasted
only six months – was arranged from the top downwards.' Adorno's comment
on this was that

> there is something genuinely paranoid about the fact that experiences that
> do not fit into the pattern of persecution mania are remodelled in such a
> way that the system is correct after all. That the American soldiers were not
> inhuman is something that the participants in the experiment can see for
> themselves, but they categorically refuse to concede that there was no obli-
> gation on the victor to help the Germans after all that had happened or that
> the supplies that were available in the country in the early months of 1945
> would almost certainly not have been enough to meet this obligation. They
> want to feel persecuted and tormented and so they invent a command from
> on high, one from mysterious powers, allowing them to combine their agree-
> able experiences of the soldiers, their memory of the hunger that they
> genuinely suffered and their displacement of their own guilt on to others.[57]

Adorno interpreted the participants' statements in such a way that they are
bound to appear as irrational paranoid reactions. The phrase 'arranged from
the top downwards', with its apparent reference to a hierarchy of commands
within the occupying powers, was bound to strike him as risible because he

misinterpreted it as a belief in 'mysterious powers'. Above all, however, Adorno's own interpretation of what had happened lacked any sense of internal logic. On the one hand, the good will of the occupying forces was affirmed (it was simply that there were insufficient supplies), while on the other the absence of this good will was justified after the event (in view of Germany's crimes, there was no obligation to help). As a result the actual help that was given was bound to seem an act of mercy that could be interpreted only on the strength of a fundamentally humanitarian outlook but which, in itself, when judged by the enormity of Germany's guilt, was not compelling. Here, it may be added, there may have been a rational nucleus to the rejection of guilt on the part of many participants in the group experiment. Anyone who had to consider that a confession of guilt might be used, if necessary, to justify a new famine policy was bound to think twice about what he or she said.

For it is beyond doubt that the famine suffered by the Germans in the immediate post-war period was the result of a deliberate policy. It was not a lack of food supplies that was the cause but a refusal to allow the Red Cross's relief supplies to be received by the defeated country. The minutes of the Potsdam Conference had made it clear that the living standards of the Germans were to be kept low. Urgent appeals from the International Red Cross to allow them to deliver relief supplies were turned down. Donations from the Red Cross were refused by the military authorities during the winter of 1945/6, and the relief organizations were told to send them to other parts of Europe that needed help 'even though large Irish and Swiss donations had been specifically earmarked for Germany', as we read in a study by Alfred de Zayas.[58] Not until March 1946 could donations reach the American zone, not least thanks to the intervention of British intellectuals such as Bertrand Russell and Victor Gollancz – the latter had published a polemic under the title *The Ethics of Starvation* that caused something of a stir in the West.

A further subject of controversy was the situation of prisoners-of-war immediately after the German capitulation. During the summer of 1945 the situation was determined by the fact that Switzerland, which had been the protecting power of German prisoners-of-war up to 8 May 1945, the day on which the surrender was signed, was now excluded, a step that was justified by the Allies on the grounds that the German Reich no longer existed. In short, the prisoners-of-war were without a protecting power, with the result that they were deprived of the right to inform independent observers about their situation. Secondly, the prisoners were divided into new categories. Not only were there prisoners-of-war who were still covered by the terms of the Geneva Convention, but also two new groups, 'surrendered enemy persons' and 'disarmed enemy persons', who simply fell outside the Convention. Members of the civilian population in Germany who gave food to prisoners-of-war were punishable by death. The exact number of prisoners-of-war who starved to death is contested by historians. Be that as it may, the way in which the American and French prisoners-of-war were fed and accommodated was such that people were soon drawing open comparisons with the Nazi camps. The psychoanalyst Alexander Mitscherlich, who later conducted research into the mentality of prisoners returning home, has the following to say on the subject: 'That they were inhumanely treated, that they were forced to starve under wretched living conditions and that they were tortured is seen as unjust by the prisoners, a crime against humanity that puts them in the same category as the victims of the concentration camps. And it leads to the conclusion that "the others" do exactly the same as that for which they are blamed.'

Mitscherlich did not question the veracity of the accounts from the camps but merely criticized the resultant attempt at self-exoneration. This was not true of Adorno. The question of guilt came up in the group experiment, where he mentions the claim that 'the Americans treated prisoners-of-war brutally'[59] and goes on to repeat the assertion of one particular deserter, who was in fact merely repeating what was common knowledge after 1945: 'What happened next was more than terrible, and I can imagine that when people here speak about concentration camps, no one in a concentration camp here can have experienced anything worse than what they did to us.'[60] Adorno's trick in invalidating this statement (the only remark on the subject that is mentioned in the study) consists in revealing the speaker as a dyed-in-the-wool National Socialist, which he probably was in any case, for he later goes on to complain that he and his comrades were forced to watch a film on the Nazi camps. In this way Adorno succeeded in shifting the facts into the area of a projection. A situation which Mitscherlich, presumably drawing on his practical experience as a therapist, had depicted in a subtly differentiated way was not a problem for Adorno. For him, there was no knot that needed to be untied.

Adorno adopted the same approach to the subject of Dresden. A former member of the German Airforce reported on the Allied attack on the city (the name is never spelt out but invariably replaced by three dots) and ventured the view that this was a war crime as there was no military need to destroy the city. Adorno accused him of indulging in 'precise calculations',[61] thereby invalidating the remark, for 'calculations' were beneath the level of moral reflection. Another speaker is then quoted who claimed to have seen members of the armed forces in Dresden, thereby freeing the attack from any suspicion of a crime. Considerations of justice, which one is entitled to expect from a keen mind like Adorno's, played no part in the discussion. No doubt this omission stemmed from fear for the future of German democracy, but it still remains a gap in his moral response.

In lectures that he gave fifteen years later under the title 'On the Doctrine of History and Freedom', Adorno came back to the question of the significance of the destruction of German towns and cities. On this occasion his aim was to show that the 'overall social process', by which he meant capitalist modernization, was winning through in the longer term. The air attack on Germany served to elucidate this point:

> There is no doubt that the bombing raids on German towns and cities during the last war had absolutely nothing to do with slum-clearance measures and the 'Americanization' of the urban landscape or with advances in hygiene and the like. Perhaps because the old town centres, some of which dated back to the Middle Ages, were destroyed and burnt down on account of their greater combustibility, their effect none the less amounts to that remarkable attempt to bring German towns and cities closer to their American counterparts, not least in terms of their appearance, something that is all the more striking in that we simply cannot assume any so-called historical influence here.[62]

The tone of this lecture is not easy to interpret. On the one hand, the philosopher lays claim to a cool, universal-historical overview before which the details relating to events and their meaning pale into insignificance. Capitalist modernism arises quite literally like a phoenix from the ashes of Germany, too, once the final obstacles have been removed. But there was more to be said on the subject, and Adorno sensed this, hence his use of the words 'destroyed and burnt down'. One notices a moment of nervousness, but it is soon over. The lecturer refuses to explore the implications of his remark but returns to his agenda.

No one can deny that in the material included in 'Guilt and Defence', Jews and 'displaced persons' of the post-war period are sometimes described with a degree of prejudice and hostility that is positively frightening, but no less clear is the interpreter's carefree tendency to subsume under the suspicion of anti-Semitism remarks that do not belong there. The fact that the social research conducted here operated in the spirit of the Americans is evident above all from the question of German rearmament. At the height of the Cold War, when Korea had become a tinderbox, German rearmament was in the interest of the United States. Anyone who spoke out against it in the Federal Republic, as did the later Federal President Gustav Heinemann, may have had entirely honourable motives, but such remarks were suspect when they were part of the material analyzed by Adorno.

As was always the case when Adorno fell back on psychoanalytical interpretations, these interpretations failed to convince even those who were sympathetic to his aims. Just as Schoenberg rejected Adorno's psychopathological critique of Stravinsky, so on this occasion it was the philosopher Helmuth Plessner who remained unconvinced. Plessner, who had filled in for Adorno during his period with the Hacker Foundation in the United States, shared his colleague's reservations concerning stick-in-the-muds, but he found the study's psychological interpretations untenable. When he saw the first results in Frankfurt, he told Horkheimer: 'To be honest, Max, I'm fairly disappointed. The people produce virtually only excuses or the old clichés. And I don't care for the amateurish approach to psychoanalysis in the way the material is assessed.'[63]

14   The Frankfurt School

It is impossible to return to a country if one does not identify with it, no matter how problematical and how circumscribed that sense of identity might be. Assessments of their old homeland naturally played a major role in the correspondence between Thomas Mann and Adorno, of whom the latter chose to return to Germany, while the former spent the final years of his life in Switzerland. Adorno evidently blossomed in his contacts with his German students: 'Physically speaking, I feel exceptionally well, three times as fresh and fit for work as in the West,' – in other words, California – 'no longer suffering from headaches – a strange response to his homeland on the part of someone who might be termed a professionally homeless man.'[1] In 1949 he gave a lecture under the title 'Culture Resurrected'.[2] And certain passages in this lecture, which recorded his early impressions of his return to Germany, sounded so plainly optimistic that many listeners were puzzled by them. Adorno began by admitting that he had been pleasantly surprised by the intellectual climate in Germany and had had to revise his ideas concerning the country's descent into barbarism. 'The relationship with matters of the mind, understood in the widest sense of the term, is intense. It seems to me that it is greater than in the years leading up to the National Socialists' seizure of power. At that time the struggles over power politics supplanted everything else.'[3] Needless to say, Adorno's positive view of the situation was not his last word on the subject: even in 1949 he was already criticizing the Germans' lack of readiness for Utopia and for post-national commitment – this eternal complaint on the part of the eternal left. The Swiss critic Max Rychner approvingly took up Adorno's remarks, so that the latter was then left wondering whether he had ultimately made too many concessions.

While Adorno slowly and, in the case of his students, benevolently familiarized himself with the reality of the Federal Republic, Thomas Mann remained at loggerheads with his native country: 'Your comments on the country where you are currently working' – thus the cool formulation – 'took an excessively pro-German line – apparently. I knew how to read them, but so did Rychner.'[4] On another occasion he wrote to his friend: 'I do not begrudge you the Germans, but at the same time I feel only too well the satisfaction that your desire for a chance to be effective finds an outlet there.'[5] All too often in his later letters Mann reminds the reader of a sclerotic prophet of doom fulminating against the Coal and Steel Union between the Federal Republic and France, which he claimed would foster German hegemony, and against the 'Fascism' of McCarthy's policies in the United States, from which he had fled to Switzerland. In such cases it was often Adorno who maintained an impartial view of reality. In one of his letters to Mann, for example, he described as a sign of barbarism the fact that the left – notably Carl von Ossietzky's *Die Weltbühne* – had not decided between Heinrich Brüning, an authoritarian man of the centre, and Hitler before 1933: 'even in negative matters' it was important 'to draw subtle distinctions'.[6]

Then, again, one has the impression that Adorno was unable to escape from the keen competition with Mann. Apart from Ernst Jünger,[7] it was Heidegger and Wagner who unsettled him the most: 'Do you know, by the way, that attempts are being made to reopen Bayreuth, and have you considered what's to be done about it? It seems to me that Bayreuth, along with the re-acceptance of Heidegger, is one of the most worrying symptoms, to the extent that people are not prepared to examine more closely the primary factors that have emerged here.'[8] In fact only a few years were to pass before Adorno himself began to give lectures in Bayreuth and write articles for the programme booklets. Meanwhile, the much criticized Ernst Jünger had just taken a step in Adorno's direction, as the latter reported to Gershom Scholem: immediately after the war Jünger had sent word to him through Eduard Roditi to say 'how much Benjamin meant to him'.[9] Adorno was immensely successful in the new Federal Republic – far more so than he himself can have expected. In a letter written during the early 'fifties to a friend in Bremen, Friedrich Wilhelm Oelze, Gottfried Benn reports on a lively meeting with Adorno, when he had been filled with admiration for the eminent philosopher: 'I got to know Herr *Adorno*, who gave another lecture, a *highly* intelligent, not very prepossessing Jew but with the intelligence that is really only found in Jews, good Jews. We rushed up to each other, as it were, only he is still very self-centred, vain and – albeit in the legitimate sense – in need of admiration.'[10]

But it was not only the human contacts and growing recognition to which Adorno responded so positively. Anyone who upheld the thesis that the whole was untrue was operating within the purview of Hegelian philosophy, for the doctrine of critical theory concerning the untrue whole was a reversal of Hegel's proposition, 'But the true is the whole'. Anyone who thought with Hegel against Hegel had to think in the language of Hegel. Adorno spoke of the 'metaphysical surplus of the German language,'[11] and when at the same time he warned against imagining that this feature of the German language 'already guarantees the truth of the metaphysics that it suggests or of metaphysics in general',[12] it was impossible not to hear in this an intellectual and affective attachment to his mother tongue, a language which he claimed had had a decisive impact on his resolve to return to Germany. It would not have been easy to renew his links with classical German philosophy in the United States, making it inevitable that in the longer term he would have had to adapt to either the analytical or the pragmatic tradition of Anglo-Saxon philosophy. But his own philosophy would have lost something in consequence. Adorno was clear in his own mind that even 'individual and very precise terms such as that of the spirit, the moment, experience and all that resonates with them in German' could not be translated into another language without doing violence to them.[13] Just as in music he clung to a German tradition that had developed historically and that could be located in Vienna, so the same was true on a linguistic level. The German language, he argued, had a particular affinity with philosophy, especially to its speculative elements – in other words, the very elements that were vaguely suspected in the West of being dangerous:

> Historically speaking, the German language, as part of a process that still requires proper analysis, has become capable of expressing something about phenomena that goes beyond their mere essence, positivity and givenness. One can gain the most striking picture of this specific quality of the German language from the almost prohibitive difficulty involved in translating into another language the most demanding philosophical texts such as Hegel's *Phenomenology of Spirit* and his *Science of Logic*. German is not simply the signification of fixed meanings but has retained more of its power of expression than is evident to anyone who did not grow up among western languages and to whom those languages are not second nature.[14]

Horkheimer had begun his career with two studies on Kant's *Critique of Judgment*, and he spent a great deal of his life researching collective prejudice. Although he conceded that it was no doubt not fortuitous that anti-Semitism had had the most terrible consequences in Germany, apart from the first group experiment study, this finding did not play a major role in the development of theories within the Institute for Social Research. In its Horkheimerian version, critical theory

Adorno and his wife Gretel in Sils Maria in 1964

became a programme designed to introduce a moral tone to science: 'That which is good and bad,' he once wrote, 'can be derived only from theory.'[15] Even for the young Horkheimer, theory had been conceivable only as the moralizing force of society, a kind of secular priesthood, and he returned to this trend after discarding the Marxist terminology of the 'thirties. This also explains the tone of Horkheimer's post-war speeches, which expressed the hope that one could act from insight and that the right kind of action followed from the theory. Time and again he appealed to Spinoza's *Ethics* – it was the first book on philosophy that he read as a young man – and he called on his students to 'do things better in the sense that emerges from the critical account'.[16] It was the rhetoric of a civil religion that Horkheimer adopted, a rhetoric that belonged to the Germany of the post-war period when the country's spiritual crisis had to be overcome with the help of fixed bearings. One can even suppose that without these rhetorical exaggerations from the language of a civil religion it would not have been possible to encourage students to think for themselves again. In short, Horkheimer must be judged at this stage in his life by the standards of other priest figures of the post-war period, figures such as Romano Guardini, Martin Buber and Albert Schweitzer.

Adorno's impact was different from Horkheimer's. It rested above all on the fact that he could be expected to provide reliable comments in the spirit of a greater liberalization and modernization of the new Federal Republic on a whole series of cultural and political topics, including Surrealism, functionalism, sexual taboos and the current legal situation. While Horkheimer moved further and further away from contemporary concerns, Adorno set store by the most varied journalistic activities geared to the standards of modernity. And while Horkheimer removed more and more bricks from the edifice of critical theory, Adorno remained caught up within an orthodoxy associated with the doctrines that had determined his youth, namely, psychoanalysis and Marx's analysis of capitalism. And this brought its own problems. Clemens Albrecht has put forward the theory that only when Adorno took over the running of the Institute in 1960 could one speak of a 'newly intense Marxist orientation'.[17] In 1959 Jewish cemeteries had been daubed with anti-Semitic slogans and the public at large was confronted with the resurgence of National Socialism in Germany. Horkheimer noted at this time: 'I have an idea about the meaning behind this action. It originates with Nasser and his Nazi advisers, behind whom we may assume a number of groups in Germany.'[18] This conspiracy theory was by no means as wrong-headed as it might seem at first sight, for we now know that the German Democratic Republic's Ministry for State Security had a hand in the matter and was blackening the Federal Republic's name in international circles.

It was now that the Frankfurt Institute began to exercise a new round of influence. Adorno wrote two studies, 'What is the Significance of "Reappraisal of the Past"?'[19] and 'Education after Auschwitz',[20] in which he summed up his earlier ideas on the authoritarian personality. Clemens Albrecht has spoken of the process involved in 'laying the intellectual foundations of the Federal Republic', a process that began at this time with an intellectual reappraisal of Germany's National Socialist past.[21] Adorno's diagnosis sought to forge a link between socio-psychological and socio-theoretical findings, speaking of the bourgeois coldness that was typical of a competitive society and of the fetishization of technology – one of the subjects involved in the American research for *The Authoritarian Personality* had declared 'I like nice equipment' and was promptly accused of a reified, manipulative consciousness. The fact that 'Fascism lives on,' Adorno wrote in 1959, stemmed from the 'continuing existence of the objective social preconditions that led to Fascism'.[22] It was the economic system that kept people in a state of dependency and mental immaturity. And so his students were delegated with the task of carrying on the struggle against capitalism – with the subliminal promise that in this way they could requite the sins of their fathers. It was a trap. For the students of 1968 had scarcely heard the message and made a serious start on the anti-capitalist struggle when a new generation of historians appeared and showed them that Fascism and National Socialism were characterized not by too much capitalism and market economy, but by too little, and that the rebels, far from dealing with the burden of guilt, had merely avoided it once again.

The impact of the Frankfurt School was not limited to social research. A social theory that simultaneously aimed to embrace economic theory and philosophical criticism and took in wide-ranging areas of human existence, from instructions in self-observation such as are found in Adorno's own *Minima moralia*, to rules on the right way to listen to music and, finally, to psychoanalysis, had always been more than one hypothesis among many but offered integral self-understanding, an intellectual programme about the meaning of life, a milieu. Dedicated to Max Horkheimer, *Minima moralia* appeared in 1951 and marked the beginning of Adorno's great public impact in the Federal Republic. Subtitled 'Reflections from Damaged Life', it offered an account of social injustice that unfolds here in individual scenes in the manner of a panorama. According to the dedication, Adorno's aim was to proffer his reader a 'melancholy science',[23] while Gershom Scholem, one of its first readers, spoke of a 'negative theology'.[24] Its best-known maxim – 'Wrong life cannot be lived rightly'[25] – undoubtedly points in this direction. Adorno wanted to set out from the philosophical tradition of 'teaching the good life',[26] but as a Marxist he found himself confronted not by life but by its 'estranged form' and by 'the objective powers that determine individual existence even in its most hidden recesses'.[27] Our 'perspective of life has passed into an ideology which conceals the fact that there is life no longer'.[28] It was not philosophy that had shown people the nullity of the subject but the concentration camp.

In the course of these aphorisms and vignettes, Adorno justifies his own life form as a 'hothouse plant'. Resisting the traditional division of professional lives, he sees his life devoted equally to composition, musicology, literary criticism, sociology and philosophy. And the subject of this life form also exercises the office of public critic: *Minima moralia* is a programmatical text, an apologia for the intellectual. What is an intellectual? The word arose in France at the time of the Dreyfus affair and describes the educated person in his public function as a critic. In Adorno's case everything else was subsumed under this task. And if, in the opening section of the book, he speaks of the 'so-called intellectual professions', meaning those of the artist and the scholar, the word has already undergone a slight but decisive change of meaning, as neither the artist nor the scholar is a priori an intellectual. Rather, the intellectual is someone who asserts the precedence of intellectual and political commitment over artistic creativity and research.

And so the book begins with a reflection on the role of the intellectual, who is introduced as the son of well-to-do parents – the autobiographical element is barely concealed. He is condemned to loneliness. Nor is he is supported by a university. Rather, Adorno believes, those who 'bear the distasteful title of colleagues' are the most envious of him, asserting their professionalism and 'domineering competence' in the face of his intellectual independence.[29] And it is not without a certain coquettishness that Adorno mentions his own precociousness. It is still the classic workers' movement on which he can rely in the future: 'Even solidarity, the most honourable mode of conduct in socialism, is sick.'[30] The word 'solidarity' had become no more than a form of extortionism since the Hitler-Stalin Pact. 'There is even an echo of this in the sententious language of the worker who wants, as a Socialist, to "learn something", to partake of the so-called heritage, and the philistinism of the Bebels lies less in their incomprehension of culture than in the alacrity with which they accept it at face value, identify with it and in doing so, of course, reverse its meaning.'[31] Groups belonging to the political and artistic avant-garde no longer walk in step with each other. Instead, isolated individuals now have the task of bringing their concerns back together again. At the same time, the pieces that make up *Minima moralia* make it clear that the writer has only the highest opinion of his own gifts. Conversely, it is the course of the world itself that still reveals a hostile tendency in the tiniest episodes: 'The person one wishes most anxiously to keep away from one's beloved will unfailingly invite her, be it from a distance of three thousand miles, thanks to well-meaning introductions, and bring about ominous acquaintances.'[32] From here it is not far to the assumption that there is a 'sadism latent in everyone',[33] a sadism evoked in more and more new scenes, both actual and invented, extending from mere tactlessness and a fridge door that is closed too noisily to massive injustice.

The third part of the book includes autobiographical reflections on one of Adorno's love affairs in California in the 1940s. But here too the author portrays himself as someone to whom an injustice was done: 'Someone who has been offended, slighted, has an illumination as vivid as when agonizing pain lights up one's own body.'[34] His passion for the unnamed woman – she wrote filmscripts in Hollywood – is examined from every aspect before he finally returns to his lawful wife:

> The dialectician knows the unhappiness and vulnerability of the ageing spinster, the murderousness of divorce. But in anti-romantically giving objectified marriage precedence over ephemeral passion which is not preserved in a shared life, he makes himself the mouthpiece of those who practise marriage

at the expense of affection, love what they are married to, that is, the abstract property-relationship.[35]

As in *Dialectic of Enlightenment*, the injustice done to women by patriarchal society is a major theme of the collection. For long stretches it reads like Kierkegaard translated into the language of Marxism. Certainly, this is true of the thesis that 'the sickness proper to the time [consists] precisely in normality'[36] and of the belief that 'the only objective way of diagnosing the sickness of the healthy is by the incongruity between their rational existence and the possible course their lives might be given by reason'.[37] But Adorno's own – altogether Proustian – sensitivity is celebrated with narcissistic abandon. The construction of his position as a cool and superior observer is at odds with the analytical schemata that the book has to offer in the form of Marxism and psychoanalysis. Today's reader may be struck not only by the lack of genuine observations on America but may gain only an inadequate idea of the author's empirical existence: but if Adorno had been identical with the 'implied author', he would no doubt have been prevented from writing the book by sheer unhappiness.

The Institute for Social Research attracted many of the most gifted sociologists of the younger generation. They included not only Ludwig von Friedeburg and Jürgen Habermas, who were later to inherit the mantle of critical theory, but also scholars who subsequently went their own way: Gerhard Schmidchen, Friedrich Tenbruck, Erwin K. Scheuch and Ralf Dahrendorf all worked for a time in Frankfurt. Dahrendorf in particular was examining class conflicts in modern societies and thought that his work would advance here. 'On 1 July 1954,' he reports, 'I set foot for the first time in the new, purpose-built structure on the Senckenberganlage in Frankfurt, which the Institute for Social Research had chosen as its headquarters following its return from exile in America. For a young sociologist, no first job could have been more distinguished than that as Professor Horkheimer's assistant.'[38] He was given a friendly welcome by Adorno, albeit with the request that he edit the tiresome material from the group experiment. The Institute wanted to make amends for the débâcle caused in the University by the first public presentation of the material. But Dahrendorf soon realized that any attempt to do this was a waste of effort: 'The group experiment (over which many others were to cudgel their brains) was ultimately not particularly profitable from a methodological point of view or even in terms of its content. . . . Where anything new had been attempted, it proved unsuitable; and what was suitable produced few new findings.'[39] Soon Dahrendorf himself became the Institute's sociological interpreter; harking back ironically to the early Marx, he speaks of a 'holy family' that functioned as a point of reference for a generation lacking all sense of direction.

Friedrich Tenbruck was another writer who knew the Institute from the inside and who has drawn attention to the peculiarly powerful position of Adorno and Horkheimer that resulted from their moral authority as émigrés:

> It was different for the students, who found themselves weighed down by the inherited guilt of being German, a point on which their politicians prefered to maintain an embarrassed silence. And so they turned to the Institute for Social Research in their attempt to be enlightened about the disaster and to be assured that it would not be repeated, but soon they found themselves appointed initiates, absolved of authoritarian inherited guilt and finally called upon to act as fellow guardians. More and more generations came here in search of absolution from their guilt at being German and were freed from self-reproach and safeguarded against the complaints of foreigners, all of which was achieved without the need to confess but through a profession of faith in the school and its community.[40]

For his part, Dahrendorf saw how the directors were engaged in playing various roles, saw the 'ambiguity of "critical theory" and the ability, while adapting to a market economy and a western orientation, to give the impression of being in fact anti-capitalist and anti-American'.[41]

Adorno and Horkheimer struck Dahrendorf as intellectual gurus whose conversations must occasionally have seemed unintentionally comical to outsiders:

> 'An intelligent student had previously told me that Aristotle's relationship between *dynamis* and *energeia* reminded him of Einstein's relation between "mass" and "energy".' The speaker was Horkheimer, who wanted to talk not about the student but about himself and who therefore added the punchline: 'Then I said to him, "Yes, but with Einstein energy is also mass!"' At this, Adorno replied with all the signs of reverential delight in the profundity of this insight: 'Max, you're right, with Einstein it's an equation!' The two men were literally close to embracing one another.[42]

On another occasion, when the Institute was planning a kind of relaunch of its journal and had already acquired an article by the art sociologist Arnold Hauser that talked a lot about class, Dahrendorf wondered about the precautions that were taken in discussing this difficult subject. Horkheimer, he recalled, had wanted to remove the unfortunate word: '"Why class? It's not necessary to shock people deliberately." (Brecht's *Tui* novel wittily includes a section in which the "argument of the Tuis over the existence of classes" is resolved by a competition organized by the emperor that decides that there are no classes.) As it was my intention to write my postdoctoral dissertation on social classes and class conflicts, I drew my own conclusions.'[43] After barely a month Dahrendorf decided that Frankfurt was the wrong place for him – he told Horkheimer's wife that the reason for this was because 'all manner of possible and impossible chores' had been foisted on him.[44] 'We should not grieve unduly over Dahrendorf,' Horkheimer wrote to Adorno on 24 August 1954. 'If he runs off because of a better offer, we shan't have lost too much.'[45]

An additional reason for the renegade researcher's decision to leave was that he was 'no longer all that amused' by the directors' treatment of their fellow workers. A refugee from the German Democratic Republic, Heinz Maus, was given a post 'but on a reduced salary and with no visible presence'.[46] Much the same later happened to Jürgen Habermas, whose political views met with violent opposition on Horkheimer's part, leading Dahrendorf to comment coolly that 'his interests in any case forced him to undertake his postdoctoral dissertation with professors who were less intimidated by the zeitgeist'.[47] During the 1950s Horkheimer's political circumspection turned into massive mistrust, so that he believed, for example, that Paul Massing, a colleague whom he had formerly valued very highly, had been asked by the American authorities to sound him out and blacken his name as someone who could not be relied on in the Cold War. Everything that could be construed as a reference to the teachings of the class struggle was henceforth to be expunged from the Institute's publications. In a long letter that he wrote to Adorno from Montagnola on 27 September 1958, Horkheimer gave vent to his fury against Habermas, his attack on his assistant not only capturing the spirit of the early Federal Republic but, in human terms, constituting a document of wounding causticity, a tone motivated, perhaps, by Horkheimer's fear over his American citizenship, which he had lost and which he continued until 1963 to attempt to regain.

Habermas had published an article 'On the Philosophical Discussion about Marx and Marxism' in the *Philosophische Rundschau* in 1957. Horkheimer read into it a theory of revolution, while at the same time claiming that Habermas had been a 'student propagandist' in the campaign against nuclear weapons. There was a 'danger', he argued, that Habermas would 'set the tone at the Institute'.[48] Revolution for Habermas was 'a kind of affirmative idea, an absolute that has been put out of its misery'. If new revolutionary movements were to be formed, Horkheimer went on, liberation would not be the result, but a new terroristic tyranny – very much in the spirit of the classical doctrine of the cycle of constitutions. What should be defended, therefore, was not the sublation of philosophy in revolution but 'the last surviving remnant of bourgeois civilization'.[49] In writing this, Horkheimer had forgotten and repressed his own past. Now it would look as though the Institute for Social Research had never been anything more than a refuge for liberal Western humanism. 'What concerns H[abermas] is Marxist theory and practice. Even during the years when National Socialism was on the increase, during the Third Reich, we knew that the idea of salvation through revolution was futile. To proclaim that this is now something topical, without reflecting on the consequences of "being addressed", the failure of which H. criticizes in Marx, can only encourage the work of the gentlemen in the East on whom he declares war but to whom it would in fact be handed over or else it would play into the hands of the Fascists within the country.'[50] The end of Horkheimer's letter finds him using the same Marxist concepts as those that Habermas had employed, but now they are maliciously caricatured: 'No doubt he has a good, nay, brilliant career ahead of him as a writer, but he would cause great harm to the Institute. Let us proceed to sublate the present situation and in a spirit of kindness persuade him to sublate and realize his philosophy somewhere else.'[51] Adorno added a number of critical marginalia to this letter, sometimes question marks, on other occasions the objections 'Too quickly!', 'No, unjust!' and 'Well –',[52] but above all noting that Habermas 'probably did *not*' mean a naïve theory of revolution. But the situation was virtually beyond hope. Habermas wrote his postdoctoral dissertation in Marburg, where his supervisor was Wolfgang Abendroth, a left-wing socialist political scientist. His thesis, *Structural Change in Public Life*, was to become a classic, while Habermas himself went on to become Horkheimer's successor in Frankfurt – a nice touch of irony on the part of history.

The more that actions are guided by the certainty that they fulfil a moral mission, the greater is the tendency to rise above bourgeois customs in practical matters, to refuse to compromise and not to be squeamish about one's choice of means. A good historico-philosophical conscience is the best possible basis for everyday Machiavellianism. Many of the staff at Frankfurt University and the Institute for Social Research were made to feel this by Horkheimer and Adorno. Leo Löwenthal, for example, who loyally stood guard over the Institute's journal and who had remained in the United States at the end of the war, approached the Institute in the late fifties in an attempt to assert his pension rights. The Institute ignored his appeal and a lawyer was called in. From then on, Löwenthal was ostracized by the staff in Frankfurt. Not even Adorno could escape from the maelstrom of this conflict. Löwenthal wrote to him on 6 September 1963, congratulating him on his sixtieth birthday but making no secret of his disappointment at their estrangement: 'It makes me infinitely sad that it was easy for you to allow the terrible things that passed between Max and me to have such a one-sided effect on you that you'd forgotten my face in Pontresina. . . . One acquaintance after another was appalled at the "Stalinist historiography" that you seem to be constantly pursuing in relation to my contribution to the Institute and to the ideas that we have in common.'[53] The Frankfurt jurist and philosopher Wolfgang Preiser, who was received by Löwenthal in the most generous way in New York in the early 1950s, recalled thinking that on his return to the Federal Republic he would invite Löwenthal to take up a guest professorship in Frankfurt, with the result that he turned to Horkheimer. 'The way in which he flatly turned down my suggestion with explanations hedged in with qualifying clauses and pacifying phrases still fills me with a deep sense of indignation whenever I recall it.'[54] Adorno and Horkheimer also prevented Golo Mann from being appointed to a chair in Frankfurt. Both men had excellent contacts with the Ministry of Culture in Hesse and drew attention to the historian's subliminal anti-Semitism that they claimed to have noticed – Mann later got his own back when he commented that the heads of the Frankfurt School were 'good-for-nothings'.

The Institute introduced itself to a wider public in 1956 with a volume titled *Sociological Digressions*. The publisher was the Europäische Verlagsanstalt, which was later to publish the Institute's dissertations under the title 'Frankfurter Beiträge zur Soziologie', which were intended to continue the tradition of its journal. It was a joint undertaking by the Institute that was set in train by Adorno and Horkheimer. The article headed 'Society'[55] contains an outline of sociology as an emancipatory science, with society given precedence over the state and economy. This presupposed a preliminary decision. If evil exists and if there is a negative force in world history, this stems not from our anthropological constitution, in other words, from our essential nature but from 'irrational rule'.[56] Falling back on the history of eighteenth- and nineteenth-century ideas, the authors interpreted 'society' as a battle term in the sense of 'tendencies critical of the state'.[57] Anyone who sets out from the idea of institutions is already, therefore, intellectually degenerate: 'Something that is secondary, the institution, becomes the first consideration in the minds of people who live under institutions, while they continue to suppress from their conscious lives what is in fact the prime consideration, their actual process in life.'[58] The pessimistic diagnosis of 'progressive regression' due to rationalization is contrasted with a hesitantly optimistic diagnosis to the effect that social conflicts may threaten the standard of civilization that has been reached but can also point beyond it in a positive way.[59] Marx, Comte and Spencer were the inspiration behind this particular view of sociology, which revealed itself as a belated product of the nineteenth century. Only once is a contemporary – Talcott Parsons – mentioned by name.

Although *Sociological Digressions* contains chapters on 'Prejudice' and 'Ideology', it has nothing on religion. We can speak of a classic case of sociology: true being is that of individuals and their claims to happiness; state and institutions in general are secondary forms derived from them, forms which, if necessary, must be changed. Political philosophy, we read here, is the 'veil' that covers the 'vital process' of society.[60] This vital process is interpreted first and foremost as the type of economy that for its part points to the right of disposal over the means of production. Only one conclusion can be drawn from this airy definition of society: that it must be changed. Society itself is a kind of tabula rasa: people in it live without traditions, without religion, without nations and without a state.

Against this, it may be claimed that every historically identifiable society begins by sacralizing the basic rules of its relationships – gods such as Zeus, Jupiter or Wotan, who protect treaties, hospitality, fair exchange and so on, defeat the deities of the previous world in mythological narratives. In other words, the assertion of that which is right and lawful demands sacrality, cult and dominion, strict penalties against the criminal, the individual's renunciation of his or her instinctive desires in favour of the whole and, finally, armed protection of the specific social life forms against external enemies. Thus even the pure concept of society leads to the idea of powerful institutions, more especially when people are not prepared to give up minimum standards of justice – and then humanity in particular would demand that the institutions remain solid. This was the position that Arnold Gehlen maintained in the 'fifties and 'sixties, a thinker who repeatedly engaged in gentlemanly debates with Adorno on both radio and television. As Wolf Lepenies has written, they themselves described their joint broadcasts as '*Haupt- und Staatsaktionen*', a term that has no obvious equivalent in English: it derives from the plays performed by travelling players in Germany in the seventeenth and early eighteenth centuries. The *Hauptaktion* was serious, the *Staatsaktion* coarsely comic. Today the phrase is used only in the idiom 'to make a song and dance about something'. Lepenies also noted that Gehlen and Adorno 'would argue if their fees for these appearances turned out not to be "impressive enough"'. In many instances the two men agreed. 'I too am convinced by the abdication of the subject,' Gehlen wrote to Adorno on 31 August 1962, 'likewise by the superiority of evil – with or without the confirmation corroded away; we are living in the age of "going on for its own sake", in a situation in which everything has become paralyzed and nowhere shows any signs of thawing: quite the opposite, it is only just beginning. More and more frequently I find the expression "*s'engourdir*" in recent French writings. I call this "crystallization". As for the relationship between the two social philosophers, Lepenies noted that, 'as Adorno once wrote, they behaved like two enormous mastiffs that went their own way without biting each other'.[61]

Adorno's confrontations with Gehlen may be seen as an argument between an emancipatory theory of society and a more conservative one, while his discussions with Karl Popper involved a clash between two positions, both of which demanded to be regarded as 'critical'. And both parties could appeal to enlightenment, Popper to its scientific aspect and the process involved in the understanding of nature, Adorno to the theories of emancipation that dated from the eighteenth century. At a conference organized in Tübingen in 1961 by the German Society for Sociology, Popper delivered a paper on the 'Logic of the Social Sciences', to which Adorno offered a formal response. Whereas Popper interpreted the concept of criticism as an element of scientific understanding that advanced only through falsification, Adorno repeated his old thesis that society was in itself 'largely irrational', so that the concept of criticism needed to be interpreted more widely.[62] This was the first time that the Frankfurt School saw itself confronted by an adversary who could not be dismissed as backward and provincial but who had grown up on the same soil of modernity. Popper, too, had been a socialist in his youth but following his experiences of the destructive consequences of revolutionary movements he had come to the conclusion that the only solution lay through cautious, gradual reforms that contained within them the possibility of correction. He rejected a fundamental change in society. In this way he became a theorist to whom the Social Democrats under Helmut Schmidt could later appeal. For its part, this party had long since turned its back on fundamentalist socialism with the Godesberg Programme of 1959 and decided definitively in favour of the reformist way forward, a course that had triggered a bitter struggle within the party in the years around 1903. But Adorno refused to give up the idea of a fundamental change to society even if he was less ready than ever to give more details about the future. It was no longer change and the retention of the status quo that were now regarded as opposites. Rather, change had proved to be at odds with reform and basic opposition. The 'sixties had dawned.

15 Resistance as a Message

Adorno's lecture series 'On the Doctrine of History and Freedom' dates from the winter of 1964/5. Germany and the Western world stood on the threshold of a radical protest movement which in the Federal Republic was cued in by Adorno. In the notes that he made for his first lecture he wrote that it was no longer possible to speak of freedom: 'Objectively' one could not do so

> because of the increasingly dense network of society in East and West, the greater concentration and administration that more and more reduces people to functions. Freedom is limited to self-preservation. Even the people at the top are functions of their function. Subjectively because of ego weakness, dependence on consumption, conformism. Impossible to speak any longer of progress in the consciousness of freedom, even in the case of the progressive democratization of forms, which is resisted not only by the content of social power but by people's apathy. Indifference to freedom. Neutralization of consciousness. Depoliticization of science.[1]

This was a comprehensive and unequivocal diagnosis of the present day. And it gave the people to whom it was addressed the certainty that moral autonomy could be found only in acts of resistance, for life in society as it then existed could not offer this possibility, being morally void in each of its aspects. Even worse was the fact that those involved were incapable any longer of gaining an insight into this state of affairs. Johann Fichte would have spoken of a new era of total sinfulness. The institutions and social forms in which morally mean-ingful actions might unfold had been invalidated and 'irrational things such as family and nation'[2] were scarcely worth discussing any longer. Adorno did not believe that democracy was possible in a nation state: nations were 'fundamen-tally hardened against reason' and 'anachronistic'.[3] The very idea of responsible action within existing society was ideologically and critically invalidated. Entrepreneurs were 'character masks' of economic constraints and denied any creative possibilities: 'If he calculates and takes his entrepreneurial measures, an entrepreneur will not be guided by his character but by calculation, balance sheets, budgets and planning for the next cycle. . . . And this is true mutatis mutandis of all the functions that people generally have to perform, especially today. Even the most powerful minister will in general find himself restricted to transferring documents from his "pending" tray to his "out" tray.'[4] Anyone who thinks he is acting in this society is deluding himself and performing a literally senseless task.

This self-delusion has become universal. The 'historical obligation that is placed on people now affects the innermost recesses of their psychological lives'.[5] The man who is efficient at his job is in fact inwardly deformed, unable to see the extent to which he is acting against his own objective interests: 'For that reason they are able, on principle, to become socialized only as non-rational beings, even largely as irrational beings or, as one would say clinically, neurotic, through repression, through regression, through all the mutilation compulsions for which psychology has a name.'[6] With the exception of an élite of critical theorists, no one understood what was happening any longer: 'This means that people simply do not know what the world has made of them, because if they knew, they would be different and could not be turned into what the course of the world has just made of them.'[7] And Adorno speaks of 'infantilism especially among adults'.[8] In the earlier empirico-sociological studies on *The Authoritarian Personality* and 'Guilt and Defence', large-scale collective neuroses had been explained in terms of specific symptoms, whereas now they no longer needed any substantive criterion but applied simply to 'what exists'. Self-blindness was now universal. All that remained in this frenzy of disappearance was the abstract concept of 'resistance', the emotional resonances of which filled Adorno's lectures with vibrant life. Such resistance becomes boundless, for where existing conditions are condemned in their totality, resistance must be total. The subliminal message lay in the twofold meaning of the word: parental failure to resist National Socialism could be made good by resistance in the present – this, at least, is how his listeners were bound to understand Adorno and this is how they did indeed understand him. 'Resistance to scientific activity' was the 'task that has been left to philosophy,' we read at the very beginning.[9] And this was soon interpreted as an invitation to politicize science.

Time and again Adorno recalled the period of National Socialism, his lectures forging a link between the events of 20 July 1944 (one of the participants in the Stauffenberg Conspiracy was Fabian von Schlabrendorff, whom Adorno had met and whom he mentions and quotes) and the individual's task to avoid 'conformism'.[10] In the background is the catastrophe of Auschwitz. An attitude

Adorno in his apartment in the Kettenhofweg in Frankfurt in 1967

of protest is justified on the basis of the experience of National Socialism. 'If such a protest is substantial,' Adorno argued, it 'always involved a certain degree of reason. If, for example, an individual rebelled against the Third Reich, it was not just a moral feeling. If he was a politically thinking person, then he must – and I think I may even claim this for myself and my first experiences of Hitlerite Fascism – he must, I say, have been aware that the policies of the Nazis ushered in what has been called a policy of disaster.'[11]

Adorno was taking a risk in advancing this view. He himself became bogged down in a performative contradiction between radical rhetoric and institutional necessities that was soon to affect him, too. Following a tour of Germany in the autumn of 1958 Siegfried Kracauer wrote to Leo Löwenthal, reporting with some indignation on a conference in Munich on cultural criticism:

What on earth is cultural criticism? Teddie seems partly responsible for this intellectual commotion [last word in English in the original], which carries on in a radical fashion and is wholly inconsequential. He's also writing such a lot, and some of the things I saw are wrong on a high level, hackneyed profundity and a radicality that is doing all right for itself. (Not everything:

a few pages on Eichendorff are really beautiful and brilliant.) If I'd seen him, I'd have told him all this myself.[12]

Kracauer repeated his criticisms in February 1960, again in a letter to Löwenthal: after reading Adorno's *Aspects of Hegelian Philosophy*, which he described as 'really very intelligent and dazzling',[13] he expressed an opinion that already looks forward to the reproaches of the student movement:

> But here too he operates according to exactly the same principle – first he tramples everything down, then he smooths it all out again. And, completely impermissibly, the concept of Utopia is used as a purely defining concept that has absolutely no content to it. Alas, he doesn't see Utopia. I know of no other example of apparently invasive criticism that has so little power to engage with its subject. Ultimately everything remains as before, and basically he feels very comfortable with this. (Keep this to yourself: it's no doubt too late in any case to want to change Teddie.)[14]

Even Max Horkheimer began to adopt a more sceptical approach to the business of abstract negativity, noting in 1965 that

> Beckett is dealing with the same thing as critical theory: depicting the sense-lessness of this society and this life, protesting against it and yet subsuming within his protest the thought of something better. Adorno says the opposite to each of his analyses. But in spite of this dialectic, which is being taken to extremes, what he says remains untrue. For the truth cannot be said. And on a personal level he remains uninvolved. But what matters is somehow to realize the truth that one has.[15]

An observer as precise and as competent as the poet and composer Jürgen von der Wense – a proponent of modern music who, although he did not know Adorno personally, none the less read his publications with great attention to detail – wrote to a friend in March 1963 in a language reminiscent of that of carpenters and alchemists: 'Adorno's style recalls certain towers that are twisted in the shape of spirals because the imperial stem to which the groin rafters are morticed and tenoned is missing. But as for the matter itself, he is always right, a good alloy of copper and arsenic. But the effect is simply the product of his own vanity. A word must be magic and all-pervasive!'[16] The 'Grand Hotel Abyss' to which Lukács refers in the new edition of his *Theory of the Novel* in the early 'sixties was now inhabited, while here and there groups were slowly forming who had taken literally Adorno's invitation to offer resistance. Adorno faced them like the sorcerer's apprentice no longer able to control the elemental forces that he had unleashed.

Even the brutality with which the Frankfurt students confronted Adorno from the winter term of 1968/9 onwards may have been built into critical theory – unintentionally, no doubt. If it is true that every action develops its moral potential not primarily in a universal sphere but in a particular sphere, namely, within the family, in concrete responsibility for an area of work and in political practice bound up with the nation state; if, in short, morality in its formative process is dependent on particular social forms, then anyone who invalidates these limited forms of action, rendering them suspect and declaring them irrelevant is guilty of removing from morality the very ground on which it can flourish. What that person leaves behind is a hypermorality that can no longer define its own limits and which can therefore veer abruptly in the direction of brutality.

At the same time, it was very much Adorno's criticism that lent credibility to his claim to represent an ongoing tradition. Like Horkheimer, Adorno was bound to high German culture of the nineteenth century to a degree that is almost impossible for us to imagine today. It is enough to read his fragmentary study of Beethoven, on which he worked from the 'thirties onwards, to discover an almost literally desperate love: he recognizes in the composer a man of unbridled, violently authoritarian anger and judges him harshly, but he also sees in him a kindred spirit in terms of the tenderest and highest emotions. His attempt to confront Beethoven speaks of his love for Germany as well as the sufferings that Germany caused him, and it is scarcely fortuitous that he never completed a work that in its conceptual design repeated everything that the sociologist had already established about the opposite poles of authoritarian personality and unprejudiced character. One of Adorno's pupils, Albrecht Wellmer, summed up this impact as follows: 'With Adorno, it again became possible in Germany to be intellectually, morally and aesthetically present and at the same time not to hate Kant, Hegel, Bach, Beethoven, Goethe or Hölderlin.' By the same token, it is impossible not to be moved by some of the things that Horkheimer, too, wrote about the music of Anton Bruckner and the poems of his Swabian compatriot, Justinus Kerner. As a result, the doctrines of critical theory were interpreted in two different ways, on the one hand as a radical critique of existing conditions, while on the other – and this is especially true of the writings of Walter Benjamin – they provided access to the history of German ideas, a history that would perhaps have been buried sooner than was in fact the case. If we are justified in speaking of dialectics, then it is here: by making Auschwitz the focus of his thinking, Adorno also made it possible for his readers and listeners to cling to their love of the German language and of German philosophy and music.

As for philosophy, Adorno's main concern during the 1960s was his critical engagement with Heidegger and above all with the language of Heidegger. He had seen this as a challenge as long ago as the early 'thirties, and now the moment for open confrontation had come. Heidegger, too, had formulated a fundamental critique of the present and had analyzed its technicist tendencies. The resultant work revolved around the problem of historical time and the individual event, while his later writings abounded in idiosyncratic coinages that were gleaned from all sides, dissected, recombined and insistently repeated, assuming in the process the semblance of primordial words. One such word was 'Ge-Stell', which was intended to describe not something set up [aufgestellt] on its own but to epitomize all the different types of thought and behaviour that constitute modern technology. Heidegger believed that every problem should be examined according to its technical solubility, to the exclusion of all other possibilities. In short, it was a thesis about technocracy or at least one that could easily be translated into such terms. From here it is not far to the 'one-dimensional' human being of Heidegger's pupil Herbert Marcuse. But Adorno, who confronted Heidegger critically in his lectures on 'Ontology and Dialectics' during the winter term of 1960/61, produced something rather different from it: the 'framework'.[17] An error over a key concept does not necessarily inspire confidence. Evidently the details concerning Heidegger's later philosophy were of only moderate interest to Adorno.

A point that Adorno had first made in his dissertation on Husserl – his attempt to come to terms with the concept of 'givenness' – now returned in expanded form in his critical engagement with Husserl's pupil, Heidegger. Adorno's argument was based on an individualistic concept of the empirical consciousness within whose framework all meaning was to form. From this point of view, it was difficult to avoid the initial suspicion of ontology, namely, that it was concerned only superficially with investigating basic structures of existence, whereas in fact a false order was being ideologically glossed over. As a result, Adorno was able to stage his lectures on ontology as a political struggle between reaction and progress. What we find here are the two front-line positions of the emergent Federal Republic. On the one hand everything is archaic, rural, substantialistic, the 'path through the fields', the obscure provinces and ultimately myth, which Adorno treats in a fundamentally ironical way in his lectures: Heidegger's philosophy, so runs the message, is anachronistic, that of a backwoodsman. In short, it is humbug. And on the other hand there is all that is modern, rational, transparent and urban.

But Adorno signally failed to understand Heidegger's philosophy, and it is a source of particular regret that, having criticized Heidegger in his lectures on ontology, he did not go on to examine Heidegger's real achievements in formulating such basic terms of history as that of the 'event'. Adorno's *Jargon of Authenticity*, which was published in 1967 and which constituted a linguistic critique of existentialist philosophy in general and of Heidegger in particular, proved to be one of its author's most successful books. But its consequences were devastating. For several decades Heidegger was not just an object of criticism among the German intelligentsia. Rather, people thought that in smiling at his language they were already above him. Even Günter Grass parodied Heidegger's German in his novel *Dog Years*, but when he read from the work in Israel to an audience that included two of Adorno's friends, Werner Kraft and Gershom Scholem, he encountered a frostier response than he may have expected. Werner Kraft picks up the story: 'Turning to Scholem, Ernst Simon said that in spite of everything he thought that Heidegger was a great philosopher of historical impact, and he asked Scholem whether he thought the same. After reflecting for a moment, the latter said yes, he thought so too.'[18] It required the authority of Jacques Derrida to rediscover Heidegger's philosophy as a subject for meaningful discussion in the 'seventies and 'eighties.

Adorno had initially been able to convince others by linking together the language of existentialist philosophy with its empty use in public discourse. Words devoid of meaning such as 'concern' (*Anliegen*), 'commission' (*Auftrag*) and 'encounter' (*Begegnung*) that feigned a mixture of authority and humanity – ideally both at once – demanded not only criticism but satire. A 'Stencilled Speech for Festive Occasions' that he included in *Jargon of Authenticity*[19] threw arresting light on public speaking in the Federal Republic, for it was indeed the case that the language of down-at-heel existentialism served to draw a veil over social conflicts. But had not such an outstanding representative of existentialist philosophy as Karl Jaspers written a critical commentary on the movement's development in Germany and in his study *Where is the Federal Republic Heading?* provided a detailed analysis of the debates over lifting the time limit under which National Socialists could still be tried for their crimes? Could Heidegger really be reduced to the level of an 'impartial contemplative of essence',[20] to quote Adorno's wilfully jocular formula? Was the idea of 'being thrown into a particular place' in Heidegger's *Being and Time* really 'according to the taste of fascism'?[21] Had Heidegger deliberately 'overlooked the law of value which is asserting itself'[22] when criticizing the use of the word 'one' as an anonymous social authority and had he thus proved to be a poor reader of Marx?

Adorno's philosophy, music and theory of art had this in common: they were all related to language. But at least on a stylistic level, the linguistic character that he envisaged was literary, representing not only a civilizatory ideal *vis-à-vis* philosophy but also an alien measure. One can speak of a Latin, 'Romance' corrective to idealistic philosophy, and there is no doubt that this is how Adorno himself saw it when he recalled classical rhetoric in his *Negative Dialectics* in 1966: 'The vilification of Cicero and even Hegel's aversion to Diderot bear witness to the resentment of those whom the trials of life have robbed of the freedom to stand tall, and who regard the body of language as sinful.'[23] Schopenhauer had already combined a critique of the philosophy of Hegel, Fichte and Schelling with the idea of urbane prose and the essay as a literary form. And as with Schopenhauer, it was the intellectual who was the yardstick by which the language of philosophy was judged. At the same time, Adorno had no wish to share the positivist contempt for language: philosophy, *Negative Dialectics* made clear, was not just a method, it was also bound up with 'its linguistic nature', with 'texts'.[24] More than that: language involved more than just the silent reading of the text but also the sound of the voice, to which Adorno devoted a number of reflections in a brief but significant review – an idea that must have seemed obvious to the son of a singer.[25]

The idea behind *Negative Dialectics* is that of a metaphysical truth that may no longer speak dogmatically about its objects, God, freedom and immortality. Following the disaster that had overtaken Germany, any direct reference to 'meaning' had become questionable. Among the circumlocutions for the truth, the one that mattered most was arguably that which stated that it could be interpreted only as 'fragile'.[26] And Adorno turns his back not only on the naïve proclamation of eternal verities but also on simple nihilism. The 'unthinkable' aspect of death proves stronger.[27] Rather, Adorno attempts to salvage these metaphysical thoughts in an extreme concretion of experience, albeit one that can no longer offer the certainty of faith. Here it is particularly worthwhile following his argument in detail. The section 'Dying Today' in *Negative Dialectics* culminates in a theory of landscape:

What is a metaphysical experience? If we disdain projecting it upon allegedly primal religious experiences, we are most likely to visualize it as Proust did, in the happiness, for instance, that is promised by village names like Applebachsville, Wind Gap, or Lords Valley. One thinks that going there would bring the fulfillment, as if there were such a thing. Being really there makes the promise recede like a rainbow. And yet one is not disappointed; the feeling now is one of being too close, rather, and not seeing it for that reason. And the difference between the landscapes and regions that determine the imagery of a childhood is presumably not great at all.[28]

One should be 'entranced in one place without squinting at the universal'.[29] 'Landscape' becomes the password that grants access to metaphysics. And only in 'experience'[30] can one still hope to become aware of its contents. It 'is, and it is not'[31] is Adorno's beautiful way of formulating what is left of the promises made by the older philosophy. He resists the 'total liquefaction of everything thinglike'[32] by appealing to the wealth of sensual experience: 'Yet the surplus over the subject, which a subjective metaphysical experience will not be talked out of, and the element of truth in reity – these two extremes touch in the idea of truth.'[33] In this way the end of *Negative Dialectics* circles around metaphysics, approaching it, only to move away again.

Time and again it was poetic, imagined, composed mountain landscapes that delighted Adorno, the 'man of the mountains'. In an essay on the final scene of Goethe's *Faust* published in his *Notes on Literature*, he describes his place of rescue:

> As at my feet the chasm descending
> Rests on the deep abyss below,
> Or as the thousand streamlets blending
> Plunge in dread fall, and foaming flow,
> Or as the trunk, the forest gracing,
> Lifts its own strength so nobly tall,
> So is almighty love embracing
> All it has made, to cherish all.
> (Trans. Philip Wayne)

These lines are about a setting, a hierarchically structured landscape that rises up in tiers. But what happens in it – the plunging waterfall – seems as though the landscape is telling the story of its own creation by allegorical means. The being of the landscape pauses as a parable of its becoming. . . . As the word of natural history appeals to ruined existence as love, there opens up the aspect of the reconciliation of the natural. In recalling its own natural being, it rises above its addiction to nature.[34]

Even Goethe's greatness is devoted to landscape: 'The first [difficulty to be overcome] would no doubt be a peculiar quality of greatness that should not be confused with monumentality but that appears to defy a more precise definition. Perhaps it is closest to the feeling of breathing a sigh of relief in the open countryside.'[35] The reader may be surprised by the frequent association between landscape and death in Adorno's thinking, an association already found in his early essay on Schubert. In the same way we find him writing about Sils Maria, the Swiss village associated with Nietzsche that Adorno was fond of visiting: 'The advantage that the Engadine countryside has over the petty bourgeois landscape in terms of illusion-less truth is made up for by its imperialism, its consent with death.'[36] And in discussing Schoenberg's First Chamber Symphony, he recalls how 'a conductor once felicitously compared the field of resolution at the end of the great development section with a glacier landscape.'[37]

There is something curiously right, therefore, about the title that the poet Paul Celan gave to his story about a failed meeting with Adorno: 'Conversation in the Mountains'. It dates from August 1959. Celan had bought a copy of Adorno's *Notes on Literature* the previous spring and read the philosopher's essay on Heine, underlining passages that dealt with the poet's alienation within the German language. In July 1959 Celan took his wife and son to Sils Maria, where he had arranged to meet Adorno. 'But Celan returned early to Paris, and so – "not accidentally," he said – missed seeing Adorno.'[38] In inscribing an offprint of 'Conversation in the Mountains', Celan mentioned Sils Maria, 'where I was to meet Herr Prof. Adorno, who I thought was a Jew'.[39] Celan's text includes echoes not only of Georg Büchner's short story *Lenz* ('On 20 January Lenz went walking through the mountains') but also of Nietzsche's *Thus Spake Zarathustra* ('When Zarathustra was thirty years old, he left his homeland . . . and went into the mountains'). Celan had also translated Kafka's 'Excursion into the Mountains' into Romanian,[40] and he knew Martin Buber's 'Conversation in the Mountains' of 1913. 'One evening', Celan begins

> the sun, and not only that, had gone down, then there went walking, stepping out of his cottage went the Jew, the Jew and son of a Jew, and with him went his name, unspeakable, went and came, came shuffling along, made himself heard . . . went walking like Lenz through the mountains, he, whom they let live down below where he belongs, in the lowland, he, the Jew, came and he came.[41]

It is Jew 'Groß' and Jew 'Klein' who meet in the mountains:

> Groß came up to Klein, the Jew, bade his stick be silent in front of Jew Groß's stick. So the stone was silent too, and it was quiet in the mountains where they walked, himself and that one. So it was quiet, quiet, up there in the mountains. It wasn't quiet for long, because when one Jew comes along and meets another, then it's goodbye silence, even in the mountains. Because the Jew and Nature, that's two very different things, as always, even today, even here.[42]

But it is with nature – the names of plants – that the conversation continues. When Adorno read 'Conversation in the Mountains', he told Celan that the latter should have stayed on in Sils Maria as he would then have had a chance to meet the 'real Jew Groß', by which he meant Gershom Scholem, who also happened to be staying there.[43] Even so, we may note a hint of reservation in Celan's remark that he 'thought' Adorno 'was a Jew'. As John Felstiner comments, this was intended as a dig at Adorno for abbreviating his father's name of Wiesengrund – a curious criticism on the part of Celan, whose own assumed name was an anagram of his family name of Ancel.

Celan is the poet who, more than any other, confronted the question of the genocide of the Jews – and not only in his famous *Deathfugue*. In another poem, dating from 1945, we read: 'The angels are dead and the Lord has gone blind in the region of Acra, / there's none in the night who will guard for me those who have gone to their rest there.'[44] The reader encounters a world ruled over by destruction. But it is in *Deathfugue*,[45] with its barely tolerable tension between the gently rocking rhythm of its language and the utter horror of the events it describes, that he discusses directly the world of the camps and crematoria. The line 'Der Tod ist ein Meister aus Deutschland' – 'Death is a master from Germany' – became famous, not to say emblematic, for it was a phrase that struck home, touching the Germans' most sensitive and painful spot, that of their own distinctive work ethic, the quality product, 'craftsmanship' and mastery, the Mastersingers and Master Eckart. If the self-awareness of the Germans can be summed up in a single word, then it is arguably in the word 'Master', which now, thanks to the poet's authority, answers for Germany's programme of murder and is contaminated for ever after.

Celan wrote *Deathfugue* in the mid-'forties. His father and mother had both been victims of the SS, and he himself had been interned in a labour camp. *Deathfugue* is now seen as one of the great poetic expressions of the policy of extermination. Adorno may not have read it when in the 1950s he formulated an equally emblematic sentence that points in the opposite direction:

> The more totalitarian that society becomes, the more reified the mind and the more paradoxical its attempt to break free from reification on the strength of its own self. Even the most extreme consciousness of fate threatens to degenerate into gossip. Cultural criticism finds itself faced by the final step in the dialectics of culture and barbarism: to write a poem after Auschwitz is barbaric, and this also erodes the realization that states why it has become impossible to write poetry today. As long as it remains self-possessed, the critical mind is unequal to the task of absolute reification that

presupposed the progress of the spirit as one of its elements and that is now on the point of absorbing it completely.[46]

As Joachim Seng has shown, Celan knew this challenging thesis, commenting on it in a note dating from the time of his volume of poetry *Atemwende*: 'No poem after Auschwitz (Adorno): what sort of an idea of a "poem" is being implied here? The arrogance of the man who hypothetically and speculatively has the audacity to observe or report on Auschwitz from the perspective of nightingales and song thrushes.'[47] By the time that he came to write *Negative Dialectics*, Adorno had read *Deathfugue* and was familiar with Celan's later, more austere poetic language, prompting him to withdraw his original dictum: 'Perennial suffering has as much right to expression as a tortured man has to scream; hence it may have been wrong to say that after Auschwitz you could no longer write poems.'[48]

Even so, poet and philosopher remained estranged. When Claire Goll, the widow of the poet Iwan Goll, accused Celan of plagiarism in the 'sixties, the latter began to regard himself as the victim of a new anti-Semitic campaign. 'This whole affair,' he wrote to Adorno on 23 January 1962, 'is a kind of Dreyfus affair. Among those implicated is the so-called intellectual élite.'[49] Adorno did not respond, either to the senseless reproach of plagiarism or to the poet's extreme reaction, and Celan, who for a time during the Goll affair found it impossible to distinguish between long-standing friends and patrons on the one hand and enemies both real and imagined on the other, suspected a kind of complicity between Adorno and criticism of his poetry, a suspicion to which he gave expression in the following untranslatable lines: 'nicht / ab-, nein wiesen- / gründig, / schreiben sie, die / Aber-Maligen, dich / vor / die / Messer'.[50] (Here Celan puns on the word 'abgründig', meaning 'cryptic', and Wiesengrund's name, which is a poetic word in German for 'meadow': literally, the lines mean: 'Not cryptically, no as Wiesengrund, they, the revenants, write you before the knives.') But Celan mistrusted not only his friends but also his own family, resulting in his attempt to murder them. As a result, Adorno's reluctance to have any closer contact with him is entirely understandable. He did not write the essay on Celan that he was planning, or the book that the poet evidently wanted. But his *Aesthetic Theory* contains sentences that point in the direction that his reading was taking him. Here he describes Celan as 'the most important contemporary representative of German hermetic poetry'.[51] It is not *Deathfugue*, however, that forms the starting point of Adorno's tribute but the later works: 'Celan's poems want to speak of the most extreme horror through silence. Their truth content itself becomes negative. They imitate a language beneath the helpless language of human beings, indeed beneath all organic language: It is that of the dead speaking of stones and stars.'[52] This is not incorrect, but it is still not an exactly inspired verdict, sounding as it does a little glib and hackneyed. The poet and critic Werner Kraft, who was a friend of Benjamin and Scholem and who advocated a total ban on images of the extermination camps, with the result that he remained sceptical towards Celan's poetry, describes a scene in which the background to this situation becomes a little clearer:

> I remember a conversation with Adorno in Frankfurt in which I said that Celan reminded me of someone who gulps down what has been produced even before it is out. To this, Adorno said that it was remarkable, but his wife was always saying the same. Then he mentioned his planned essay on Celan. But I can't help thinking that not only his wife, who was entirely capable of making up her own mind, thought this about Celan but above all he himself by pretending that it was his wife.[53]

But there is no denying the truth of Kraft's observation that in the 'sixties Adorno took a far greater interest in other poets, who evidently meant more to him. Adorno edited a selection of Rudolf Borchardt's poems for Suhrkamp and used a line of Borchardt's – 'Ich habe nichts als Rauschen' (I have nothing but rustling) – as a motto for an essay on Hegel. And he corresponded with Wilhelm Lehmann – nowadays regarded only as a nature poet – on the subject of poetic experience. In short, Adorno's actual poetic preferences seem to have been more conservative than his *Aesthetic Theory* maintains.

Even so, the profound ambivalence that Celan felt for Adorno gives us an idea of the forces that were beginning to tug at Adorno from all sides. While earlier friends such as Ernst Krenek had thought that they felt a powerful sense of Adorno's Jewishness, he was now subjected to the opposite reproach, and whereas he was criticized by Krenek and others for his left-wing orthodoxy, there were soon others for whom he was not left-wing enough.

Adorno's *Notes on Literature* played a substantial part in his public influence in areas beyond that of social philosophy. He published three volumes of these studies during his lifetime, with a fourth appearing after his death. They cover the whole of the bourgeois age – Classicism, Romanticism and Modernism – and are devoted not only to German literature from Goethe and Eichendorff to Heine, Stefan George, Thomas Mann and Karl Kraus but also to French literature from Balzac to Proust, Valéry, the Surrealists and above all Samuel Beckett, in whose works Adorno saw the authentic, resistant art of modernity following the disaster of the Second World War. Finally, these volumes include loving yet critical portraits of the men who influenced his youth: Ernst Bloch, Georg Lukács, Walter Benjamin and Siegfried Kracauer. It is clear from them how much Adorno was attached to Europe. So comprehensive is the absence of English-language literature and poetry that it seems almost beyond belief that Adorno ever lived in Oxford, New York and Los Angeles. With the exception of two early essays on Dickens and Priestley that he refused to have reprinted and a brief reference to Evelyn Waugh in *Minima moralia*, Ango-Saxon literature is not mentioned. There is an essay on Aldous Huxley in the collection *Prisms*, but the tone is that of a cultural critic rather than a literary critic. And the American writers who caused a sensation in Germany after the war – Hemingway, Steinbeck and Faulkner – seem barely to have affected Adorno. It is unnecessary to add that Socialist Realism and the related counter-classicism that was proclaimed above all in the German Democratic Republic and associated with the names of Maxim Gorky, Romain Rolland and Martin Andersen-Nexö play no part here, and the same is true of literature written during the war years, including the books of Ernst Jünger.

The inclusion of French literature in Adorno's canon must be seen, in fact, in a political light. Ever since the anti-Napoleonic Wars of Liberation at the beginning of the nineteenth century, many Germans had regarded French civilization as a hostile element, with the Catholic conservative writer Constantin Frantz, for example, demanding that Germany should escape from the influences of its western neighbour. This in particular was Germany's vocation, Frantz wrote in 1859, 'because, of all the continental countries, Germany alone possesses the requisite gifts and powers of spirit and mind to bring about a more noble form against which French civilization will be powerless'.[54] Adorno wrote against this tradition, too, in his *Notes on Literature*. One of the decisive essays in this collection and one that was later to become a bone of contention with students in Berlin was his analysis of the Classicism of Goethe's *Iphigenia in Tauris*. It was, as it were, Adorno's last word on a subject that had exercised him from an early date and to which he was to return in major studies and in almost throwaway remarks on nature and landscape throughout much of the rest of his life: the problem of 'natural history'. According to Adorno, an enlightenment 'that eludes itself and does not preserve in self-reflection the natural connection that distinguishes it from freedom becomes guilty of a crime against nature, which is part of the mythical natural framework. . . . Reconciliation is not the total opposite of myth but embraces justice towards myth.'[55]

The *locus philosophicus* of such reconciliation is art. In his *Aesthetic Theory*, which he was unable to complete, Adorno took critical stock of the modern age since his birth in 1903, and he realized that this modern world was growing old. Once again he recalls the years of his childhood as a time of transition culminating in modernity, and he remembers Frank Wedekind's satirical novel *Mine-Haha*, which was published in fragmentary form in 1903, and Guillaume Apollinaire's apostrophization, that same year, of the twentieth century as the 'century of speed'. But there is no denying the note of resignation that he felt in the face of present-day art: 'The sea of the formerly inconceivable, on which around 1910 revolutionary art movements set out, did not bestow the promised happiness of adventure. Instead, the process that was unleashed consumed the categories in the name of that for which it was undertaken.'[56]

Adorno believed that instead of using their opportunities for freedom, artists had set out prematurely in search of new organizational models. But there was literally no escape. 'Art must turn against itself, in opposition to its own concept, and thus become uncertain of itself right into its innermost fiber.'[57] In retrospect, Adorno realized that the age to which he belonged was one of 'schools'. He speaks of the age of 'isms', Expressionism, Fauvism, Cubism, Brecht's epic theatre and Surrealism. These isms had taken the place of tradition, they were its secularized form, 'schools in an age that destroyed them as traditionalistic'.[58] They replaced the authority of tradition by something matter-of-fact. But – and Adorno had no illusions on this score – this age was now over, and any reference to the 'avant-garde' now had something of the 'comic quality of aged youth'.[59] *Aesthetic Theory* is thus as much a justification of his own generation as an attempt to come to terms with transience, the 'fatal aging of the modern'.[60] Political and aesthetic progressiveness had long since drifted apart. Adorno reacted critically to every idealist attempt to revive the progressiveness of the twenties. Just as he reacted to the situation at the time of his birth and made the onset of modernism his model, so he reflected towards the end of his life on the fact that this situation was soon to disappear. If there was any need of the proof of intellectual power, this fact alone would have been one of the most impressive.

But there is one idea above all that Adorno develops in his *Aesthetic Theory*, that of the similarity between art and language. According to Adorno, art groped for the language of things,[61] which was not entirely accessible to any human language. Hofmannsthal's 'Lord Chandos Letter' (1902) is a key work of modern literature and is mentioned by Adorno as one of many pieces of evidence.[62] Music is like language, we read on one occasion. The theory of traditional musical form recognized the existence of the sentence, phrase, period and punctuation. 'Questions, exclamations, subordinate clauses are everywhere, voices rise and fall, and, in all of this, the gesture of music is borrowed from the speaking voice.'[63] When Beethoven demands that a bagatelle from his op. 33 be played 'with a certain speaking expression', he was merely emphasizing, in his reflection, an ever-present aspect of music, we read in the same passage. Adorno saw music as a language lacking in judgment, and even modern music did not dispense with its similarity to language but continued to preserve it as a specific and yet hidden statement. But was this not more than aesthetics? Was it perhaps an overwhelming sense of gratitude to his mother's voice, the voice of Maria Calvelli-Adorno, in whom he must have been aware of something of music's similarity to language and whose name he may have preferred to his father's for that very reason? For it was this union of language and art in singing that Adorno later tried to rediscover not only in the Second Viennese School, whose members habitually set poetry to music, but even for a time in National Socialist speech-song.

It was with the music of his youth in his ears that Adorno reacted to the works of a younger generation of composers, dismissing them as anticyclical and out of season. While increasingly eccentric compositional principles vied all around him with increasingly bold provocations of chance, he recalled the great figures of his youth, writing a series of essays and monographs on Schreker and Zemlinsky, Mahler and Berg, and not even shying away from the reproach that he was a 'Romantic'. He struggled to make contact with the younger generation, notably Ligeti, and in the case of Dieter Schnebel he evinced a touching concern that extended to a personal level. But young composers understood him less and less. The writer on aesthetics Bazon Brock recalled:

> I was at the Academy of Music in Frankfurt when Adorno turned up there one day and accompanied a singer at the piano. It was his own pieces that she sang. The only impression that I still have of the whole thing is Adorno getting up from his piano stool at the end of the performance, coming down to the front of the stage and bowing. I'm sorry, but with Adorno the ageing process of music was already grotesque. To a certain extent one always had the impression when he spoke of Stockhausen or Henze that he simply did not know what modern music is. But for us, Stockhausen and Henze was like meeting our own washed-out grandfathers. For us, Cage was what mattered. Adorno didn't see that. He lived in a fictional world within which his reflections were not inaccurate, reflections that as a philosopher he brilliantly put forward, for example on alienation problems in artistic creativity. But the leading cultural theorist of his day did not take part in the important developments of the fifties, either in the theatre or in music or in the visual arts.[64]

16   Student Conflict

In the end it was those who were closest to Adorno and who had learnt most from him who turned against him. Jacob Burckhardt's insight that in a crisis those who have triggered that crisis with their critique of the existing situation are the first to fall behind and be flattened by the second and third wave of the revolution is also true in the present case.

By the early 'sixties the world seemed entrenched in a confrontational situation, encouraging commentators to speak of 'post-history'. The erstwhile revolutionary doctrine that had promised a different future had been integrated into the apparatus of power in the East, where Marxism had lost its appeal, just as psychoanalysis had done in the West, where it had become a bourgeois fashion. History, stopped in its tracks, seemed to bar the way to action, and it was subversive theories, above all, that were everywhere seen as instruments of conformism. Where could the way out be found? Evidently it was necessary to adopt a twofold perspective: the freer, anarchical impulses to act that stressed pleasure and that had now become possible in liberal affluent societies in the Western world had to be joined by an ultra-orthodox reading of the classic texts of Marx and Freud, allowing their original subversive and revolutionary potential to re-emerge once again. It was at this time, accordingly, that we first find the alliance between Dadaist performance art and Marxist orthodoxy that became typical of the student movement. The modernism that had begun to gain acceptance as a cultural phenomenon during the 'fifties now found a new generation to support it. And this generation was no longer willing to play by the old rules. A purer tone evolved, not only in pop music. For Adorno, who was even more pained by the 'raucous followers of Elvis Presley' than by jazz listeners, this was pure torment: Storm Troopers in jeans.[1] Ascetic abstraction in art was now a thing of the past. Colour was once again shown off to advantage, and American pop artists such as Andy Warhol discovered the world of the commodity as a subject for art. The age of affluence that had dawned in the 1950s now bore fruit. Happiness seemed more attainable and, above all, more immediate. Capitalism was no longer associated with a 'Protestant ethic', with its emphasis on discipline and renunciation of the instincts, but with a wealth of merchandise and enjoyment. Procrastination was frowned upon.

The generation of those who, as children, had survived the nightly bombing raids and then witnessed the staggering pace of post-war reconstruction thought everything was possible. There were already theories of automation that promised a dramatic reduction in the time spent at work. Traditional culture had been eroded. And every political party spoke of 'reform', not least with a view to solving what was called the 'education disaster'. Masses of students were streaming into subjects such as sociology that promised comprehensive orientation. At the same time, all was quiet on the political front, at least on the surface. The post-war generation had not only come to terms with existing conditions but regarded its own achievements with pride. There was a wide concensus concerning the Federal Republic's constitution, even if individual political steps were contested. But the long era of Adenauer – described in a widely-read book of the period as the 'Christian Democrat state' – was drawing to a close. Political protest on the part of intellectuals, and not just left-wing thinkers, was triggered by the *Spiegel* affair, when the magazine's editor, Rudolf Augstein, was arrested on suspicion of treason.

Adorno's themes returned, seeming more topical than ever. Suhrkamp launched the edition that bears its name in May 1963. One of the most success-ful series of all time, it became synonymous with the country's intellectual awakening and initially ran to twenty titles, including Adorno's *Eingriffe* (Inter-ventions), Benjamin's *Städtebilder* (Municipal Portraits), Beckett's *Waiting for Godot*, Ernst Bloch's *Tübingen Introduction to Philosophy* and Brecht's *Life of Galileo*. Even a station bookshop could inform the publisher: 'You will undoubtedly be astonished to learn which titles are selling best with me – Bloch, Wittgenstein, Adorno, Benjamin, in that order.'[2] The literary historian George Steiner coined the term 'Suhrkamp culture' to describe the return of émigré intellectuals to public consciousness in Germany.

The full significance of a capitalist consumer society and culture industry was now recognized in all quarters, but criticism, too, became more vocal, finally turning against its originator. The Socialist League of German Students was not alone in slaving away at Marxist theory, an obsession that led to its expulsion from the German Socialist Party. Through his pupils Alfred Schmidt and Oskar Negt, Adorno was in contact with this group. From the United States came news of new forms of student protest and of the 'Free Speech Movement' in Berkeley, a movement that had attracted attention with its 'go-ins' and 'sit-ins'. The members of small artistic and intellectual circles brooded on forms of action that took as their starting point the Dadaist and Surrealist avant-garde. The international art movement Fluxus was founded in 1962 and immediately caused a stir with its 'happenings'. By the mid-'sixties the two trends had come together, with the new forms of action joining forces with the neo-Marxist experiments of the New Left. As chance would have it, the leading representatives of both groups – the kingpin of the Socialist League of German Students, Hans-Jürgen Krahl, and the action artist Hans Imhoff – were among Adorno's students.

The publishing house of Fischer had its finger on the pulse of the age and in 1961 suggested bringing out a new edition of *Dialectic of Enlightenment*. Both Adorno and Horkheimer had long resisted the idea of its reissue – the text lay in the basement of the Frankfurt Institute and was accessible only to the initiated – and until then no one had thought that this most radical and uncompromising formulation of critical theory could be read as a description of what was currently happening in Germany. But Horkheimer and Adorno continued to oppose the idea of a new edition and accordingly withheld their consent. First, they asked the book's original dedicatee, Friedrich Pollock, to check through the text, and on 24 January 1961 Pollock reported on his findings in a letter to Horkheimer: 'For the most part my question marks and crosses indicate reservations about an excessively frank language. . . . In general I have come to the very sad conclusion that the content of "Dialectic" is not suited to mass dissemination. Conversely, individual chapters, partly reworked, should be republished in the planned collection.'[3] Herbert Marcuse felt differently. In the summer of 1962 he wrote to Horkheimer and Adorno, jubilantly welcoming the idea of a new edition: 'Although you already know this, I'd still like to tell you that it's a tremendous book that has merely become more tremendous in the nearly twenty years since it was written. Nothing that has been published in the meantime by those nice sociologists and psychologists comes close to even one of the footnotes in your book. . . . And so: a NEW EDITION! And a dedicated copy of the new edition for me!'[4]

Negotiations with Fischer dragged on until 1969, by which date the student movement had long since disseminated pirated copies of the Amsterdam edition. But even before then, and to the dismay of its two authors, the idea contained in *Dialectic of Enlightenment* had already found topical expression. Anyone who was a student in Munich or Tübingen, Stuttgart or Berlin in May 1964 could have read a remarkable poster on walls and fences in the vicinity of their local university: 'Lost' was the heading of the leaflet that had been produced by a group calling itself Subversive Action. And it was signed 'Th. W. Adorno,

6 Frankfurt am Main, 123 Kettenhofweg'. The text was by Adorno himself, typographically transformed into a manifesto:

THE CULTURE INDUSTRY HAS SUCCEEDED IN TRANSFORMING SUBJECTS INTO SOCIAL FUNCTIONS AND DONE THIS SO UNDIFFERENTIATEDLY THAT THOSE WHO ARE COMPLETELY SEIZED BY THIS, NO LONGER MINDFUL OF ANY CONFLICT, ENJOY THEIR OWN DEHUMANIZATION AS SOMETHING HUMAN, AS THE HAPPINESS OF WARMTH.[5]

This passage is taken from *Dialectic of Enlightenment*. And it was with this poster that the estrangement between Adorno and his greatest admirers began. Anyone interested in the pamphlet could write, poste restante, to Munich, citing the password 'Antithesis'. The elder statesmen of Marxism had no answer to the playfully provocative way in which the younger generation treated their theories.

Ernst Bloch wrote to Adorno from Tübingen in June 1964: 'Dear Teddie, I feel the need to write to you and say that, if you want, I shall make myself available. Specifically, I heard from a student at a seminar this evening that you have filed a petition against the good-for-nothings responsible for the "Lost" report. I read the good-for-nothings' poster recently on an underpass: it is also said to have been posted up near the University. It's all beyond me.'[6] Somewhat later Bloch wrote again to report that he had asked around about the 'Munich bastards' and continued to fulminate against the 'good-for-nothings who call you a fool',[7] offering to find out the names of the miscreants. Adorno had thus become both the inspirational mentor and the first victim of the new student movement. He reported the culprits to the authorities when the University of Stuttgart sent him a bill for the cost of removing the posters. Dieter Kunzelmann and Frank Böckelmann were fined for infringing the press laws. They had previously tried in vain to 'talk to Adorno directly'.[8]

Kunzelmann was one of the leaders of the group behind the handbill. It is no exaggeration to describe him as the first and decisive German representative of the actionist protest movement. He was not yet twenty when, fleeing from his job as a trainee bank clerk in the Franconian town of Coburg, he went to Paris to live as a tramp and encountered a big city from beneath. The old market at Les Halles still existed at this date, and here he was able for a time to hold his head above water by doing odd jobs. Kunzelmann nurtured a romantic sympathy for the failures and outcasts of society. The son of the director of a building society, he was proud to sleep under bridges: the banks of the Seine had not yet been turned into expressways. 'The risk involved in escaping from domestic wellbeing and bourgeois security and in leading an extreme life on the street left deep traces,'⁹ he recalled in his autobiography. In Schwabing he joined the Situationalist Internationale, an avant-garde group of artists and intellectuals which in 1959 had published a manifesto on 'Unitarian Urbanism' protesting against the alienation of urban architecture. People should resist the 'passive spectacle, the basis of our culture' and the tendency to turn art into a museum for tourist purposes. And the group advocated the 'maintenance of a playful urban space' beyond the reach of 'police decrees'. For the present, this was all theoretical. But it was not long before disturbances broke out in Schwabing, with the confrontations between young visitors to pavement cafés and the police during the summer nights of 1962 proving a dry-run for what was to follow.

'Cannon of the Revolution' was the title of one of Kunzelmann's texts from this period, beautifully illustrated like all radical artists' manifestos. It echoed the cultural critique of the current situation: 'Towns and cities become sand castles for grown-up children; every person owns a space Volkswagen; states become tennis balls hit across planets by transobjective forces for our general amusement.'¹⁰ Following initial contacts between the radicalized Bohemian world and the anti-authoritarian Young Turks of the Socialist League of German Students who had turned their back on traditional Marxism, it was decided, according to Kunzelmann, to concentrate all their resources on a single city, and 'on account of its locational advantages this could only be Berlin'.¹¹ Another of the insurgents, Bernd Rabehl, describes Kunzelmann's appearance at this time: 'He was jumpy, kept plucking nervously at his beard, his conversations made no logical sense, and he played neither the man of culture nor the one who sees through others.'¹² Commune One, which Kunzelmann founded in Berlin with Fritz Teufel and Rainer Langhans, was an experiment in destroying the bourgeois family by carnevalistic means.

And this was something for which critical theory had already prepared the ground. As Adorno had explained in his lectures on history and freedom, the family and the nation were 'irrational' institutions. At the Institute for Social Research, the writings of the early French Socialist Charles Fourier (1772–1837) had been excavated and translated during the mid-'sixties. The vocalizing of a head-in-the-clouds, socialist Utopia, they propagated new, commune-like forms of harmonious social coexistence. It was Fourier who demanded the liberation of the wife from the family as the gauge of a nation's culture:

Can one see even a glimmer of justice in the lot inflicted on women? Is the young woman not a commodity offered for sale to anyone prepared to haggle over her acquisition and sole ownership? Is her consent to the bond of matrimony not utter contempt, forced upon her by the tyranny of prejudices that have assailed her from her childhood onwards? People try to persuade her that her chains are made of flowers, but can she delude herself over her degradation, even in those countries such as England that are puffed up with philosophy and where men have the right to take their wives to market with a rope around their necks and sell them like a head of cattle to whoever is willing to pay the price for them? In general the thesis may be proposed that social progress goes hand in hand with progress in the emancipation of woman and that the decline in social order goes hand in hand with the removal of the woman's freedom. An increase in women's prerogatives is the universal principle of all social progress.

This is an early expression of the theses contained in *Dialectic of Enlightenment* concerning the fate of women under the rule of Western man. The Surrealists, too, had admired Fourier, with André Breton, for example, penning an ode to the eccentric cultural reformer.

Elisabeth Lenk was a student of Adorno's and had also belonged to the circle around Breton. During the 1960s she helped to build a new bridge between critical theory and the Surrealists. Her correspondence with Adorno revolves around the poets and thinkers of unleashed passions, with Adorno's own passion momentarily striking a more practical note: 'I have never,' he told Lenk using the familiar 'Du' form of address, 'I have genuinely never met a woman whom I consider as brilliantly gifted as you, in the areas that are closest to me; and please do not put this down to my infatuation, to which it merely contributes yet further.'[13] And shortly afterwards: 'I lack the words to tell you how much I am looking forward to going away with you, we'll work it out together.'[14] Elisabeth Lenk's note is short and to the point: 'This dream holiday never took place.'[15] And it was not long before Adorno was using the formal 'Sie' again, a formality that Lenk had never abandoned. Flatteringly, she praised his 'pouvoir de séduction', but this power was limited to reports and examinations. Contact with Elisabeth Lenk once again brought out the Surrealism element in Adorno. When a mutual acquaintance was murdered, he pretended for a moment to have Breton's powers of prophecy: 'Even so I can recall that when I wanted to invite Aliette and heard that her address was unknown, for a fraction of a second I had a feeling that something was wrong.'[16] Only for a moment did Adorno succumb to this surreal experience, after which he started back: 'But, of course, something like that can also be a projection after the event.'[17]

The Vietnam War provided further justification for the protests. Horkheimer stuck demonstratively to the side of the United States, whose mission to save the free world from the dangers of Eastern Communism he had made entirely his own. To the horror of his students he declared in the America House in Frankfurt in May 1967: 'Whenever it is a question of waging war in America – now listen carefully – a question of waging war, it is not so much to defend the fatherland but is essentially about defending the constitution, defending human rights.'[18] He reminded critics of the United States 'that we would not be here and could not speak freely if America had not intervened and ultimately saved Germany and Europe from the most terrible totalitarian terror.'[19] Adorno, by contrast, maintained contact with the student opposition, not least during the protests against the emergency laws. When the student Benno Ohnesorg was shot by an armed policeman during the Shah of Persia's visit to Berlin on 2 June 1967, Adorno was clearly shocked at his sociology lecture. But by now there was open conflict between teachers and students. On 9 June 1967, only a week after Ohnesorg was shot, Jürgen Habermas spoke at a conference on 'University and Democracy' in Hanover, describing the new forms of protest as 'left-wing Fascism' and finding himself violently contradicted by Rudi Dutschke.

Be that as it may, the tone now became coarser, and jokes were turned into insults. Kunzelmann's Commune had found imitators in Berlin, where Commune II appealed to Wilhelm Reich's theories on sexual liberation. People admired the cultural revolution in China and refused to be deterred by its attendant reign of terror. On 7 June 1967, only five days after Ohnesorg's death, Adorno delivered a lecture on the 'Classicism of Goethe's Iphigenia' in the main auditorium of the Free University in Berlin, once again expatiating on his idea of a non-sacrificial humanism, while Commune II distributed mocking leaflets: 'The big cheese of science is coming! What's old Adorno to us? Why should we care about a theory that disgusts us because it does not say how we can best set fire to this shitty university and a few America Houses with it.'[20] Peter Szondi, who introduced the lecture, invited those students who did not wish to listen to it to leave the hall. When Adorno began, banners were unfurled: 'Iphigenists of the world, unite!' and 'Berlin's left-wing Fascists greet Teddy the classicist.' Red jellybabies in the shape of bears were handed out, underlining the students' contempt for 'Teddie'. The chairman of the General Student Committee, Hartmut Häußermann – now urban sociologist at Humboldt University – wrote to Adorno to apologize, but in a very roundabout way: 'The dividing line between a demonstrative expression of opinion (which in our view too was entirely legitimate before the start) and a disruption that resembled violence is one that our fellow students seem not to have observed closely enough.'[21] Adorno wrote to Szondi to say that Häußermann's apology was 'almost like a second insult'.[22]

In spite of all this, there was one sensitive point on which we must agree with the protest movement's criticism of Adorno: his edition of the writings and letters of Walter Benjamin contains a number of cover-ups. Problematical letters, including ones to the expert on constitutional law Carl Schmitt and to the philosopher Ludwig Klages, were not included in the edition on political grounds. Schmitt and Klages were men of the right, and any record of contact between them and Benjamin could have given rise to confusion. A passage on the Marxist doctrine of 'civil war' in Benjamin's review of a collection of essays on the First World War by Ernst and Friedrich Georg Jünger was removed from the new edition without any indication of its omission – how ironical in view of Ernst Jünger's letter to Adorno in which the former speaks of his admiration for Benjamin. The rebellious students began to rediscover the origins of critical theory in the class struggle at a time when the theory's originators had turned their backs on at least its militant terminology.

In his essay 'Marginalia to Theory and Practice', Adorno responded to the spectacular demonstrations organized by the Socialist League of German Students. He had now broken with the protesters, whose leaders struck him as skilled disputants but also as brutal and narcissistic, activistic and delusional. There was in fact a structural problem here affecting Adorno's sociology, which draws its strength from the tension between a social foreground that is perceived as entirely hostile and the extensive conceptual background against which systematic tendencies – staticity and dynamics, late capitalism and industrial society – are discussed. The vanishing point, as it were, was the concept of reconciliation that Adorno defined in *Negative Dialectics* as 'remembrance of the much that is no longer hostile'. Wherever Adorno saw conflicts, he could no longer recognize dignity and humanity, and it was only logical, therefore, that in his empirical investigation into the 'authoritarian personality', he regarded the opinion that there will always be conflicts as a cynical expression of a 'generalized hostility'. Even his early study of the teacher-pupil relationship regarded social conflict as a form of malicious, spiteful hostility. In his final contribution to sociology, which he wrote with Ursula Jaerisch in 1968, 'Notes on Social Conflict Today', the consumer society of the 'sixties was more or less identically diagnosed and said to manifest 'crushed and misdirected aggressions', 'squabbles' and, once again, 'envy'.[23] Adorno's demand that social conflicts be observed in a way that also took account of their gestural element had already been realized by *Minima moralia* in the America of the 1940s. What we find here is a nation of domestic tyrants, bickering wives and shameless teenagers, all of whom were later written off as 'antidemocratic individuals with powerfully aggressive features'. If the sociology of Georg Simmel, which still presupposed the legal certainty of Wilhelmine Germany, could interpret argument as something that enriched a person's life, even the microscopic forms of conflict suggested delusion and the will to destroy to Adorno. Simmel's aim of demonstrating that the interplay between opposing vibrations was a higher form of education reflected the self-consciousness of German Jews in the years around 1900. Adorno, who was much younger, saw only an apologetic tendency here. Subjected to all that his generation experienced, his sociology became rigidified, a phenomenology of hostilities. The students who attended Adorno's lectures on sociology during the summer term in 1968 were bound to be as mystified as their teacher by the conflicts to which they were heading. Once again Adorno vehemently rejected the idea that social conflicts could involve an 'intrinsic quality of society'[24] – but in denying this idea, he was at the same time blocking the way to a genuine analysis. When the demonstrations reached the Institute for Social Research six months later, Adorno could see only a repeat of what he had always seen in conflictual situations: 'characters tied to authority' that were 'aggressively directed outwards'. Thus we read in his 'Marginalia on Theory and Practice'.[25]

But not only the students were involved. Everyone now began to tear at Adorno, and from all sides he was assailed by criticisms of his individualistic position. György Ligeti, who had fled to the West from Hungary, reproached him for making too many concessions to the Marxist students, while Günter Grass wrote to him to complain that he had not declared himself more clearly in favour of social democracy. Grass's poem, 'Adorno's Tongue', expresses his disenchantment:

> He sat inside the heated room
> Adorno with the silver tongue
> Sat playing with the silver tongue.
>
> Then butchers bounded up the stairs
> They climbed the stairs with steady steps
> And ever closer came the butchers.
>
> Adorno then took out his rounded
> Polished rounded pocket mirror
> In which his silver tongue was mirrored.
>
> The butchers did not knock, however,
> But opened up Adorno's door
> With knives and did not knock.

Adorno was alone just then,
Alone with just his silver tongue,
It lay in wait for paper and the word.

As butchers over steps they left
The house, and bore the silver tongue
Away with them, they bore it home.

Much later, when Adorno's tongue
Was cut in pieces, coated tongue
Arrived and sought the silver tongue,

Too late.[26]

In Frankfurt, Adorno was still able, at least for a time, to maintain a dialogue with his radical students, and it was not until the winter term of 1968/9 that the situation degenerated into an 'active strike' that included the occupation of various buildings, including the Institute for Social Research. The directors called in the police to evacuate the building, and Adorno brought a charge for trespass against Hans-Jürgen Krahl. Krahl had been born in 1943 and was marked by the war, having lost an eye in an air raid. Among the younger generation of philosophers, he was in line to take up Adorno's theory and make it more radical. In his statement to the court, he described his life as an 'odyssey through the organizational forms of the bourgeois class',[27] entirely along the lines laid down by Adorno in his battle with the 'jargon of authenticity'. He had grown up in the provinces on the right of the political spectrum: 'In Lower Saxony, or at least in the parts that I come from, there still survives to a large extent something that can be described as an ideology of the earth, and so when I went through the process of political education, I too could initially operate only within the framework of the German Party and even the Welf Party.'[28] And he went on: 'It was an enormous step in the direction of enlightenment when in 1961 I founded the Young Union and joined the Christian Democrats in my home town of Alfeld.' He later became an active Christian and then a member of a duelling fraternity, from which he was eventually thrown out. After that he joined the Socialist League of German Students. Central to his thinking was the idea of the organization. He knew from his own experience how they function in detail, how loyalties are formed and how they can later be lost, how organizations are formed and how they fall apart. What Lukács had done for the Communist movement of the 1920s with his study 'Methodisches zur Organisationsfrage', Krahl now wanted to do for the student protest movement. If he were to write a philosophy, he proudly declared, it would not fall beneath the level of Lukács's text.

At the height of the student revolt: Ludwig von Friedeburg, Adorno, Hans-Jürgen Krahl and K. D. Wolff in the Volksbildungsheim in Frankfurt in the autumn of 1968

Krahl's opposition to the society of the Federal Republic was undoubtedly conditioned by his homosexuality, which forced him into the position of an outsider. Behind his rhetoric on the role of the organization lies something of the homoeroticism of the League of Youths that rises up against the world of its elders. He had come to the cities from a village society with its hint of myth in order to devote himself to science. There was a tragic irony to his premature death in a car accident on 16 February 1970, a technological death around which no myth could accrue. Capitalism had struck him as a 'senseless' social order, with the world market becoming its destiny. Krahl left behind him only fragments of a philosophy, and it was only in the final months of his life that he abandoned Marxism – neither Auschwitz nor the developments of present-day capitalism seemed to him to be understandable in terms of Marxist theory. Often it was only in disjointed sentences that he was able to express himself: he envisaged a theory in the widest sense of the term but it was developed against the background of the breakneck, precipitate developments of the years between 1966 and 1970. Reports by his friends suggest that he also hoped to find a degree of personal stability in organisations – his own behaviour bordered on the antisocial and he had a serious alcohol problem. The inability to be part of an organization struck him as 'demoralizing'[29] and led to 'self-destruction' and to the 'syndrome of antisocial behaviour'.[30]

Krahl placed 'organization' on the very spot where art had stood in Adorno's estimation. On 1 February 1969, Krahl was arrested during the 'active strike' in the Institute for Social Research: Ludwig von Friedeburg had called in the police to evict the students who were occupying the building. Charged with coercion and trespass, he was taken into custody awaiting trial, but within a week he had been released on conditional bail. At his trial in July 1969 Krahl and Friedeburg accused each other of hysteria. 'But with his supervisor Adorno, he was more circumspect,' reported the *Frankfurter Allgemeine Zeitung* on 19 July: 'When the feud between the left wing and its mentor finally seemed to have found its way into court, with its contest between the theorist and those who have drawn "actionistic consequences" from his ideas, the philosopher said that the case revolved simply around the fact that in spite of being asked three times to do so, Krahl had not left the Institute.'[31] Krahl cross-examined his supervisor and asked him what made him think that the Institute was being occupied. According to the *Frankfurter Allgemeine Zeitung*, 'there then developed a lengthy discussion of the "phenomenology of occupation". The students, Adorno explained, had turned the corner of the Dantestraße, marching quickly, not in any formation, but in a coherent manner. On the basis of recent events, he knew that they were planning an occupation.'

According to the *Süddeutsche Zeitung* of 23 July, Adorno finally declared that he was going on holiday and could give no further evidence to the court during the coming weeks. 'Pursued by furious looks and with a number of powerful insults ringing in his ears, the philosopher . . . left the court on the arm of a devoted female student.' The same newspaper also reported that Adorno was seen to smile at Krahl in a superior manner. Krahl was given a three months' suspended sentence and fined three hundred marks. As mitigating circumstances, the court noted that he was 'of an idealistic disposition'. The latter is also said to have appeared to Adorno in a dream at this time – the account has come down to us only by word of mouth, but even if it is untrue, it is certainly *ben trovato*. The militant student sat like an incubus on Adorno's chest, waving a knife in his face: 'Is that not an act of terror, Herr Krahl?' asked the teacher, to which the pupil offered a reply that seems to come straight from Adorno's own theory: 'You're personalizing the situation.'

The action artist Hans Imhoff, meanwhile, placed artistic immediacy and a greater degree of mediation at the point where for Adorno the 'work' had stood. Like Krahl, he too had had Adorno as his supervisor, his stated subject being

'Hegel's Concept of Experience'. Here he had argued for an increase in Hegel's 'absolute knowledge' in poetic understanding. In around 1967 he declared in one of Adorno's seminars that in a free society art would be 'positive'. Even on the level of categories, this went to the very heart of the 'negative' utopian philosophy of art that Adorno had developed, while still being an extension of Adorno's own dialectics. 'Positive' was not intended to be understood in the banal sense of a propagandist advocacy of all that currently existed. Rather, it implied the re-evaluation of the empirical subject, which now declared itself the highest artistic manifestation in its sheer presence. Nor was this an isolated case in the mid-'sixties, when Timm Ulrichs exhibited himself in a glass case. Imhoff drew up an aesthetics of action art that had been prefigured by the Fluxus movement, happenings, and in all that was known about Situationism and the members of anti-bourgeois protest movements in the Netherlands, and which now acquired its conceptual finishing touches in Frankfurt.

Another of Adorno's pupils, the philosopher Werner Becker, described Imhoff as a physical embodiment of the 'non-identical' envisaged by Adorno's theory. 'For months,' wrote a Marxist critic of the strictest persuasion, 'bourgeois arts correspondents took delight in him.' And so they did. In November 1968, Saarland Radio reported that Imhoff had been so successful with his actions that he had 'become popular in a way that most poets here can only dream of becoming in their lifetimes'. Even when Imhoff decided in the autumn of 1968 not to disrupt that year's Büchner Prize awards, the press thought that this was worth reporting. And one cannot say that the ideas of action art were totally alien to Adorno. In his late volume, *Aesthetic Theory*, he sought access to this most contemporary of modern art forms:

> By conspicuously and willfully ceding to crude material, art wants to undo the damage that spirit – thought as well as art – has done to its other, to which it refers and which it wants to make eloquent. This is the determinable meaning of the meaningless intention-alien element of modern art, which extends from the hybridization of the arts to the *happenings*. It is not so much that traditional art is thereby sanctimoniously condemned by an arriviste judgment but that, rather, the effort is made to absorb even the negation of art by its own force.[32]

Imhoff had been born in February 1939 and by 1968 was no longer sufficiently naïve to believe in the political aims of the movement. He took part in the general euphoria, but as an individual, acting on his own initiative, with his own signed publications, which imitated, caricatured and outdid the language of the student demonstrators and critical theory, adopting it to suit his own ends,

'Art must be positive': the action artist Hans Imhoff at an event organized by the publishing house of Suhrkamp. In the background are Martin Walser (left) and Günter Eich

which at that time were hard to define. His leaflets, which appeared in series, included learned and richly allusive mottoes, turning something that had no status as a literary form and that was normally severely practical into a highly esoteric and aesthetic form that Imhoff later collected together and published in a de luxe edition titled *Antisocial Behaviour*. One of these leaflets was dedicated to Adorno: 'POETRY AS AN ELEMENT IS THE SUM TOTAL OF THE SPEECH-FORMING ORGANS IN THEIR REALIZATION OF THE REPRODUCTION OF THEMSELVES AS FATE,' we read here, the words reproduced in capitals in the manner of a manifesto.[33] Poetry was directly associated with articulation and at the same time with fate. While actionism in Vienna at this time was bloody in practice and Catholic and Dionysian in its tendency, Imhoff was interested in the legacy of German idealism, including philosophy, society and, above all, poetry. For a time Imhoff worked with sequences of random syllables as the building blocks of articulate speech: 'lamt kalet rent zwed pin ser lers por are twet egw rers'. This pure sound, extending over six pages, forms the content of *Prometheus Redeemed* and goes back to the sound poems of Filippo Tommaso Marinetti and the European avant-garde, and perhaps unconsciously, too, to

Jakob Böhme, who had wanted to forge a link between language and the cosmos in order to create a unity between sound and meaning. 'Frankfurt now has its own form of non-theatre that goes far beyond anti-theatre,' the *Frankfurter Allgemeine Zeitung* reported on 12 February 1968, when *Prometheus Redeemed* was performed in the city. The critic of another newspaper commented on the 'language, chopped up, as it were, into firewood': 'But the performance never let up in terms of its earnestness, entirely as though it was a matter of pedagogically driving home important information from a dialect area on the northern slopes of the Himalayas.' In fact, Imhoff later studied the scriptural language of ancient India and translated prayers from the Vedic. His work, completely destroying language and then reconstructing it equally completely, in each case in a strict form specially invented for it, answered one of the challenges facing his generation. People who had spent the first years of their lives without their fathers, whom they were later forced to welcome home as strangers, had been deprived of an entire dimension of language and engagement. By 1945 they were old enough to suspect that a whole new discourse now had to be learnt. It was against this background that Imhoff became a poet. If he was able to depict processes at the very edge of linguistic chaos, it was because he had honed his concept of form.

For his actions Imhoff was particularly fond of turning up at events where the progressive *Zeitgeist* was celebrating its own achievements. His appearance at an event organized by the publishing house of Suhrkamp has since become famous. When the poet and radio dramatist Günter Eich tried valiantly to deliver himself of what *Der Spiegel* described as a 'predominantly left-wing text' – 'I wake up and am at once in a crisis' – Imhoff was heard to interject: 'Even on a formal level, that doesn't work . . . can't you see?'[34] With his carefully timed disturbances, Imhoff made sure that those who were laughing were on his side. When he interrupted Jürgen Habermas's lecture on 14 November 1968, when he preferred to speak of 'Hans Imhoff's inaugural lecture', the stage was set for high comedy: 'Today I am beginning on an entirely Socratic note: whom are you entreating, O wondrous man? In Plato: O daimonie?' Habermas remained in the style familiar to him from the members of the Socialist League of German Students: 'What do you want then? Let's discuss it.' Imhoff: 'Oh dear, in that case I think we'd rather hear the rest of the lecture.' After a brief exchange, the following memorable dialogue unfolded. Habermas: 'Since Herr Imhoff will not bow to a majority decision . . . ' Imhoff (interrupting Habermas): 'That's straight out of the newspaper, I see you've prepared yourself. Perhaps I shall bow after all.' Habermas smiled for a moment, regained his composure, postponed his lecture and left the lecture theatre. Voice of an advanced student (who has risen from his seat, very agitatedly): 'But Herr Professor, I'd like you to remain.' (Laughter in the hall.) Imhoff (calling after Habermas in his embarrassment): 'Do stay.' Final scene: Imhoff packs away the notice, while the students hesitantly start to disperse. Groups of them form to discuss the matter.[35] Imhoff later documented each of his actions in the form of publications, with his 'Mitscherlich Action' even being annotated by members of the Sigmund Freud Institute. Taken together, these writings provide a genre picture of the late 'sixties that is unique in terms of its intelligence and sheer comedy.

On 13 June 1969 Adorno wrote to the dean of the Faculty of Philosophy: 'Spectabilis, in accordance with the regulations, I am informing you that my lecture was again broken up yesterday. The action that broke it up was directed by Herr Imhoff and a Herr Widmann. Herr Imhoff began by performing one of his well-known clown's acts, after which Herr Widmann – in spite of my objection and without my having the opportunity to say anything – took over the chair for a so-called discussion on the right of order.'[36] The writer and critic Arno Widmann, who is now editor-in-chief of the *Berliner Zeitung*, recalls in fact that the action on which he collaborated with Imhoff was not clownlike in character – Adorno's explanation was evidently based on his knowledge of other actions – but was intended as a protest against the University's new right of order. Some of the students had pleaded for a discussion of the disciplinary measures involved here and suggested that a vote be taken on whether to continue the lecture – but in general he and Imhoff had been 'absolute fans' of Adorno. But Adorno interpreted the situation very differently in his letter to the dean: 'It is not unimportant that the students began to show a kind of solidarity against me at the very moment that I declared my intention to inform the household management of the events. No one was in a position to explain how the two troublemakers could otherwise have been removed. Whereas it was an altogether violent assault, there would have been complaints about violence if any countermeasures had been taken.'[37] Widmann recalls that, following the incident, Rudolf zur Lippe had interceded with Adorno and arranged a seminar on *Dialectic of Enlightenment*, to which Adorno is said to have looked forward.

On the whole, however, the atmosphere in Frankfurt was now poisoned, and the summer term witnessed another, tasteless demonstration. On 22 April several women forced their way into Adorno's lecture in a scornful reversal of the hopes for women's emancipation that had found expression in *Dialectic of Enlightenment* and *Minima moralia*. Leaflets were distributed in the hall, headed 'Adorno as an institution is dead', while three female students clad in leather jackets surrounded him, strewing flowers, performing a dumb show and, in a final attempt to harass the man they were parodying, baring their breasts.[38] The death wish expressed in the leaflet was soon to come true.

By the time that Adorno died in August 1969, the normative potential of his theory was already exhausted. The heroic modernism of 1903 had had its day. The argument over art that Adorno had started in the 1960s, between Hans Thoma on the one hand and Ernst Wilhelm Nay on the other, was a non-starter as modernism had comprehensively won the day, with music long since having struck out in a completely different direction from that of Webern's ascetic successors. Men had walked on the moon – it was no longer an Expressionist fantasy as it had been in the poem from Adorno's youth. The message in the bottle that had been sent out by Adorno and Horkheimer had reached its intended readers, but the bottle had now shattered. Social theory, with its goals of universal emancipation, began to move away from culture; and the sort of association with the German language and German music that had still been decisive for Adorno was now regarded as outdated. The abstractions of exchange and money became the ideology of a world without symbols, of a universality without culture.

Epilogue: The Abandoned Room

The countryside of the Valais in southern Switzerland combines Alpine and Mediterranean features, while German- and French-speaking towns and villages lie side-by-side. The region is favoured by an agreeable climate, with the visitor being able to count on pleasant temperatures and little rain. Viniculture flourishes as it does nowhere else in Switzerland. In the eighteenth century, at a time when the countryside was being discovered, Jean-Jacques Rousseau praised the Valais in the twenty-third letter in Part One of *La nouvelle Héloïse*: even the purity of the mountain air brought with it a sense of inner peace, while the region's grandeur, beauty and variety were a source of perpetual stimulation. 'Finally, this play has I know not what kind of magic about it, something supernatural that enthrals both spirit and senses; one forgets everything, one forgets oneself, one no longer knows who one is.' It was also the vast range of different types of scenery within such narrow confines that impressed Goethe on his journey through Switzerland: 'The sight of the beautiful valley of the Valais,' he wrote on 8 November 1779, 'inspired a number of good and lively thoughts.'

Rainer Maria Rilke, who settled in Muzot after the First World War, described the 'wonderful Valais'[1] in a letter to a female friend:

> I was imprudent enough to come down here to Sierre and Sion; I've told you what a singular magic these places exerted on me when I first saw them a year ago at the time of the grape-gathering. The fact that Spain and Provence are so strangely blended in the landscape affected me deeply even then: for both those countries appealed to me in the last years before the war more powerfully and more decisively than anything else; and now to find their voices united in a wide-spreading Alpine valley in Switzerland! And this echo, this family likeness is not imaginary. Only the other day I read in a treatise on the plant-world of Valais that certain flowers appear here which are otherwise only to be found in Provence and Spain; it is the same with the butterflies:

thus does the spirit of a great river (and for me the Rhône has always been one of the most marvellous) carry gifts and affinities through country after country. The valley is so broad here and so magnificently filled with little eminences within the frame of the great bordering mountains, that it affords the eye a continual play of most bewitching modulations, like a game of chess with hills. As though hills were still being shifted about and grouped – so creative is the rhythm of what you see, an arrangement new and startling with every change of standpoint, – and the old houses and castles move all the more pleasingly in this optic game since most of them have the slope of a vineyard, the woods, the glades or the grey rocks for a background, blent into it like the pictures on a tapestry; for a sky that is absolutely indescribable (almost rainless) has its share high up in these perspectives and animates them with so ethereal a radiance that the remarkable correlation of object to object, just as in Spain, seems to shadow forth at certain hours the tension we think we can perceive between the stars in a constellation.[2]

What Rilke describes here is the rural counterpart of a subtly differentiated work of art, with the Valais as the epitome of natural beauty.

In his *Critique of Judgment*, Kant writes:

A man who has taste enough to judge the products of fine art with the greatest correctness and refinement may still be glad to leave a room in which he finds those beauties that minister to vanity and perhaps to social joys, and to turn instead to the beautiful in nature, in order to find there, as it were, a voluptuousness for the mind in a train of thought that he can never fully unravel. If that is how he chooses, we shall ourselves regard this choice of his with esteem and assume that he has a beautiful soul, such as no connoisseur and lover of art can claim to have because of the interest he takes in his objects.

During the summer of 1969 Adorno fled from the situation in Frankfurt, which had become intolerable for him, and sought refuge in the natural beauty of the Valais and, in particular, of Visp, a village six hundred metres above sea level with a wonderful view of the Matterhorn. Nearby, in Raron overlooking the Rhône, lies Rilke's grave. On 22 July 1969, Adorno's secretary, Elfriede Olbrich, wrote to Alfred Sohn-Rethel: 'Professor Adorno left yesterday on vacation, in a completely overwrought state and much the worse for wear. He asks me to thank you for your letters. He also asks you most kindly not to be cross with him for not having written to you himself; these lines are intended merely as a sign of his gratitude and friendly indebtedness to you.'[3]

Adorno loved the Matterhorn. At Easter 1921 he wrote: 'In our experience of nature the formation of the world takes place in the ego; a formed world enters meaningfully into a formed ego, radiant in the reflected glow of the divine'

Still incomplete was Adorno's *Aesthetic Theory*, a work that had been intended to salvage natural beauty in the face of the idealistic philosophy of art, and anyone who looks at the final weeks of Adorno's life is bound to be struck by the close correspondences between his earliest thoughts and those from the end of his life. The title of the essay that he wrote for his school-leaving examination had been 'Nature: A Source of Elevation, Instruction and Recuperation'. 'The word "nature"', we read here, 'in its most general sense means the totality of unconscious existence as such.'[4] 'To enter nature' signifies 'seeking out unconscious existence at the very place where it is most clearly revealed in the phenomenal world.'[5] This is followed by the earliest expression of Adorno's theory of culture: civilized man had dedicated himself to pure awareness and had invented the machine, and this had led to an awakening of the desire 'to recapture the lost unconscious'.[6] Anyone who sought out nature wanted 'unconscious existence in contrast to conscious civilization'.[7] Here man recovers and by reflecting on the laws of nature all around him, he acquires understanding and recognizes that 'all existence is meaningful'.[8] Later, in *Aesthetic Theory*, Adorno speaks of 'the application of reason to landscape'.[9] Ultimately, the experience of nature can 'raise the individual from the isolation of selfness into a meaningful wholeness, into the cosmic, it can *elevate* him'.[10] The sense of proportion that it gives relativizes the meanings that force their way to the forefront of our conscious minds. In this way nature leads man 'beyond the conceivable to the inconceivable and forces him to feel reverence'.[11] Only in nature does the isolated individual experience the law 'against which he would like to rebel every hour of his life, working away unconsciously, and he is overcome by the presentiment that this great law dictates the course of his soul just as it prescribes the path of the stars. Then he knows that he is one with the stars and all the unconscious things around him that are full of the spirit-law and as heavy as fruit on the tree that is God'. A man who has 'repressed' the 'irrational' now feels it with all his senses, and he who 'lost his soul in the conscious finds it again in the unconscious'.[12]

The emotional tone of these lines belonged to Adorno's youth. Was the theory that he developed an attempt to find a language for the ideas that he had grasped at that time – a language that would stand up to the critique of the mature thinker? For in his *Aesthetic Theory*, too, he laments the fate of the category of the naturally beautiful, even if that lament is couched in terms that have in the meantime grown more sober. It 'was repressed,' writes Adorno,[13] reverting to his nostalgic longing for the irrational and pleading that 'the case of natural beauty' be taken to the court of appeal.[14] But to reflect on nature meant returning to the basis of aesthetic experience. What beauty gives to nature is the chance to 'take a breath', according to these later drafts.[15] One of the conclusions of *Dialectic of Enlightenment* and its thesis that the domination of nature was a disaster for man was that nature, as an object in its own right, had to be reappraised as an object of philosophical and aesthetic contemplation: 'Verlaine's "la mer est plus belle que les cathédrales" is intoned from the vantage point of a high civilization.'[16] But equally obvious was the objection to images familiar from the culture industry of purple heath and 'even paintings of the Matterhorn'.[17] Was it the distinction between the authentic experience of a mountain – a 'Conversation in the Mountains' of the kind that Celan had envisaged – and its mass-produced representation that exercised Adorno in

Visp? Elisabeth Lenk has drawn attention to the fact that for Adorno this region must have been an ideal individual landscape. *Aesthetic Theory* contains the following crucial sentence about Zermatt, where the Matterhorn appears as though it is 'a child's picture of the absolute mountain, as though it were the only mountain in the whole world'.[18] Adorno died on 6 August 1969, 'following an excursion to his beloved Matterhorn,' recalled Elisabeth Lenk. Once again we are reminded not only of his comment to Monika Plessner, 'I'm a man of the mountains',[19] but also of a passage in a letter that he wrote when he was twenty-two: 'The mountains would be the right thing for me . . . and I'm not afraid of any lack of originality if I plan to divide my later life between the South Tyrol and Vienna.'[20]

In *Negative Dialectics* we find the remarkable sentence: 'The moment in which nature and history become commensurable with each other is the moment of passing.'[21] Anyone who goes into the country, Adorno wrote in his school-leaving examination,

> must have keen eyes and keen ears: but then he will encounter, quietly and wide-eyed, all the secret things that had slipped through the fine mesh of his net of ideas. That is why nature is loved by all those people who go out in search of secret things much as the gypsies go out stealing – poets and musicians and good-for-nothings, but also those who wrestle with the ultimate and most secret truths with the wakeful courage of bold ideas; they all loved nature, Goethe and Hölderlin, Schubert and Mahler, Eichendorff and Nietzsche and Maupassant; all these dissimilar human beings lost themselves in order to find themselves, they found their souls, they were raised to their homeland.[22]

Notes

Abbreviations

GS: Theodor W. Adorno, *Gesammelte Schriften*, ed. Rolf Tiedemann (Frankfurt am Main 1997)

B-A-MH: Theodor W. Adorno and Max Horkheimer, *Briefwechsel Band I: 1927–1937*, ed. Christoph Gödde and Henri Lonitz (Frankfurt am Main 2003)

B-A-WB: Theodor W. Adorno and Walter Benjamin, *Briefwechsel 1928–1940*, ed. Henri Lonitz (Frankfurt am Main 1995); trans. by Nicholas Walker as *Theodor W. Adorno and Walter Benjamin: The Complete Correspondence 1928–1940* (Cambridge 1999) (page numbers of both editions)

B-LL-SK: Peter Erwin Jansen and Christian Schmidt (eds.), *In steter Freundschaft: Briefwechsel Leo Löwenthal und Siegfried Kracauer 1921–1966* (Lüneburg 2003)

B-A-AB: Theodor W. Adorno and Alban Berg, *Briefwechsel 1925–1935*, ed. Henri Lonitz (Frankfurt am Main 1997)

B-A-TM: Theodor W. Adorno and Thomas Mann, *Briefwechsel 1943–1955*, ed. Christoph Gödde and Thomas Sprecher (Frankfurt am Main 2002)

GS(MH): Max Horkheimer, *Gesammelte Schriften*, ed. Alfred Schmidt and Gunzelin Schmidt Noerr (Frankfurt am Main 1988–96)

FAB: Frankfurter Adorno Blätter

Prologue

1. *GS*, xvi.282; trans. by Rodney Livingstone as *Quasi una fantasia: Essays on Modern Music* (London 1992), 35.
2. *GS*, xx/2.524.
3. *GS*, vi.15; trans. by E. B. Ashton as *Negative Dialectics* (New York 1973), 3.

Chapter One

1. Heinz Ludwig Arnold (ed.), *Text und Kritik: Theodor W. Adorno* (Munich 1977), 16.
2. Immanuel Kant, 'Anthropologie', *Schriften zur Anthropologie, Geschichtsphilosophie, Politik und Pädagogik*, ed. Wilhelm Weischedel (Frankfurt am Main 1964), 666.
3. Viktor Hehn, *Italienische Ansichten und Streiflichter* (Munich n.d.), 78.
4. Arnold, *Text und Kritik* (note 1), 16–17.
5. *GS*, iv.201–2; trans. by E. F. N. Jephcott as *Minima moralia: Reflections from Damaged Life* (London 1978), 177.
6. Arnold, *Text und Kritik* (note 1), 16.
7. Thomas Mann, 'Die Entstehung des Doktor Faustus', *Reden und Aufsätze* (Frankfurt 1990), iii.173; trans. by Richard and Clara Winston as *The Story of a Novel: The Genesis of Doctor Faustus* (New York 1961), 45.
8. *GS*, xvii.303.

9. *GS*, x.302–3.
10. *GS*, x.303–4.
11. Soma Morgenstern, *Alban Berg und seine Idole: Erinnerungen und Briefe* (Lüneburg 1995), 119.
12. *GS*, iv.254–5; (*Minima moralia*), 223.
13. *GS*, xvi.117–18.
14. *GS*, xx.758.
15. *GS*, xx.756–7.
16. *GS*, xx.758.
17. *GS*, xx.759.
18. *GS*, xx.759–60.
19. Theodor W. Adorno, 'Zur Lehre von der Geschichte und von der Freiheit', *Nachgelassene Schriften* (Frankfurt am Main 2001), iv/13.250.
20. *GS*, iv.219; (*Minima moralia*), 192.
21. *FAB*, viii (1999), 85.
22. *FAB*, viii (1999), 85.
23. *FAB*, viii (1999), 86.
24. *GS*, iv.219; (*Minima moralia*), 192–3.
25. *GS*, xx.715.
26. *GS*, iv.220; (*Minima moralia*), 193.
27. *GS*, xx.722.
28. *GS*, xx.722.
29. *GS*, xx.725.

Chapter Two

1. Siegfried Kracauer, *Schriften*, ed. Karsten Witte and others (Frankfurt am Main 1971—), v/1.229.
2. ibid., v/1.229.
3. ibid., v/1.232.
4. Elisabeth Lenk, 'Hauptgeschäfte, Nebensachen: Begegnungen mit, Briefe von Theodor W. Adorno', *Frankfurter Allgemeine Zeitung* (23 Oct. 1999).
5. Kracauer, *Schriften* (note 1), vii.255.
6. ibid., vii.256.
7. ibid., vii.256.
8. ibid., vii.261.
9. *GS*, xi.388.
10. *GS*, xi.388.
11. *B-LL-SK*, 44.
12. *B-LL-SK*, 45.
13. *B-LL-SK*, 28.
14. *B-LL-SK*, 28.
15. *B-LL-SK*, 51.
16. *B-LL-SK*, 54.
17. *B-LL-SK*, 54.
18. Kracauer, *Schriften* (note 1), i.125.
19. Ingrid Belke and Irina Renz (eds.), *Siegfried Kracauer 1889–1966* (Marbach am Neckar 1988).
20. Quoted from 'Ausgerichtet sei der Mensch. Siegfried Kracauers soziologische Reportagen "Die Angestellten": Kritik einer Legende', *Frankfurter Allgemeine Zeitung* (24 Jan. 2001).
21. ibid.
22. ibid.
23. ibid.
24. ibid.
25. ibid.
26. ibid.
27. ibid.
28. Péter Esterházy, *Harmonia caelestis* (Berlin 2001).
29. Georg Lukács, *Die Seele und die Formen* (Neuwied and Berlin 1971), 179; trans. by Anna Bostock as *Soul and Form* (London 1974), 124.
30. ibid., 181, 126.
31. ibid., 185, 128.
32. ibid., 185, 129.
33. ibid., 197, 134.
34. ibid., 229, 160.
35. ibid., 230, 160.
36. ibid., 237, 165.
37. Georg Lukács, *Lenin* (Neuwied and Berlin 1969), 7.
38. Ernst Nolte, *Streitpunkte* (Berlin and Frankfurt 1994).
39. Lukács, *Die Seele und die Formen* (note 29), 245; (*Soul and Form*), 171.
40. Thomas Mann, *Der Zauberberg* (Frankfurt am Main 1995), 509–10; trans. by H. T. Lowe-Porter as *The Magic Mountain* (London 1999), 372.
41. ibid., 524, 382.
42. ibid., 536–7, 392.
43. Theodor W. Adorno, 'Ontologie und

Dialektik', *Nachgelassene Schriften* (Frankfurt am Main 2002), iv/7.384–5.

44. *GS*, xix.42.
45. *GS*, xi.556.
46. *B-LL-SK*, 24.
47. *GS*, xi.557.
48. *GS*, xi.557.
49. *GS*, xi.556.
50. *B-LL-SK*, 32.
51. Soma Morgenstern, *Alban Berg und seine Idole: Erinnerungen und Briefc* (Lüneburg 1995), 119.

Chapter Three

1. *GS*, i.17.
2. *GS*, i.27.
3. *GS*, i.76.
4. *B-LL-SK*, 57–8.
5. *GS*, xix.23–4.
6. *GS*, xix.29.
7. *GS*, xix.26.
8. *Theodor W. Adorno / Ernst Krenek: Briefwechsel 1925–1935*, ed. Wolfgang Rogge (Frankfurt am Main 1974), 46 (letter of 7 Oct. 1934).
9. Rolf Tiedemann, 'Gretel Adorno zum Abschied', *FAB*, iii (1994), 148–51. Tiedemann's article is also the source of the following information about Gretel Adorno.
10. Thomas Mann, 'Die Entstehung des Doktor Faustus', *Reden und Aufsätze* (Frankfurt 1990), iii.173; trans. by Richard and Clara Winston as *The Story of a Novel: The Genesis of Doctor Faustus* (New York 1961), 44.
11. *B-LL-SK*, 28.
12. *GS*, xviii.270.
13. *GS*, xviii.266.
14. *GS*, xviii.269.
15. *GS*, iv.248; trans. by E. F. N. Jephcott as *Minima moralia* (London 1978), 218.
16. *GS*, iv.248; (*Minima moralia*), 217–18.
17. *GS*, xiv.369.
18. *GS*, xiv.356.
19. *GS*, xiv.356.
20. *GS*, xiv.357.
21. *GS*, xiv.357.

22. *GS*, xiii.340; trans. by Juliane Brand and Christopher Hailey as *Alban Berg: Master of the Smallest Link* (Cambridge 1991), 13.
23. *GS*, xix.11.
24. *GS*, xix.11.
25. *GS*, xix.13.
26. Soma Morgenstern, *Alban Berg und seine Idole: Erinnerungen und Briefe* (Lüneburg 1995), 117.
27. ibid., 118.
28. ibid., 118.
29. ibid., 118.
30. ibid., 119.
31. ibid., 184.
32. ibid., 168–9.
33. ibid., 171.
34. Dieter Schnebel, 'Einführung in Adornos Musik', *Adorno und die Musik*, ed. Otto Kolleritsch (Graz 1979), 15.
35. ibid., 16.
36. ibid., 16.
37. Morgenstern, *Alban Berg* (note 26), 123.
38. ibid., 123.
39. *GS*, ii.258.
40. *GS*, xvii.313.
41. *GS*, xvii.315.
42. *GS*, xvii.317.
43. Ernst Krenek, *Im Atem der Zeit: Erinnerungen an die Moderne* (Hamburg 1998), 454.
44. ibid., 729.
45. ibid., 782.
46. Mann, 'Die Entstehung des Doktor Faustus' (note 10), iii.175; (*The Story of a Novel*), 47.
47. *GS*, xvii.18.
48. *GS*, xvii.23.
49. *GS*, xvii.24.
50. *GS*, xvii.33.
51. *GS*, xvii.33.

Chapter Four

1. Max Weber, *Gesammelte Aufsätze zur Religionssoziologie* (Tübingen 1988), iii.6.
2. Stanley Rothman and S. Robert Lichter, *Roots of Radicalism: Jews, Christians, and the New Left* (Oxford 1982).

3. Theodor Lessing, *Untergang der Erde am Geist: Europa und Asien* (Hanover 1924), 271–2.
4. See Norman Cantor, *The Sacred Chain: A History of the Jews* (New York 1994).
5. Georg Simmel, *Soziologie: Untersuchungen über die Formen der Vergesellschaftung* (Berlin 1958), 511–12.
6. *GS(MH)*, xiv.332.
7. Bertolt Brecht, *Werke* (Berlin and Weimar 1995), xxvii.94.
8. Ulrike Migdal, *Die Frühgeschichte des Frankfurter Instituts für Sozialforschung* (Frankfurt am Main 1981), 12.
9. ibid., 18.
10. ibid., 19.
11. ibid., 20.
12. ibid., 44.
13. *GS(MH)*, xviii.570.
14. *GS(MH)*, xv.80.
15. *GS(MH)*, xv.80.
16. *GS(MH)*, xv.82.
17. *GS(MH)*, iii.31.
18. *GS(MH)*, iii.26.
19. Walter Benjamin, *Gesammelte Schriften*, ed. Rolf Tiedemann and Hermann Schweppenhäuser (Frankfurt am Main 1972–89), i/3.1000.
20. *GS(MH)*, iii.33.
21. *GS(MH)*, iii.33.
22. *GS(MH)*, xi.301.
23. *GS(MH)*, xi.342.
24. *GS(MH)*, x.247.
25. *GS(MH)*, xviii.592.
26. *GS(MH)*, xviii.592.
27. Conversation with Erich Fromm in *Die Zeit* (21 March 1980).
28. Erich Fromm, *Das jüdische Gesetz: Zur Soziologie des Diaspora-Judentums* (Weinheim 1989), 40.
29. ibid., 42.
30. ibid., 43–4.
31. ibid., 30.
32. Erich Fromm, *Psychoanalysis and Religion* (New Haven and London 1950), 84.
33. Fedor Stepun, 'Formen deutscher Sowjetophilie', *Sinn und Form* (2002), 216.
34. ibid., 217.
35. *Zeitschrift für Sozialforschung*, i (1932), 98.
36. *Zeitschrift für Sozialforschung*, i (1932), 274.
37. *Zeitschrift für Sozialforschung*, i (1932), 117.
38. *GS*, xviii.733; trans. by Wes Blomster as 'On the Social Situation of Music', *Essays on Music*, ed. Richard Leppert (Berkeley 2002), 395.
39. *GS*, xviii.767; ('On the Social Situation of Music'), 424 (trans. emended).
40. *GS*, xviii.734, 396.
41. *GS*, xviii.737, 398.
42. *GS*, xviii.737, 398.
43. *GS*, xviii.736 and 738, 398 and 399.
44. *GS*, xviii.746, 406.
45. *GS*, xviii.747, 407.
46. *GS*, xviii.747, 407.
47. *GS*, xviii.751, 410.
48. *GS*, xviii.751, 411.
49. *GS*, xviii.752, 411.
50. *GS*, xviii.731, 393.
51. *GS*, xviii.732–3, 394.

Chapter Five

1. Ernst Krenek, *Im Atem der Zeit: Erinnerungen an die Moderne* (Hamburg 1998), 729.
2. Heinz Ludwig Arnold (ed.), *Text und Kritik: Theodor W. Adorno* (Munich 1977), 12.
3. *GS*, xx.594.
4. *GS*, xx.595.
5. Petra Kohse, *Marianne Hoppe: Eine Biographie* (Berlin 2001), 77.
6. *GS*, xx.542.
7. Carl Dreyfus, 'Bericht über den Ausflug', *Neue Schweizer Rundschau*, xxiii/4 (1930), 279ff. and 'Fröhlicher Abend', *Der Querschnitt*, xi/5 (1931), 611ff.
8. *GS*, xviii.749; trans. by Wes Blomster as 'On the Social Situation of Music', *Essays on Music*, ed. Richard Leppert (Berkeley 2002), 409 (trans. emended).
9. *GS*, xi.630.
10. *GS*, xi.630.
11. *GS*, xx.588.
12. *GS*, xx.595.

13. *GS*, xx.591.
14. *GS*, xx.595–6.
15. *GS*, xx.597.
16. Quoted in 'Der Kitsch, der Tod und die Krise', *Frankfurter Allgemeine Zeitung* (30 May 1998).

Chapter Six

1. Karl Marx, *Das Kapital: Kritik der politischen Ökonomie* (Berlin 1972), i.85; trans. by Ben Fowkes as *Capital: A Critique of Political Economy* (London 1990), i.163.
2. ibid., i.97, i.176–7.
3. ibid., i.94, i.173.
4. ibid., i.86–7, i.165.
5. *GS*, i.345–65.
6. *GS*, i.345.
7. *GS*, xx.173.
8. *GS*, xx.173–4.
9. Hans Puttnies and Gary Smith, *Benjaminjana* (Gießen 1991), 102–3.
10. *B-A-WB*, 234, 178.
11. *B-A-WB*, 108, 80.
12. *GS*, xx.175.
13. *GS*, ii.256.
14. *GS*, iii.72; trans. by Edmund Jephcott as *Dialectic of Enlightenment* (Stanford, California, 2002), 42.
15. *GS*, ii.78; trans. by Robert Hullot-Kentor as *Kierkegaard: Construction of the Aesthetic* (Minneapolis 1989), 53.
16. *GS*, ii.152, 107.
17. *GS*, ii.172, 121.
18. *GS*, ii.181, 127.
19. *GS*, ii.173–4, 122.
20. *GS*, ii.199–200, 140.
21. *GS*, ii.199, 140.
22. *B-A-AB*, 249.
23. *Philosophisches Jahrbuch der Görresgesellschaft*, xlviii (1935), 396.
24. *Kant-Studien*, xl (1935), 327.
25. Gershom Scholem and Walter Benjamin, *Briefwechsel 1933–1940*, ed. Gershom Scholem (Frankfurt am Main 1985), 36.
26. ibid., 109.
27. *GS*, i.335.
28. *GS*, i.341.

29. *GS*, i.338.
30. *GS*, i.338.
31. Kurt Mautz, *Der Urfreund* (Paderborn 1996), 41.
32. ibid., 42.
33. ibid., 43.
34. ibid., 44.
35. ibid., 44.

Chapter Seven

1. *GS*, iv.117; trans. by E. F. N. Jephcott as *Minima moralia: Reflections from Damaged Life* (London 1978), 104.
2. Heinz Ludwig Arnold (ed.), *Text und Kritik: Theodor W. Adorno* (Munich 1977), 19.
3. ibid., 18.
4. *B-A-AB*, 279.
5. *GS(MH)*, xv.99.
6. Theodor W. Adorno, *Zur Lehre von der Geschichte und der Freiheit: Nachgelassene Schriften* (Frankfurt am Main 2001), iv/13.31–2.
7. *B-A-AB*, 286.
8. Soma Morgenstern, *Alban Berg und seine Idole: Erinnerungen und Briefe* (Lüneburg 1995), 257.
9. *B-A-AB*, 286–7.
10. *GS*, xix.250.
11. Arnold, *Text und Kritik* (note 2), 18.
12. ibid., 19.
13. *GS*, xix.598.
14. *GS*, xix.237–8.
15. *GS*, xix.238.
16. *GS*, xix.246.
17. *GS*, xix.247.
18. *GS*, xix.252.
19. *GS*, xix.252.
20. *GS*, xix.252–3.
21. *GS*, xix.331.
22. Arnold, *Text und Kritik* (note 2), 20.
23. *GS*, xix.332.
24. *GS*, xviii.795; trans. by Susan H. Gillespie as 'Farewell to Jazz', *Essays on Music*, ed. Richard Leppert (Berkeley 2002), 496.
25. *B-A-AB*, 276.
26. *B-A-AB*, 279.
27. *GS*, xvii.319.

28. *B-A-AB*, 291.
29. *GS*, xvii.128.
30. *GS*, xvii.128.

Chapter Eight

1. Theodor W. Adorno and Ernst Krenek, *Briefwechsel 1925–1935*, ed. Wolfgang Rogge (Frankfurt am Main 1974), 44.
2. *GS*, xx.46–118.
3. *GS*, xx.119–34.
4. *GS*, v.7–245.
5. The sources for Adorno's period in Oxford have been assembled by Andreas Kramer and Evelyn Wilcock, 'A preserve for professional philosophers: Adornos Husserl-Dissertation 1934–37 und ihr Oxforder Kontext', *Deutsche Vierteljahrsschrift für Literaturwissenschaft und Geistesgeschichte*, lxxiii (1999), 115–61 (special issue entitled *Wege deutsch-jüdischen Denkens im zwanzigsten Jahrhundert*).
6. Adorno and Krenek, *Briefwechsel* (note 1), 23.
7. *B-A-MH*, 19.
8. *B-A-MH*, 68.
9. Heinz Ludwig Arnold (ed.), *Text und Kritik: Theodor W. Adorno* (Munich 1977), 20.
10. *B-A-MH*, 82–3.
11. Arnold, *Text und Kritik* (note 9), 20.
12. ibid., 20.
13. *B-A-MH*, 85.
14. *B-A-MH*, 87.
15. *B-A-MH*, 208.
16. *B-A-MH*, 279.
17. *GS*, xx.95.
18. *GS*, xx.95.
19. *GS*, xx.95.
20. *GS*, xx.96.
21. *GS*, xx.96.
22. *GS*, xx.52.
23. *GS*, xx.84.
24. *B-A-MH*, 357.
25. Alfred Sohn-Rethel, *Ökonomie und Klassenstruktur des deutschen Faschismus* (Frankfurt am Main 1973).
26. See Carl Freytag, '"Kann man leben von seinem Genie?" Alfred Sohn-Rethel in Heidelberg', Reinhard Blomert and others (eds.), *Heidelberger Sozial- und Staatswissenschaften: Das Institut für Sozial- und Staatswissenschaften zwischen 1918 und 1958* (Marburg 1997).
27. *B-A-MH*, 170.
28. *GS*, xvii.102.
29. *GS*, xiii.16; trans. by Rodney Livingstone as *In Search of Wagner* (London 1981), 17. (As many reviewers have pointed out, the title of the otherwise exemplary English translation was apparently foisted on the translator by his publisher, and it is not entirely appropriate as Adorno was not searching for Wagner but was convinced that he had already found him. The present translator has preferred a more literal alternative: *Essay on Wagner*.)
30. *GS*, xiii.25; (*In Search of Wagner*), 27.
31. Bertolt Brecht, *Werke* (Berlin and Weimar 1995), xxvii.49–50.
32. *GS*, i.79–322.
33. *GS*, ii.573.
34. *B-A-MH*, 539.
35. *B-A-MH*, 541.
36. *B-A-MH*, 541.
37. *B-A-MH*, 542.
38. *B-A-MH*, 553.
39. *FAB*, viii (1999), 96.
40. *B-A-MH*, 537.
41. *B-A-WB*, 329, 252.
42. *B-A-MH*, 301.
43. *B-A-WB*, 264, 202.
44. *GS*, x.215.
45. *GS*, xiii.145; (*In Search of Wagner*), 156.
46. Shortly after the First World War, Benjamin planned to translate some of the prose pieces of the Catholic writer Charles Péguy. Between 1900 and his death in 1914 Péguy wrote for and edited the polemic *Cahiers de la quinzaine*.
47. *GS*, xiv.14–50; trans. anonymously as 'On the Fetish-Character in Music and the Regression of Listening', *Essays on Music*, ed. Richard Leppert (Berkeley 2002), 288–317.
48. *B-A-MH*, 131.

49. *B-A-MH*, 134.
50. *B-A-MH*, 374.
51. *B-A-MH*, 440.
52. *B-A-MH*, 442.
53. *B-A-MH*, 513.

Chapter Nine

1. *GS*, x.703–6.
2. *GS*, xx.585–6.
3. *B-A-WB*, 348, 267.
4. *B-A-WB*, 389, 298.
5. *GS*, x.706–7.
6. *GS*, x.707.
7. *GS*, xiv.181–98.
8. *GS*, xiv.184.
9. *GS*, xiv.184.
10. *GS*, xiv.185–6.
11. *GS*, xiv.196.
12. *GS*, iv.53; trans. by E. F. N. Jephcott as *Minima moralia: Reflections from Damaged Life* (London 1978), 48.
13. *GS*, iv.54; (*Minima moralia*), 48.
14. *GS*, xx.574.
15. *GS*, xx.575.
16. *GS*, iv.54; (*Minima moralia*), 49.
17. *GS(MH)*, xii.512.
18. *GS(MH)*, xii.513.
19. *GS(MH)*, xii.513–14.
20. *GS(MH)*, xii.514.
21. *GS(MH)*, xii.514.
22. *GS(MH)*, xii.515.
23. *GS(MH)*, xvii.97.
24. *GS(MH)*, xvii.98.
25. *GS(MH)*, xvii.152.
26. *GS(MH)*, xvii.141.
27. *GS(MH)*, xvii.141.
28. *GS(MH)*, xvii.210.
29. *GS(MH)*, xvii.211.
30. Bertolt Brecht, *Werke* (Berlin and Weimar 1995), xxvii.12–13.
31. ibid., xvii.159.
32. Hans Bunge, *Fragen Sie mehr über Brecht: Hanns Eisler im Gespräch* (Munich 1970), 188.
33. Ernst Bloch, *Briefe 1903–1975*, ed. Karola Bloch and others (Frankfurt am Main 1985), 443.
34. *GS*, xx.190.
35. ibid., 530.

36. Soma Morgenstern, *Alban Berg und seine Idole: Erinnerungen und Briefe* (Lüneburg 1995), 353.
37. *GS(MH)*, xii.561.
38. *GS(MH)*, xii.567.
39. *GS*, viii.392.
40. *GS*, viii.394.
41. *GS(MH)*, xii.576.
42. *GS(MH)*, xii.569.
43. *GS(MH)*, xii.576.
44. *GS*, xx.575–6.
45. Bunge, *Fragen Sie mehr über Brecht* (note 32), 22.
46. *GS*, xv.32; trans. as *Composing for the Films* (London 1994), 24.
47. *GS*, xv.32, 24.
48. *GS*, xv.33, 24.
49. *GS*, xv.33, 25.
50. *GS*, xv.34, 26.
51. *GS*, xv.35, 26–7.
52. *GS*, xv.36, 28.
53. *GS*, xv.36, 28.
54. *GS*, iii.293; trans. by Edmund Jephcott as *Dialectic of Enlightenment* (Stanford, California, 2002), 212.
55. *GS*, x.365. The actor was Harold Russell (1914–2002), who won two Oscars for his role in *The Best Years of Our Lives*.
56. Thomas Mann, *Tagebücher 28.5.1946 – 31.12.1948*, ed. Inge Jens (Frankfurt am Main 1989), 166.
57. ibid., 166.
58. *GS*, xv.145.
59. *GS*, xv.144.
60. Bunge, *Fragen Sie mehr über Brecht* (note 32), 189.

Chapter Ten

1. *GS*, iii.15; trans. by Edmund Jephcott as *Dialectic of Enlightenment* (Stanford, California, 2002), xvii.
2. *B-A-MH*, 166.
3. *GS*, iii.141, 94.
4. *GS*, iii.141, 94.
5. *GS*, iii.143, 96.
6. *GS*, iii.144, 96.
7. *GS*, iii.145, 97.
8. *GS*, iii.145, 98.
9. *GS*, iii.155, 106.

10. *GS*, iii.179, 126.
11. *GS*, iii.40, 17.
12. *GS*, iii.36.
13. *GS*, iii.130; (*Dialectic of Enlightenment*), 86.
14. *GS*, iii.131, 86.
15. *GS*, iii.131, 87.
16. *GS*, iii.132, 87.
17. *GS*, iii.137, 91.
18. *GS*, iii.135, 89.
19. *GS*, iii.201, 145.
20. *GS*, iii.203, 146. It may be added that the idea of Jesus as a magus revered as an idol goes back to the Talmud and specifically to Baraita Sanhedrin 43a: 'On the eve of Passover Yeshua the Nazarean was hanged. For forty days before the execution took place, a herald went forth and cried, "He is going forth to be stoned because he has practised sorcery and enticed Israel to apostasy. Any one who can say anything in his favour, let him come forward and plead on his behalf." But since nothing was brought forward in his favour he was hanged on the eve of Passover.'
21. *FAB*, viii (1999), 237.
22. Theodor W. Adorno, *Dissonanzen: Musik in der verwalteten Welt* (Göttingen 1956).
23. *GS*, xvii.12.
24. *GS(MH)*, xvii.332.
25. *GS(MH)*, xii.175.
26. Leo Strauss, *Persecution and the Art of Writing* (Chicago 1988).
27. *GS*, iii.64; (*Dialectic of Enlightenment*), 37.
28. *GS*, iii.64, 38.
29. *GS*, iii.65, 38.
30. *GS*, iii.66, 39.

Chapter Eleven

1. *B-A-TM*, 80.
2. *B-A-TM*, 99.
3. *B-A-TM*, 34.
4. This is the wording of the text by Mann that Suhrkamp used in promoting *Philosophy of Modern Music*.
5. Thomas Mann, 'Die Entstehung des Doktor Faustus', *Reden und Aufsätze* (Frankfurt 1990), iii.173; trans. by Richard and Clara Winston as *The Story of a Novel: The Genesis of Doctor Faustus* (New York 1961), 43.
6. ibid., 172, 42.
7. ibid., 172, 42.
8. ibid., 172, 42–3.
9. ibid., 174, 45.
10. ibid., 176, 48.
11. ibid., 207, 94–5.
12. Thomas Mann, *Doktor Faustus: Das Leben des deutschen Tonsetzers Adrian Leverkühn erzählt von einem Freunde* (Frankfurt am Main 1980), 321; trans. by John E. Woods as *Doctor Faustus: The Life of the German Composer Adrian Leverkühn As Told by a Friend* (New York 1997), 253.
13. ibid., 451, 354.
14. Thomas Mann, *Tagebücher 1944 – 1.4. 1946*, ed. Inge Jens (Frankfurt 1986), 296.
15. ibid., 13.
16. ibid., 100.
17. ibid., 282.
18. ibid., 257.
19. Thomas Mann, *Tagebücher 28.5.1946 – 31.12.1948*, ed. Inge Jens (Frankfurt am Main 1989), 69.
20. ibid., 20.
21. ibid., 245.
22. ibid., 221.
23. ibid., 304.
24. ibid., 322.
25. Arnold Schoenberg, *Style and Idea* (Berkeley 1984), 386.
26. Joseph Auner, *A Schoenberg Reader: Documents of a Life* (New Haven 2003), 336–7.
27. Hans Heinz Stuckenschmidt, *Arnold Schoenberg: His Life, World, and Work*, trans. Humphrey Searle (New York 1978), 508.
28. Heinz Ludwig Arnold (ed.), *Text und Kritik: Theodor W. Adorno* (Munich 1977), 77.
29. *GS*, xii.128; trans. by Anne G. Mitchell and Wesley V. Blomster as *Philosophy of Modern Music* (London 1994), 136.
30. *GS*, xii.120, 126–7.

31. *GS*, xii.37, 30.
32. *GS*, xii.37, 30–31.
33. *GS*, xii.37, 31.
34. *GS*, xii.37–8, 31.
35. *GS*, xii.103, 107.
36. *GS*, xii.110, 115.
37. *GS*, xii.110, 115.
38. *GS*, xii.111, 115.
39. *GS*, xii.111–12, 116.
40. *GS*, iv.91; trans. by E. F. N. Jephcott as *Minima moralia: Reflections from Damaged Life* (London 1978), 81.
41. *GS*, viii.373–91.
42. *GS*, xii.185; (*Philosophy of Modern Music*), 204.
43. *GS*, xii.135, 145.
44. Stuckenschmidt, *Arnold Schoenberg* (note 27), 508.

Chapter Twelve

1. T. W. Adorno, Else Frenkel-Brunswik, Daniel J. Levinson and R. Nevitt Sanford in collaboration with Betty Aron, Maria Hertz Levinson and William Morrow, *The Authoritarian Personality* (New York 1950), 1.
2. ibid., 1.
3. ibid., 228.
4. See Rolf Wiggershaus, *Die Frankfurter Schule* (Munich 2001), 418.
5. Bertolt Brecht, *Werke* (Berlin and Weimar 1995), xxvii.213.
6. Karl Marx, 'Zur Judenfrage' in Karl Marx and Friedrich Engels, *Werke* (Berlin 1976), i.372; trans. by Joseph O'Malley as 'On the Jewish Question' in Karl Marx, *Early Political Writings*, ed. Joseph O'Malley (Cambridge 1994), 52.
7. Brecht, *Werke* (note 5), xxvii.213.
8. Adorno *et al.*, *The Authoritarian Personality* (note 1), 709.
9. ibid., 695.
10. ibid., 226–35.
11. ibid., 659.
12. ibid., 667.
13. ibid., 711.
14. ibid., 718.
15. ibid., 720.
16. ibid., 723.

17. Theodor W. Adorno, *Studien zum autoritären Charakter*, trans. Milli Weinbrenner (Frankfurt 1995), 455. (This section on Martin Luther Thomas's radio addresses was added to the German edition and did not appear in the 1950 American edition.)
18. Adorno *et al.*, *The Authoritarian Personality* (note 1), 725.
19. ibid., 724.

Chapter Thirteen

1. *Jahrbuch für Soziologiegeschichte 1993* (Opladen 1995), 270.
2. *GS(MH)*, xvii.85.
3. *GS(MH)*, xviii.30.
4. *GS(MH)*, xvii.282.
5. *GS(MH)*, xvii.379.
6. *GS(MH)*, xvii.378.
7. *GS(MH)*, xvii.392.
8. *GS(MH)*, xvii.401.
9. *GS(MH)*, xvii.402.
10. *GS(MH)*, xviii.16.
11. *GS(MH)*, xviii.16.
12. *GS(MH)*, xviii.17.
13. *GS(MH)*, xviii.21.
14. *GS(MH)*, xviii.29.
15. *GS(MH)*, xviii.48.
16. *GS(MH)*, xvii.465.
17. Monika Plessner, 'Miteinander reden heißt miteinander träumen: Gruppenstudie mit Horkheimer', *Frankfurter Allgemeine Zeitung* (28 Sept. 1991).
18. Herbert Marcuse, *Feindanalysen*, quoted in *Frankfurter Allgemeine Zeitung* (18 July 1998).
19. *GS(MH)*, xvii.933.
20. *GS*, xx.390.
21. *GS*, xx.391.
22. *GS*, xx.392.
23. *FAB*, viii (1999), 95.
24. *FAB*, viii (1999), 96.
25. *FAB*, viii (1999), 98.
26. *FAB*, viii (1999), 98.
27. *FAB*, viii (1999), 99.
28. *FAB*, viii (1999), 101.
29. *FAB*, viii (1999), 101–2.
30. *FAB*, viii (1999), 102.
31. *FAB*, viii (1999), 102.

32. *FAB*, viii (1999), 105.
33. *FAB*, viii (1999), 106.
34. *FAB*, viii (1999), 107.
35. *FAB*, viii (1999), 107.
36. *FAB*, viii (1999), 106.
37. *FAB*, viii (1999), 106.
38. *FAB*, viii (1999), 108–9.
39. *FAB*, viii (1999), 109.
40. *FAB*, viii (1999), 109.
41. *FAB*, viii (1999), 110.
42. *FAB*, viii (1999), 109.
43. Plessner, 'Miteinander reden' (note 17).
44. *GS*, ix/2.131.
45. *GS*, ix/2.136.
46. *GS*, ix/2.136.
47. Plessner, 'Miteinander reden' (note 17).
48. *GS*, ix/2.320.
49. Plessner, 'Miteinander reden' (note 17).
50. Thomas Mann, open letter published in *Der Tag und Berliner Lokal-Anzeiger* (30 May 1919).
51. Marianne Weber, *Max Weber: Ein Lebensbild* (Munich and Zurich 1989), 667.
52. Sebastian Haffner, *Anmerkungen zu Hitler* (Frankfurt am Main 1981), 75.
53. *GS*, ix/2.237.
54. T. W. Adorno, Else Frenkel-Brunswik, Daniel J. Levinson and R. Nevitt Sanford in collaboration with Betty Aron, Maria Hertz Levinson and William Morrow, *The Authoritarian Personality* (New York 1950), 681.
55. ibid., 681.
56. *GS*, ix/2.245.
57. *GS*, ix/2.247.
58. Alfred de Zayas, *Nemesis at Potsdam: The Anglo-Americans and the Expulsion of the Germans* (London 2/1979), 133.
59. *GS*, ix/2.244.
60. *GS*, ix/2.244.
61. *GS*, ix/2.242.
62. Theodor W. Adorno, 'Zur Lehre von der Geschichte und von der Freiheit', *Nachgelassene Schriften* (Frankfurt am Main 2001), iv/13.37.
63. Plessner, 'Miteinander reden' (note 17).

Chapter Fourteen

1. *B-A-TM*, 49.
2. *GS*, xx.453–64.
3. *GS*, xx.453.
4. *B-A-TM*, 67.
5. *B-A-TM*, 75.
6. *B-A-TM*, 103.
7. *B-A-TM*, 47–8.
8. *B-A-TM*, 80.
9. Gershom Scholem, *Briefe Band II: 1948–1970*, ed. Thomas Sparr (Munich 1995), 239.
10. Gottfried Benn, *Briefe an F. W. Oelze 1950–1956*, ed. Harald Steinhagen and Jürgen Schröder (Frankfurt am Main 1982), 208.
11. *GS*, x.701.
12. *GS*, x.701.
13. *GS*, x.700.
14. *GS*, x.700.
15. *GS(MH)*, xiv.221.
16. *GS(MH)*, vii.21.
17. Michael Bock, Günter C. Behrmann, Harald Homann, Clemens Albrecht and Friedrich H. Tenbruck, *Die intellektuelle Gründung der Bundesrepublik: Eine Wirkungsgeschichte der Frankfurter Schule* (Frankfurt am Main and New York 1999).
18. *GS(MH)*, xiv.100.
19. *GS*, x.555–72.
20. *GS*, x.674–90.
21. Bock *et al.*, *Die intellektuelle Gründung der Bundesrepublik* (note 17), 7.
22. *GS*, x.566.
23. *GS*, iv.13; trans. by E. F. N. Jephcott as *Minima moralia: Reflections from Damaged Life* (London 1978), 15.
24. Scholem, *Briefe* (note 9), ii.29.
25. *GS*, iv.43; (*Minima moralia*), 39.
26. *GS*, iv.13, 15.
27. *GS*, iv.13, 15.
28. *GS*, iv.13, 15.
29. *GS*, iv.21, 21.
30. *GS*, iv.56, 51.
31. *GS*, iv.58–9, 53.
32. *GS*, iv.185, 163.
33. *GS*, iv.185, 163.
34. *GS*, iv.187, 164.

35. *GS*, iv.282, 246.
36. *GS*, iv.65, 58.
37. *GS*, iv.66, 59.
38. Ralf Dahrendorf, *Über Grenzen: Lebens-erinnerungen* (Munich 2002), 169.
39. ibid., 170–71.
40. Friedrich Tenbruck, 'Adornos und Hork-heimers besondere Rolle', *Frankfurter Allgemeine Zeitung* (25 Jan. 1990).
41. Dahrendorf, *Über Grenzen* (note 38), 172.
42. ibid., 172.
43. ibid., 173.
44. *GS(MH)*, xviii.273.
45. *GS(MH)*, xviii.274.
46. Dahrendorf, *Über Grenzen* (note 38), 173.
47. ibid., 173.
48. *GS(MH)*, xviii.445.
49. *GS(MH)*, xviii.444–5.
50. *GS(MH)*, xviii.443.
51. *GS(MH)*, xviii.447.
52. *GS(MH)*, xviii.451.
53. *B-LL-SK*, 248.
54. Wolfgang Preiser, 'Spät, aber nicht zu spät', *Frankfurter Allgemeine Zeitung* (23 Oct. 1989).
55. Institut für Sozialforschung (ed.), *Soziologische Exkurse: Nach Vorträgen und Diskussionen* (Frankfurt am Main 2/1972), 22ff.
56. ibid., 25.
57. ibid., 26.
58. ibid., 25.
59. ibid., 36.
60. ibid., 23.
61. *Süddeutsche Zeitung* (12 April 2003).
62. *GS*, xviii.280–81.

Chapter Fifteen

1. Theodor W. Adorno, 'Zur Lehre von der Geschichte und von der Freiheit', *Nach-gelassene Schriften* (Frankfurt am Main 2001), iv/13.11.
2. ibid., iv/13.92.
3. ibid., iv/13.152.
4. ibid., iv/13.164.
5. ibid., iv/13.102–3.
6. ibid., iv/13.105.

7. ibid., iv/13.106.
8. ibid., iv/13.108.
9. ibid., iv/13.14.
10. ibid., iv/13.87.
11. ibid., iv/13.94.
12. *B-LL-SK*, 212.
13. *B-LL-SK*, 227.
14. *B-LL-SK*, 227–8.
15. *GS(MH)*, xiv.338–9.
16. I am grateful to Axel Matthes for gener-ously placing this unpublished letter at my disposal.
17. Theodor W. Adorno, 'Ontologie und Dialektik', *Nachgelassene Schriften* (Frank-furt am Main 2002), iv/7.15.
18. Werner Kraft, *Kleinigkeiten* (Bonn 1985), 56.
19. *GS*, vi.472; trans. by Knut Tarnowski and Frederic Will as *The Jargon of Authenticity* (London and New York 2003), 72.
20. *GS*, vi.477, 78.
21. *GS*, vi.479, 81.
22. *GS*, vi.482, 85.
23. *GS*, vi.66; trans. by E. B. Ashton as *Negative Dialectics* (New York 2003), 56.
24. *GS*, vi.65, 55.
25. *GS*, xx.510–11.
26. *GS*, vi.385; (*Negative Dialectics*), 393.
27. *GS*, vi.364, 371.
28. *GS*, vi.366, 373.
29. *GS*, vi.366, 373.
30. *GS*, vi.365, 372.
31. *GS*, vi.368, 375.
32. *GS*, vi.367, 374.
33. *GS*, vi.368, 375.
34. *GS*, xi.133–4.
35. *GS*, xi.133.
36. *GS*, x.327.
37. *GS*, x.163.
38. John Felstiner, *Paul Celan: Poet, Sur-vivor, Jew* (New Haven 2001), 139.
39. ibid., 139.
40. ibid., 140.
41. Paul Celan, *Gesammelte Werke* (Frank-furt am Main 2000), iii.169; trans. from Felstiner, *Celan* (note 38), 141.
42. ibid., iii.169, 141.
43. Joachim Seng, 'Die wahre Flaschenpost:

Zur Beziehung zwischen Theodor W. Adorno und Paul Celan', *FAB*, viii (1999), 151.

44. Celan, *Gesammelte Werke* (note 41), iii.31; trans. from Felstiner, *Celan* (note 38), 44.

45. ibid., i.39, 31–2.

46. *GS*, x.30.

47. Seng, 'Die wahre Flaschenpost' (note 43), 163.

48. *GS*, vi.355; (*Negative Dialectics*), 362.

49. Seng, 'Die wahre Flaschenpost' (note 43), 190.

50. ibid., 152.

51. *GS*, vii.477; trans. by Robert Hullot-Kentor as *Aesthetic Theory* (London 2002), 322.

52. *GS*, vii.477; (*Aesthetic Theory*), 322.

53. Kraft, *Kleinigkeiten* (note 18), 61.

54. Constantin Frantz, *Untersuchungen über das Europäische Gleichgewicht* (Berlin 1859), 146–7.

55. *GS*, xi.512.

56. *GS*, vii.9; (*Aesthetic Theory*), 1.

57. *GS*, vii.10, 2.

58. *GS*, vii.45, 25.

59. *GS*, vii.44, 25.

60. *GS*, vii.509, 342.

61. *GS*, vii.96, 60.

62. *GS*, vii.31, 16.

63. *GS*, xvi.649; trans. by Susan H. Gillespie as 'Music, Language, and Composition', *Essays on Music*, ed. Richard Leppert (Berkeley 2002), 113.

64. Bazon Brock, 'Gespräch mit Werner Klüppelholz', *Was ist musikalische Bildung?* (Kassel 1984) (Musikalische Zeitfragen no. 14).

Chapter Sixteen

1. *GS*, xiv.112.

2. *40 Jahre Edition Suhrkamp* (Frankfurt am Main 2003), 37.

3. *GS(MH)*, xviii.502.

4. *GS(MH)*, xviii.533.

5. Frank Böckelmann and Herbert Nagel (eds.), *Subversive Aktion: Der Sinn der Aktion ist ihr Scheitern* (Frankfurt am Main 2002), 145.

6. Ernst Bloch, *Briefe 1903–1975*, ed. Karola Bloch and others (Frankfurt am Main 1985), 453.

7. ibid., 453.

8. Böckelmann and Nagel, *Subversive Aktion* (note 5), 146.

9. Dieter Kunzelmann, *Leisten Sie keinen Widerstand! Bilder aus meinem Leben* (Berlin 1999), 148.

10. Böckelmann and Nagel, *Subversive Aktion* (note 5), 46.

11. Kunzelmann, *Leisten Sie keinen Widerstand!* (note 9), 159.

12. ibid., 163.

13. Theodor W. Adorno and Elisabeth Lenk, *Briefwechsel 1962–1969*, ed. Elisabeth Lenk (Munich 2002), 65.

14. ibid., 65.

15. ibid., 166.

16. ibid., 137.

17. ibid., 137.

18. *FAB*, vi (1997), 196.

19. *FAB*, vi (1997), 196.

20. *FAB*, vi (1997), 122.

21. *FAB*, vi (1997), 126.

22. *FAB*, vi (1997), 126.

23. *GS*, viii.190.

24. Theodor W. Adorno, 'Einleitung in die Soziologie', *Nachgelassene Schriften* (Frankfurt am Main 1993), iv/15.115.

25. *GS*, x.774.

26. Quoted from Hartmut Laufhütte (ed.), *Deutsche Balladen* (Ditzingen 1991), 533.

27. Hans-Jürgen Krahl, *Konstitution und Klassenkampf* (Frankfurt am Main 1974), 20.

28. ibid., 19.

29. ibid., 304.

30. ibid., 305.

31. hm., 'Eine Sänfte für Herrn Adorno: Ein Philosoph im Zeugenstand gegen seinen Schüler / Die Phänomenologie der Okkupation im Gerichtssaal', *Frankfurter Allgemeine Zeitung* (19 July 1969).

32. *GS*, vii.383; trans. by Robert Hullot-Kentor as *Aesthetic Theory* (London 2002), 258.

33. Hans Imhoff, *Asozialistik*, quoted from 'Komödie der Weisheit. 1968 als Kunst:

Hans Imhoff, ein deutscher Aristophanes', *Frankfurt Allgemeine Zeitung* (30 May 1998).

34. ibid.
35. ibid.
36. *FAB*, vi (1997), 108.
37. *FAB*, vi (1997), 108–9.
38. *FAB*, vi (1997), 200.

Epilogue

1. Rainer Maria Rilke, *Briefe*, ed. Rilke-Archiv, Weimar (Frankfurt am Main 1987), ii.677; trans. by R. F. C. Hull as *Selected Letters of Rainer Maria Rilke 1902–1926* (London 1946), 319 (letter to Princess Marie von Thurn und Taxis-Hohenlohe of 25 July 1921).
2. ibid., ii.678, 319–20.
3. Theodor W. Adorno and Alfred Sohn-Rethel, *Briefwechsel 1936–1969*, ed. Christoph Gödde (Munich 1991), 164.
4. *GS*, xx.729.
5. *GS*, xx.729.
6. *GS*, xx.729.
7. *GS*, xx.730.

8. *GS*, xx.732.
9. *GS*, vii.112; trans. by Robert Hullot-Kentor as *Aesthetic Theory* (London 2002), 70.
10. *GS*, xx.732.
11. *GS*, xx.732.
12. *GS*, xx.732.
13. *GS*, vii.98; (*Aesthetic Theory*), 61.
14. *GS*, vii.99, 62.
15. *GS*, vii.100, 63.
16. *GS*, vii.103, 65.
17. *GS*, vii.105, 67.
18. Elisabeth Lenk, 'Hauptgeschäfte, Nebensachen: Begegnungen mit, Briefe von Theodor W. Adorno', *Frankfurter Allgemeine Zeitung* (23 Oct. 1999).
19. Monika Plessner, 'Miteinander reden heißt miteinander träumen: Gruppenstudie mit Horkheimer', *Frankfurter Allgemeine Zeitung* (28 Sept. 1991).
20. *B-A-AB*, 24.
21. *GS*, vi.353; trans. by E. B. Ashton as *Negative Dialectics* (New York 1973), 359.
22. *GS*, xx.733.

Index